the good cuisine

Françoise & Bernard & Alain Ducasse

Text by Catherine Vialard
Photographs by Jean-Charles Vaillant
Designed by Valérie Lhomme

Published by Ici La Press
694 Main Street South
Woodbury, CT 06798
www.icilapress.com

Printed in Singapore by Imago

Typeset by Westchester Book Composition

ISBN 1-931605-03-3

10 9 8 7 6 5 4 3 2 1

the good cuisine

Françoise & Bernard

Alain Ducasse

208 recipes
easy and inspired

ici la
PRESS

A Book with Two Faces

Françoise Bernard and Alain Ducasse. The meeting between Françoise Bernard, the editor-in-chief of "Les doigts d'or" . . . a famous culinary collection of books and magazines for homemakers, and Alain Ducasse, the six-star culinary wonder and master chef praised by his own peers.

At first glance, these two could not be more different from each other. Françoise Bernard dedicates herself to the practical concerns of her readers, and Alain Ducasse moves in the star-spangled sphere of top restaurants. Yet, both authors are the heirs of a tremendous culinary tradition. Bernard's book. *Les Recettes Faciles (Easy Recipes)* has inspired many generations of experienced cooks and novices. It has been passed down from mother to daughter for years. Ducasse has taken his talent to every continent of the world to promote French gastronomy.

They do, indeed, have much in common. Both have a fondness for vegetables. Both insist on the finding of the appropriate cooking technique to enhance each ingredient. Both share a love of the fruits from the orchard, the vegetables from the garden, the poultry from the farm, the fish from the sea as savored on the coast. Bernard visits open markets and supermarkets more often then Ducasse does—

and their differing views inevitably launch them into some heated discussions. Bernard goes straight to what is the most simple and economical. Ducasse will not hesitate to scout all over France for the wild salmon of his dreams or the most aromatic zucchini. Bernard comes from northern France and adores butter. Ducasse, who is from southern France, sings the praises of olive oil—in the end, they both always agree on one thing: quality.

Their mission in making this book was not an easy one. The authors had to select fifty-two ingredients and suggest two recipes for each. They did not choose these foods at random. Their choices were not directed by their whims or their personal preferences. They chose foods that reflect French tastes and preferences—those that people in France eat most often.

The end result is 208 gourmet suggestions—our two distinguished specialists' favorite dishes—four recipes for each selected food. Our authors have created a new model for family cooking. They have taken up the challenge of presenting everyday recipes and recipes for special occasions, too. Readers can choose a dish simply by looking up the type of food that they have in mind.

Now that the book is finished, it is time for an honest exchange of chef's secrets. Françoise Bernard joins Alain Ducasse in his "aquarium"—his small personal dining room connected to his kitchen, from where he can observe every move his staff makes.

F.B.: One thing puzzles me: Why did you want to write this book with me? Why did a famous chef like you have the idea of associating his name with Françoise Bernard, the apostle of "easy cuisine?"

A.D.: Do you think that fine cuisine is that far removed from home cooking? True, we chefs have different methods, but our concerns are the same as those of anybody else who cooks. We are limited by a budget—admittedly, it is higher than for a family meal. Just as it does to family cooks, it means a lot to us to receive our guests well and make them feel comfortable, and we are all always looking for ways and means to make our work easier. Our philosophy is basically the same as that of the homemaker. As far as I am concerned, there is no barrier between fine cuisine and family cooking. There are both sophisticated and simple dishes in my recipes and in yours. Our paths were bound to cross.

F.B.: The first time we met, you told me you had made your first chocolate mousse from the recipe in one of my books. Was this true or mere flattery?

A.D.: The simple truth. Yours was my one and only book.

F.B.: Well, this is certainly stripping me of all my illusions! I was so proud to know that the most noted Parisian chef was interested in my book when he was still a child.

A.D.: I'm afraid you misunderstood me. It was the only book in existence at the time, the book you couldn't do without.

F.B.: I feel better. It's true there are so many cookbooks out today that I often wonder how the reader can choose. This book that we just wrote together made you reconsider your methods, didn't it? Don't tell me that the recipes you are presenting here are those of the *Restaurant Alain Ducasse.*

A.D.: Of course they aren't, but the spirit is there. In these recipes, you will find my favorite ingredients, those that sing of the South. I will use no others at my restaurant in Monaco, *Le Louis XV.* Take the zucchini, for instance. I insisted on presenting the zucchinis I like best in this book—the trumpet zucchini, the violin zucchini—not to frighten readers but to remind them of the infinite diversity nature has to offer.

F.B.: I must say that I have really enjoyed the simplicity of some of your dishes. Like your whiting cooked between two plates, which is astonishingly simple.

A.D.: I am—and will always be—the kid from the Landes who grew up on a farm in Castelsarrasin. I think we all need to go back to our roots in home cooking, which is the kind of cuisine that you have always advocated. We chefs may have strayed a little too far from that. My role is to offer that little something that is missing in *cuisine bourgeoise* and family cuisine, to give it a touch of refinement and imagination.

F.B.: Isn't originality for originality's sake sometimes risky, though? I was once quite stunned by a dessert in a Parisian restaurant. I was served a pistachio ice cream sprinkled with a few grains of rock salt. The general trend is for mixtures, questioning classic flavors, and the result doesn't always taste good.

A.D.: I couldn't agree with you more. Originality must not go against the recipe and must not be purely for my own satisfaction. When I roast a rack of lamb in a buttered breadcrumb crust sprinkled with the zest of citrus fruits, I am not trying to complicate matters for the fun of it. I am offering a new vision that might help our readers better prepare their familiar dishes.

F.B.: I actually noted several very original techniques, which I will adopt from now on. For example, you have this ingenious way for preparing one bird with two recipes.

A.D.: Indeed, how many times have I heard my friends complain that the meat of a guinea hen or a pigeon is a little too dry. I came up with a dual method of cooking, because thighs and wings require different methods.

F.B.: I also enjoyed your association of cooked and raw. I like finding different textures and different temperatures in a single dish.

A.D.: That is quite important to me. It doesn't call for any more work, and it changes everything. Just imagine a caramelized apple tart sprinkled with sliced raw apples.

F.B.: This kind of idea is sure to transform a dish. I am quite happy with today's simplification of techniques. In my home, it was a sin to boil fish or to overcook string beans—come to think of it, my mother was avant-garde. Isn't this what chefs are saying today? Serve your fish pink at the bone. Do not destroy the essence of your vegetables by cooking them too long.

A.D.: Yes, this is what I keep saying. A recipe must respect the food and bring out its nuances. This is what Alain Chapel once told me, and I do not intend to change. Cooking meat must preserve the texture of the meat, and cooking a vegetable must make it tender to the right degree. . . .

"If you would kindly follow me. . . ."

[In the heat of the discussion, our "kitchen lord and lady" had forgotten that a meal was awaiting them. The intervention of the maître d' brought a delighted smile to Françoise Bernard's face.]

F.B.: Great! I must say I prefer actions to words. I will never be one of those cooks who can go on discussing a flavor or a food for hours. Even the famous gourmet Curnonsky tired of endless tasting sessions. I once told him I was surprised that he chose *tripes de Caen* right after a sublime foie gras. He then whispered in my ear, "My all-time favorite is *steak frites* [steak and French fries]."

A.D.: How right you are. Let's forget snobbery and discussions. Let's go eat!

EDITOR'S NOTES:

In measurements for butter, 1 oz. = 2 tbsp., and 8 tbsp. = ¼ lb. = 4 oz. = 1 stick. Use unsalted butter and sea salt. All pepper is freshly ground.

The symbols shown with each recipe indicate the degree of difficulty and cost of ingredients: ⚪ = very easy, ⚪⚪ = easy, ⚪⚪⚪ = difficult, ○ = inexpensive, ○○ = reasonable, ○○○ = expensive.

Contents

Crab

Françoise Bernard frequently cooks crab for her husband, who, like all true Bretons, is crazy about it. In his family, crab is always boiled. To prepare boiled crab, you have to buy and cook the crab alive. "It is cruel, but necessary," she laments. This said, she entrusts this mission to her husband. To lessen the suffering of the crabs, she first drops them in cold water.

Unfortunately, sometimes the meat disintegrates in the water, to the despair of the cook. This possibility has never pushed Françoise Bernard to recommend buying precooked crab. She is very suspicious of any ready-to-use products. She instinctively mistrusts them. Why has it been precooked? Are they trying to conceal that the fish is not that fresh? And, if it has been overcooked, the meat will be rubbery. When she gets home from the market with a few beautiful, live crabs in her basket, she abandons herself to exotic flavors.

She discovered *matoutou* crab in a West Indian restaurant near the Champs-Élysées, which Henri Salvador, a famous musician and singer, frequently visits. "The punch that we drank there, while munching acras fritters and waiting for our crab, was out of this world," she recalls. Was it because of the punch or the crab that she liked this place so much? Whatever the reason, *matoutou* crab always reminds her of that carefree evening. More traditional recipes are less to her taste, probably because she has eaten them all too often at the homes of her friends or in restaurants, where she always ends up with a crab cocktail made with grapefruit or avocado.

Alain Ducasse is not very fond of these classic recipes either. He prefers to use crabmeat as a filling, in lasagna or tomatoes, for example. He always spices it up with garden herbs—such as lemon thyme—or a spicy sauce, with a dash of cognac or sherry vinegar. A few oven-dried tomatoes add a little acidity. He confesses to a "special soft spot" for the very delicate meat of the spider crab.

Crab with Grapefruit

Pamplemousse au crabe

⌂ ∽

Françoise Bernard

Serves 4 ✦ Preparation time : 30 minutes ✦ Cooking time : 20 minutes
¼ cup (50 g) long-grain rice ✦ 1 egg yolk ✦ 1 tsp. hot Dijon-style mustard ✦ ½ cup (10 cl) oil
✦ 1 tsp. vinegar ✦ pinch of cayenne ✦ salt and pepper ✦ 2 large grapefruits ✦ 1 lb. (500 g)
crabmeat ✦ 16 green or black olives

Boil water in a saucepan. Gradually pour the rice into the boiling water and cook until done, 15 to 18 minutes. Strain the rice and rinse under cold water to cool it completely. Let it drain while you prepare the mayonnaise. **W**hisk together the egg yolk and mustard. Gradually drizzle in the oil, whisking constantly to incorporate it. Next, whisk in the vinegar, cayenne, and salt and pepper to taste. **C**ut each grapefruit in half and carefully scoop out the pulp, leaving the shell intact. Segment the grapefruit sections, detaching them from the membranes. **R**inse and drain the crab. Pit and chop 12 of the olives. Mix the rice with the mayonnaise, crab, grapefruit, and chopped olives. Just before serving, fill the hollowed-out grapefruit halves with the mixture, sprinkle with salt, and place 1 olive on top of each serving.

NOTE BY **ALAIN DUCASSE** For a more Southern taste, mix equal parts of olive oil and vegetable oil to make the mayonnaise. Choose good olives and chop them coarsely so that your guests will be able to really taste them.

Crab Lasagna with Thyme

Lasagnes de crabe au thym

⇧ ⇧ ∞

Alain Ducasse

Serves 8 ✦ Preparation time : 1 hour ✦ Cooking time : 1½ hours
2 crabs, about 1¾ lb. (800 g) each ✦ 2 spider crabs ✦ 1 head of garlic ✦ 5 lbs. (2,2 kg) tomatoes
✦ 2 carrots ✦ 1 onion ✦ 1 celery stalk ✦ 1 cup (20 cl) olive oil, plus 1 tbsp. olive oil for the
lasagna water ✦ ¼ cup (5 cl) cognac ✦ 1 cup (20 cl) dry white wine ✦ 2 tbsp. fresh lemon thyme
leaves ✦ salt and pepper ✦ 14 oz. (400 g) lasagna noodles ✦ 7 oz. (190 g) butter

Preheat the oven to 400°F (210°C). Scrub the crabs and spider crabs under cold water with a vegetable brush. Make a stock by boiling the crabs and spider crabs together in salted water for 15 to 20 minutes. Shell them, reserving the meat. Crush the shells. Peel 5 garlic cloves and slice into slivers. Finely slice 3 tomatoes, the carrots, onion, and celery. Sauté the crab shells and spider crab shells in ½ cup (10 cl) of the olive oil. Add the thinly sliced vegetables, deglaze with the cognac, and flambé the mixture. Add the wine, lemon thyme, and salt and pepper to taste. Add water to cover and cook at a slow boil for 40 to 50 minutes. Peel and seed the remaining tomatoes, reserving the skin and seeds for the stock. Heat the remaining ½ cup (10 cl) of olive oil in a frying pan. Add the peeled tomatoes, the rest of the garlic (unpeeled), and salt and pepper to taste. Bake the mixture until the water has evaporated. Lower the oven temperature to 350°F (180 °C). Cook the lasagna noodles for 3 to 5 minutes in boiling salted water with 1 tbsp. of olive oil, then drain. Remove the tomatoes from the oven, mix with the crabmeat, and add salt and pepper to taste. In a buttered baking dish, layer the noodles alternately with the tomato-crab mixture, ending with a layer of noodles. Dot with butter and place the dish in the oven for 35 minutes. Strain the stock and reduce to one-third its volume over high heat. Gradually whisk in 10 tbsp. (135 g) of butter. Crush the remaining lemon thyme leaves, and sprinkle on top. Strain the sauce and blend in a food processor. Serve a piece of lasagna in the center of each plate, surrounded by a few spoonfuls of the sauce.

It's not easy to crush crab shells! You can use a mortar or grinder-or even a hammer and a wooden cutting board covered with a large cloth.

NOTE BY
FRANÇOISE
BERNARD

Matoutou

Crabe farci à l'antillaise

⇧ ⇧ ⚬⚬

Françoise Bernard

Serves 4 ✦ Preparation time : 40 minutes ✦ Cooking time : 20 minutes
1 carrot, sliced ✦ 1 onion, sliced ✦ ¾ cup (15 cl) vinegar ✦ 3 whole cloves ✦ 1 bouquet garni ✦
10 black peppercorns ✦ 4 crabs, about 1 lb. (500 g) each, or about ¾ lb. (400 g) frozen crab,
defrosted in a little milk ✦ ¾ cup (100 g) white sandwich bread, torn into pieces ✦ ½ cup
(10 cl) dry white wine ✦ 1 garlic clove ✦ 3 small shallots or 3 scallions ✦ 1 fresh hot red pepper,
optional ✦ 5 oz. (150 g) ground pork loin ✦ 4 tbsp. dry bread crumbs ✦ 4 tbsp. (50 g) butter ✦
salt and pepper

Boil the carrot, onion, vinegar, cloves, bouquet garlic, and peppercorns in a saucepan with 4 cups (80 cl) of water and a little salt to make a court bouillon. Add the crabs and simmer for about 10 minutes. Remove from the heat and let the crabs cool in the court bouillon. When the crabs are cool enough to handle, shell them, removing the meat from the legs, claws, and body. Save the shells. **P**ut the bread pieces in a bowl and pour the wine over them. **P**eel the garlic. Chop the shallots, garlic, and pepper. Lightly sauté them and the ground pork loin in 2 tbsp. of butter. Squeeze the wine from the bread and discard the wine. Add the bread and crabmeat to the sautéed mixture. Salt and pepper to taste. Mix well. Fill the crab shells with this stuffing. Sprinkle with bread crumbs, dot with the remaining butter, then brown the stuffed crabs under the broiler.

NOTE BY **ALAIN DUCASSE** For a spicier stuffing, you can replace the ground pork loin with equal quantities of boiled ham and cured ham. The crab will taste great, because both types of ham enhance its flavor.

Stuffed Tomatoes with Crab

Tomates farcies au crabe

⬆ ⬆ ∞

Alain Ducasse

Serves 4 ♦ Preparation time : 1 hour ♦ Cooking time : 1 hour 20 minutes
8 large ripe tomatoes ♦ 4½ lbs. (2 kg) tomatoes ♦ 2 crabs, about 1¾ lb. (800 g) each ♦ 2 spider
crabs ♦ ¾ cup (15 cl) olive oil ♦ 2 onions, thinly sliced ♦ 1 carrot, thinly sliced ♦ ½ stalk celery,
thinly sliced ♦ ¼ cup (5 cl) cognac ♦ 1½ cups (30 cl) white wine ♦ 1 tsp. thyme ♦ 1 bouquet
garni with basil ♦ salt and peppercorns ♦ ¼ cup (5 cl) sherry vinegar ♦ 5 garlic cloves, unpeeled
♦ 5 oz. (150 g) arugula ♦ 15 small basil leaves ♦ 12 oven-dried tomatoes (page 231)

Peel and seed all of the tomatoes, reserving the skins and seeds. Hollow out the large tomatoes and cut the others into quarters. Scrub the crabs and spider crabs under cold water with a vegetable brush. Cook for 10 to 15 minutes in boiling salted water. Remove the meat from the shells and set aside. Crush the shells. To make the stock, sauté the shells in 3 tbsp. of the olive oil for 5 minutes. Add the onions, carrot, and celery and cook for 5 more minutes. Baste with the cognac and flambé, being careful that the flame doesn't get too high. Add the wine, thyme, bouquet garni, and tomato skins and seeds. Add water to cover, a pinch of salt, and a few peppercorns. Cook at a slow boil for 40 to 50 minutes, or until reduced to one-third its volume. Strain. Preheat the oven to 425°F (220°C). Make a vinaigrette with ⅓ cup (8 cl) of the olive oil and the sherry vinegar. Heat the remaining olive oil in a saucepan. Mix in the quartered tomatoes, garlic, salt, and pepper. Spoon into a baking dish and bake until the water from the vegetables has completely evaporated. Combine this mixture with the crabmeat, arugula, basil leaves, oven-dried tomatoes, and salt and pepper to taste. Stuff the hollowed-out tomatoes and sprinkle them with vinaigrette dressing.

You can use crabmeat or frozen crab. The taste of the dish will suffer, but you will save a great deal of time! The two kinds of tomatoes in the stuffing will give your dish a very delicate flavor.

NOTE BY **FRANÇOISE BERNARD**

Escargots

The *petit-gris* escargot, with its fine, fruity meat, is mostly found in Languedoc, Provence, and Brittany. It is called *ca-gouille* in the Charente. The large Burgundy snail, *escargot de Bourgogne*, lives in the vineyards of Burgundy; in Franche-Comté, along the Swiss border; in Savoy; and in Champagne. Going out and gathering escargots is a very pleasant country pastime, but preparing them is not always so much fun.

Escargots are something that is much more tempting to try in a restaurant than at home. Françoise Bernard fully understands why some home cooks balk at preparing snails. You must have a strong stomach and a lot of courage to let the snails live for many days without eating, watch them spit up in salt, scald them in boiling water, and finally cook them for three long hours in a court bouillon. Then you have to take them out of their shells, making sure not to break off the twisted flesh—the most nutritious and favorite part for gourmets. Out of respect for her readers, and to save them from the tedious job, Françoise Bernard has eventually given in. She now recommends canned escargots in her recipes. It is not her habit to use canned foods, but it is really more practical, especially for those people who don't live in the countryside!

As for Alain Ducasse, he has never put escargots on the menu at his restaurants. The great chef evidently does not think much of it, which is hardly surprising—he avoids anything that requires rich seasoning. And what are escargots without escargot butter, garlic, and parsley?

What people love about escargots is the sauce. Everyone is crazy about the aromatic garlic butter, which oozes from the shells and makes our heads spin. "We dunk our piece of bread in it, and it is fabulous. For me," Françoise Bernard says, "there is no better recipe for escargots than Burgundy sauce."

Escargots, Burgundy-Style

Escargots à la bourguignonne

⌂ ∞

Françoise Bernard

Serves 4 ✦ **Preparation time : 45 minutes** ✦ **Cooking time : 10 minutes**
4 dozen escargots (snails), fresh or canned ✦ **4 dozen empty snail shells** ✦ **3 garlic cloves** ✦ **1 shallot** ✦ **½ bunch parsley** ✦ **½ cup (250 g) butter, softened** ✦ **salt and pepper** ✦ **⅔ cup dry white wine**

If you wish to prepare fresh escargots, leave them in a pail for a few days without feeding them anything. On the day you are going to cook them, put them in a large pail of water, salt, and vinegar for 2 hours. Boil the escargots for 5 minutes, drain, and remove from the shells. Cut off the hard black end of the tail, or "foot." Simmer for 3 to 4 hours in a court bouillon. Finely chop the garlic, shallot, and parsley. Soften the butter with a wooden spoon to give it the consistency of a thick cream. Mix in the chopped garlic, shallot, and parsley, 1 tbsp. salt, a dash of pepper, and 2 tbsp. of wine. Drain the escargots. Fill each empty snail shell with a bit of stuffing, 1 escargot, and a bit more stuffing, packing it well. Carefully place the snails in 4 escargot or egg dishes. Refrigerate for at least 30 minutes. Just before serving, preheat the oven to 400°F (210°C). Pour 2 tbsp. of wine into each dish and bake just until the stuffing begins to bubble and foam.

NOTE BY
ALAIN
DUCASSE
I imagine that escargot butter would taste very good with almond powder and ground ham. These additions would give a special character to the taste of the escargot and add more texture. If I added these two ingredients, I would not use white wine in the stuffing.

Escargots with Garlic Butter

Escargots au beurre d'ail

⌂ ◯

Alain Ducasse

Serves 4 ✦ Preparation time : 30 minutes ✦ Cooking time : 20 minutes
9 oz. (270 g) butter, softened ✦ 1 garlic clove, minced ✦ 1 shallot, minced ✦ 4 sprigs of flat-leaf
parsley, stemmed and minced ✦ 1 heaping tbsp. mustard ✦ 1 tbsp. almond powder ✦ 4 dozen
escargots, cooked in court bouillon, or canned ✦ 4 tbsp. olive oil ✦ 4 slices of white sandwich
bread ✦ 1¾ cups (300 g) tomato confit (page 323) ✦ salt and pepper

Preheat the oven to 375°F (190°C). **M**ix 7 oz. (210 g) butter with a fork until it is light
and fluffy. Mix the garlic, shallot, and parsley with the mustard and almond powder.
Mix into the butter to make an escargot butter. **S**auté the escargots for a few minutes
in the oil, then remove from the heat and let cool. Melt the rest of the butter in a small
saucepan over very low heat. Skim the foam from the surface and transfer the clarified
butter into a bowl (discard the milky residue remaining in the bottom of the pan).
With a doughnut press or pastry cutter, cut a circle out of each piece of sandwich
bread. Fry the bread circles in the clarified butter. Spoon the tomato confit into the
bottom of 4 ramekins. Divide the escargots among them, sprinkle with garlic butter,
and top each with a piece of fried bread. Return to the oven for 5 to 8 minutes. Serve
hot.

To prepare fresh escargots, I refer our more courageous readers to Escargots, Burgundy
Style (page 18). But the rest of you should not balk at Alain Ducasse's recipe-go ahead
and use canned escargots if you prefer!

NOTE BY
FRANÇOISE
BERNARD

Escargot Canapés with Mushrooms

Canapés d'escargots forestière

⚐ ⚐ ∞

Françoise Bernard

Serves 4 ◆ Preparation time : 30 minutes ◆ Cooking time : 15 minutes
16 large button mushrooms ◆ 8 oz. (230 g) softened butter ◆ 4 dozen escargots, fresh or canned
◆ 1 cup (20 cl) dry white wine ◆ 1 garlic clove ◆ 1 shallot ◆ ½ bunch parsley ◆ 1 tbsp. almond
powder ◆ salt and pepper ◆ 4 slices of white sandwich bread

If you wish to prepare fresh escargots, see Escargots, Burgundy Style (page 18). Preheat the oven to 425°F (220°C). Clean the mushrooms and set aside the stems. Place the caps upside down in a baking dish, with a small dab of butter inside each one. Bake for 8 to 10 minutes. When the mushrooms are cooked, turn the caps over to drain them. Do not turn off the oven. Drain the escargots. Pour the wine into a small saucepan, add the escargots, and simmer over low heat. Finely chop together the mushroom stems, garlic, shallot, and parsley. Combine the chopped mixture with the remaining butter, 2 tbsp. of the escargot in wine, and the almond powder, mixing well with a fork. Season with salt and pepper to taste. Place 3 escargots inside each mushroom cap, fill with stuffing, and bake for about 5 minutes. Toast the bread slices. Serve the stuffed mushrooms on top of the warm toast canapés.

NOTE BY **ALAIN DUCASSE** Depending on the season, you can replace the button mushrooms with the large caps of young porcini mushrooms brushed with olive oil and grilled. You can also serve this dish with Porcini Marmalade (page 211).

Escargot and Porcini Pizza

Pizza aux escargots et aux cèpes

⇧ ⇧ ∞

Alain Ducasse

Serves 4 ✦ Preparation time : 50 minutes ✦ Resting time : 2 hours ✦ Cooking time : 25 minutes ✦ 2½ cups (250 g) flour ✦ 1½ packages (10 g) dry yeast ✦ ⅓ cup (8 cl) lukewarm water ✦ salt and pepper ✦ 1½ cups (30 cl) olive oil ✦ 14 oz. (400 g) porcini mushroom caps ✦ 10 tbsp. butter ✦ 1 shallot, finely chopped ✦ 1 garlic clove, finely chopped ✦ 5 tbsp. chopped flat-leaf parsley ✦ 1 lb. (500 g) cooked *petit-gris* escargots ✦ 2 slices of cured ham, diced

Pour the flour into a large bowl and make a well in the center. Stir the yeast into the water and pour it into the well. Add 1 tsp. salt and 1¼ cups (25 cl) of the olive oil. Mix and knead well. Let the dough rise in a warm place for about 40 minutes. Knead the dough again and let it rise again in a warm place for 40 minutes more. **W**hile the dough is rising the second time, preheat the oven to 400°F (210°C). **F**inely slice the mushroom caps and sauté them in the remaining oil for 15 minutes. Season with salt and pepper to taste. Soften 8 tbsp. of butter with a flat spoon. Add the shallot, garlic, and parsley and mix well. Spread a very thin layer of this herb butter on a plate and let it harden for 20 minutes in the refrigerator before cutting into 6 in. (15 cm) circles. **R**oll out the dough and cut it into 6 in. (15 cm) circles. Layer mushroom slices on each circle, one on top of the other, as you would apples in a tart. Bake for 8 minutes. Place the butter circles on top of the porcini pizzas and bake for 2 more minutes. **S**auté the escargots in the remaining butter and add the diced ham. Sprinkle the pizzas with the escargot-ham mixture and serve immediately.

To save time, use pre-made pizza dough, fresh or frozen. Better yet, order the dough from your baker—one often forgets that the baker next door can provide many services. The key is to get organized and think ahead.

NOTE BY **FRANÇOISE BERNARD**

Langoustines

Raw, fresh, and large—that's how Alain Ducasse likes his langoustines. No more than three or four to a pound. If you get five to seven in a pound, you can be sure that they are too small and won't be crunchy enough for what our Mediterranean chef is looking for. For him, the royal langoustine is the very best.

For Françoise Bernard, size matters less than freshness. Her advice is to buy live langoustines, although this is not always possible. They are a rare commodity inland. Their hard shell is deceptive—langoustines are actually very fragile and they do not travel well. "On the other hand, contrary to crayfish, for example, which we have to import, we can still hope that the langoustines we buy on our coast really come from here. The idea that either fresh or salt water seafood has traveled bothers me a bit." She prefers serving these large coastal langoustines with a rouille as a summer starter or as a seaside appetizer.

Alain Ducasse appreciates the firm texture of langoustines. He steams them *al dente*, marinated with lemon, or pan-fries them with a vegetable marinade. The head and claws make a very flavorful broth both for Françoise Bernard's American sauce and Alain Ducasse's recipe, in which the langoustines are roasted in the oven on a bed of tuna that has cooked slowly for a long time. Once, for a fancy meal, he steamed the langoustines, then topped them with caviar. Simply fabulous! Langoustines are good not only for their succulent meat—having even one on your plate makes you feel that you have been invited to a party.

Langoustines *Sauce Américaine*

Langoustines á l'américaine

⇧ ⇧ ∞

Françoise Bernard

Serves 4 ✦ Preparation time : 20 minutes ✦ Cooking time : 15 minutes
20 raw langoustines, shelled ✦ 2 tbsp. oil ✦ 1 shallot, minced ✦ 1 garlic clove, minced ✦ 3 tbsp.
cognac ✦ 1 cup (20 cl) dry white wine ✦ 2 tbsp. tomato paste ✦ 2 pinches of cayenne ✦ salt and
pepper ✦ 1 tbsp. flour ✦ 4 tsp. butter, softened

Sauté the langoustines in the oil in a pot over high heat. As soon they turn bright pink, add the shallot, garlic, and cognac. Flambé, carefully watching that the flame doesn't get too high. Add the wine, ½ cup water, tomato paste, and cayenne. Season to taste with salt and pepper. Cover and simmer for about 5 minutes. Remove the cooked langoustines with a slotted spoon and keep them in a warm place. Reduce the cooking sauce. Cut the flour into the butter and add the mixture to the sauce. Bring the sauce to a boil, stirring constantly. Pour the sauce over the langoustines and serve.

NOTE BY **ALAIN DUCASSE** One additional refinement: Peel the langoustines and add just the heads to the sauce. Serve this sauce with the langoustines, which you have cooked in another pot. You won't be disappointed.

Cold Langoustines in a Creamy Court Bouillon

Langoustines froides en nage crémée

⌂ ⌂ ∞

Alain Ducasse

Serves 4 ◆ Preparation time : 50 minutes ◆ Cooling time : 30 minutes ◆ Cooking time : 1 hour ◆ 16 raw langoustines ◆ 3 tbsp. olive oil ◆ 3 shallots, thinly sliced ◆ 1 cup (20 cl) white wine ◆ 1 cup (20 cl) light cream or half-and-half ◆ 1 carrot, peeled and diced ◆ 1 celery stalk, peeled and diced ◆ 3 scallions, peeled and diced ◆ 10 white peppercorns ◆ 10 coriander seeds ◆ ¼ cup (5 cl) heavy cream ◆ dash of Tabasco ◆ 2 lemons, juiced separately ◆ Sea salt and pepper ◆ 5 basil leaves, minced ◆ Caviar, for garnish, optional

Peel the langoustines and set aside in a cool place. Crush the claws with a mortar or grinder. To prepare the court bouillon, heat 1 tbsp. of olive oil in a pot. Add the shallots and crushed claws, then deglaze with wine. Reduce the court bouillon over medium heat to half its volume. Add the light cream. Cover, cook over low heat for 15 minutes, then strain. Sauté the carrot, celery, and scallions in some olive oil in a saucepan. Add the cream sauce, peppercorns, and coriander seeds. Let the mixture simmer over low heat until it reaches a smooth consistency—about 15 to 20 minutes. Strain again, let cool, then add the heavy cream, Tabasco, and juice of 1 lemon. Steam the langoustines for a few seconds to firm the meat. Let cool in a dish set on a bed of ice. Cut the langoustines in half lengthwise. Marinate them for 5 minutes, cut side down, in the juice of the other lemon seasoned with salt and pepper. Pour a thin stream of the court bouillon around the edges and in the center of 4 large individual soup dishes. Arrange the langoustines in a rosette pattern in each dish and sprinkle with minced basil. For festive occasions, place a spoonful of caviar on each langoustine half.

If you feel uneasy about uncooked shellfish, you might want to steam the langoustines a little longer—even though they have been marinated and have already "cooked" in the lemon juice.

NOTE BY **FRANÇOISE BERNARD**

Langoustines with Rouille

Langoustines à la rouille

⬠ ⬠ ∞

Françoise Bernard

Serves 4 ✦ **Preparation time : 30 minutes** ✦ **Cooking time : 10 minutes**
12 raw langoustines ✦ **1 bouquet garni** ✦ **salt and pepper** ✦ **7 oz. (200 g) small pasta noodles,**
such as fusilli or shells ✦ **2 tbsp. oil** ✦ **1 head of lettuce** ✦ **1 celery heart** ✦ **2 or 3 garlic cloves** ✦
1 egg yolk ✦ **1 small fresh hot red pepper, seeded and minced, or a few pinches of cayenne** ✦
1 tbsp. tomato paste ✦ **1¼ cups (25 cl) olive oil** ✦ **1 tbsp. cold water** ✦ **12 cherry tomatoes** ✦
12 black olives ✦ **12 croutons**

Place the langoustines in a saucepan of cold water with the bouquet garni and a good measure of salt and pepper. Boil, reduce heat, and simmer for 3 to 5 minutes, depending on the size of the langoustines. Remove the langoustines with a slotted spoon and set aside. Bring a large pot of salted water to a boil, add the pasta, and cook for about 10 minutes. Drain the pasta and immediately mix in the oil. Rinse and drain the lettuce leaves. Peel and cut the celery into small thin strips. To prepare the rouille, mix the peeled and crushed garlic into the egg yolk. Add salt, the hot pepper, and the tomato paste. Beat with an electric mixer until the sauce reaches a uniform consistency. Beating constantly, gradually add the olive oil—almost drop by drop at first. When the sauce begins to thicken, pour the oil in a thin stream, but do not stop beating. After all the oil has been added, slowly add 1 tbsp. of cold water to stabilize the sauce. Mix a bit of the rouille into the pasta, which may be served warm or cold. Arrange the lettuce leaves in a circle on a large dish and place the pasta in the center. Put the cherry tomatoes, the langoustines, olives, and celery strips around the outside of the plate. Serve with croutons and a sauceboat of the remaining rouille.

NOTE BY **ALAIN DUCASSE** Select beautiful, large langoustines. Cut them in two and sear them on a baking sheet in the oven. This method works wonders. It also allows you to enjoy the pink "coral" inside the heads.

Pan-Fried Langoustines and *al Dente* Vegetables

Langoustines poêlées et légumes croquants

☆ ☆ ∞

Alain Ducasse

Serves 4 ◆ **Preparation time : 50 minutes** ◆ **Cooking time : 30 minutes**
20 large (2 kg) langoustines ◆ 7 oz. (200 g) green beans, tipped ◆ 6 purple baby artichokes ◆
4 tbsp. olive oil ◆ juice of 2 lemons ◆ 3 tbsp. truffle juice, optional ◆ salt and freshly ground
pepper ◆ 10 oz. (300 g) large red tomatoes, peeled, seeded, and diced ◆ 12 purple asparagus
tips, cut on the diagonal ◆ 5 oz. (150 g) medium chanterelle mushrooms, trimmed, cleaned,
and thinly sliced ◆ 7 oz. (200 g) small fava beans, shelled ◆ ½ cup minced chervil

Peel the langoustines. Insert a toothpick lengthwise along the tails to keep them from
curling. Set aside. **C**ook the green beans for 25 minutes in salted water, then refresh
in ice water to keep their color. Cut all the beans to the same length. Cut off the tips
of the artichoke leaves and remove the artichoke stems. Cut the artichokes in half
lengthwise, then thinly slice each half. **M**ake a spicy vinaigrette with 3 tbsp. of oil, the
lemon juice, and the truffle juice, if desired. Season with salt and pepper to taste. Mix
the green beans, artichokes, tomatoes, asparagus tips, mushrooms, and fava beans.
Add about 3 tbsp. of the vinaigrette and marinate at room temperature for 15 minutes.
Season with salt and pepper to taste. **F**ry the langoustines in the remaining oil. Drain
on paper towels and grind a little fresh pepper over them. Arrange a bed of the
marinated vegetables on each plate and top with 5 langoustines. Sprinkle with the
vinaigrette and minced chervil leaves. Serve immediately.

I am less finicky about presentation than our great chef. To save time, I wouldn't bother
with the toothpicks for the langoustines. Besides, aren't langoustine tails just as pretty
when they're curled? NOTE BY **FRANÇOISE BERNARD**

Mussels

Françoise Bernard can talk about mussels forever. As far as she is concerned, the fleshy and tasty cultivated *bouchot* mussel is by far the best. It keeps its consistency while cooking, whereas the Spanish mussel "loses all its meat" and dries quickly after it's cooked. Spanish mussels are only good raw, on a seafood tray. Françoise Bernard loves the mussel soups served in the south of France. She also enjoys the North-South combination of the *mouclade* soup from the Charente region (the mussels are stuffed with garlic and cooked in a curry sauce). At home, she generally cooks mussels with cream or *à la marinière*. For the *marinière* mussels, she prepares a bed of finely chopped shallots, adds some white wine and a few dabs of butter, and lays the mussels on top. As soon as the mussels are half open, she sprinkles them with chopped parsley and serves immediately. As she says, "The guests have to wait for the mussels, not the other way around!"

The cooking juice from mussels enhances sauces and makes delicious soups. Françoise Bernard freezes the juice in yogurt jars to keep a permanent supply of small quantities. She strains it through a paper filter first. She says that there is nothing better than mussel juice—with the possible exception of cockle juice. Alain Ducasse agrees that mussel juice is succulent, but this Southerner has never put mussels in the shell on his menu.

Alain Ducasse is not a man to dwell on his gourmet memories. He does not make a display of round-bellied pots, blackened by the heat of the fire, in which his grandmother used to cook her tasty stews. Neither does he say much about the desserts he ate as a child. But there is one exception to the rule: his mother's *poulette* mussels! Their aromatic juice, delicately creamy and tasting of egg yolk, is forever engraved in his memory.

Marinière Mussels, a Specialty of Les Halles Paris Market

Moules marinière comme aux halles

⌂ ○

Françoise Bernard

Serves 4 ♦ Preparation time : 30 minutes ♦ Cooking time : 15 minutes
4½ lbs. (2 kg) cultivated mussels ♦ 2 shallots, chopped ♦ ½ cup (10 cl) dry white wine ♦ pepper
♦ 6 tbsp. minced parsley

Scrub and rinse the mussels well, discarding those that are open or have a cracked shell. Put them in a pot with the shallots and wine. Boil over high heat for a few minutes, mixing as they cook so that all of them open. As soon as they open, remove the mussels with a slotted spoon, leaving the cooking juice in the pot. Boil some water in a medium-size pot. Put the mussels on a serving platter, cover with aluminum foil, and place the platter on top of the pot of boiling water to keep the mussels warm. **S**train the cooking juice through a sieve lined with paper towels to eliminate all the sand. (Do not strain the sandy liquid at the bottom of the pan—throw it away.) Transfer the strained liquid into a saucepan and boil for a few seconds. Season with pepper. Pour the strained sauce over the mussels, sprinkle with parsley, and serve. If you have a little extra time, remove shell halves from a few of the mussels and arrange them in a rosette pattern on top of the platter as decoration.

NOTE BY **ALAIN DUCASSE** You can prepare *poulette* mussels in the same way. Lightly reduce the cooking juice, thicken with crème fraîche, and add the yolk of 1 egg to finish. Do not boil after you add the yolk.

Creamed Mussels with Saffron

Crème de moules safranée

⌂ ○

Alain Ducasse

Serves 4 to 6 ✦ **Preparation time : 45 minutes** ✦ **Cooking time : 25 minutes**
4½ lbs. (2 kg) cultivated mussels ✦ **2 large shallots, thinly sliced** ✦ **1 cup (20 cl) white wine** ✦
1 tbsp. wine vinegar ✦ **1 tsp. thyme** ✦ **1 bay leaf** ✦ **2 carrots, diced** ✦ **1 bulb of fennel, diced** ✦ **3**
tbsp. butter ✦ **1½ tsp. chopped chervil** ✦ **3 cups (60 cl) light cream or half-and-half** ✦ **¼ tsp.**
saffron ✦ **2 egg yolks** ✦ **salt and pepper**

Scrub and rinse the mussels in plenty of water. In a large stockpot, boil the shallots, wine, vinegar, thyme, and bay leaf. Add the mussels, cover, and boil over high heat until they open, shaking the pot from time to time. Transfer to a large bowl with a slotted spoon. Remove the mussels from their shells. Strain the cooking juice. Sauté the carrots and the fennel in butter until lightly colored. Add the mussels and chervil. Over high heat, reduce the juice of the mussels to two-thirds its volume. Gradually pour in the cream, stirring with a whisk. Beat in the saffron and egg yolks. As soon as you have added the egg yolks, remove the pan from the heat. Season with salt and pepper to taste. Arrange the mussels and vegetables on individual plates. Cover with the cream, which should be very hot.

The cooking juice from the mussels makes an excellent sauce and a delicious soup. This creamy juice is extremely smooth! The touch of saffron will remind you of the Charente *mouclade* soup.

NOTE BY
FRANÇOISE
BERNARD

Mussels Stuffed with Garlic

Moules farcies à l'ail

⌂ ○

Françoise Bernard

Serves 4 ✦ **Preparation time : 30 minutes** ✦ **Cooking time : 10 minutes**
48 large mussels ✦ **8 tbsp. butter, softened** ✦ **1 bunch parsley** ✦ **4 garlic cloves** ✦ **3 shallots** ✦
salt and pepper

Preheat the oven to 450°F (240°C). **S**crub and rinse the mussels, making sure that they are all closed. Steam them with a dab of butter in a large pot over high heat until they open, stirring 2 or 3 times as they cook. As soon as they open, remove them from the heat. Remove one half-shell from each mussel. **F**inely chop the parsley, garlic, and shallots. Mix the remaining butter with the chopped ingredients and add salt and pepper to taste. Put a dollop of this herb butter on each mussel. **W**hen the oven is hot, change the oven setting to broil. Arrange the stuffed mussels on a large baking sheet or individual egg dishes and broil for 2 or 3 minutes. Do not leave the mussels under the broiler too long, or they'll be tough. **T**he mussels can be prepared in advance (stuffed and arranged on the dish) and put in the refrigerator. Then, the only thing to do at the last minute is broil them. You can also sprinkle the stuffed mussels with bread crumbs before baking them.

NOTE BY
ALAIN
DUCASSE
I rarely serve mussels in their shells. I prefer using their "essence," that is, their cooking juice, which is absolutely delicious. With a little bit of cream, it becomes quite a refined sauce. The cooking juices of other shellfish—cockles, for example—are less tasty and sometimes bitter.

Poulette Mussels

Moules poulette

⚲ ○

Alain Ducasse

Serves 4 ✦ **Preparation time : 30 minutes** ✦ **Cooking time : 30 minutes**
2¾ lbs. (1,2 kg) mussels ✦ 1 leek, white part only ✦ ¼ bulb of fennel ✦ 3 tbsp. butter ✦ 5 button mushrooms, cleaned, trimmed, and diced ✦ 2 shallots, finely chopped ✦ 4 stems of flat-leaf parsley ✦ ½ cup (10 cl) white wine ✦ ½ tsp. thyme leaves ✦ ½ cup (10 cl) crème fraîche ✦ 1 egg yolk ✦ salt and pepper ✦ pinch of curry powder or saffron, optional

Scrub and rinse the mussels several times and set aside. Clean the leek and fennel and slice into long, thin strips. Sauté in 1½ tbsp. of the butter, until they turn translucent—about 3 minutes. Add the mushrooms and cook for 3 more minutes. Set aside. In a large saucepan, sauté the chopped shallots and parsley stems in the remaining butter over low heat. Pour in the wine and boil for 5 minutes. Add the mussels and cook them, covered, until the shells open—about 5 minutes. Remove with a slotted spoon, arrange on a serving platter, and cover. Strain the cooking juice into a pot. Add the thyme and reduce over high heat to half its volume. Whisk in the crème fraîche. Reduce the heat, add the egg yolk, and continue to cook, stirring constantly with a wooden spoon until the sauce becomes smooth and slightly thick. Remove from the heat just before the mixture comes to a boil. Add the sautéed vegetables. Pour the sauce over the mussels and serve hot. You can also add a pinch of curry or saffron to the sauce to give it a beautiful color.

The vegetables add a new twist to this mussel recipe. The success of *poulette* mussels depends on the sauce, which must be very creamy. You can check that you are cooking the sauce at the right temperature by using your hand. After you add the egg yolk, your hand should be able to tolerate the heat from the pot for the rest of the time that the sauce is cooking—just as for a light custard.

NOTE BY **FRANÇOISE BERNARD**

Oysters

From the beginning of time, man has tried to use oysters in cooking, at first by necessity. The oysters were salted in order to preserve them to be cooked as needed. Today, oysters arrive fresh in our cities. The old belief, which dates back to Louis XIV, that it is safe to eat oysters only during months that contain the letter R (that is, not from May to August), is now obsolete—it is not essential to cook them. This habit stayed on for quite a long time, however.

Twentieth-century cookbooks suggest cooking oysters in a cream soup, or covered in a Mornay sauce, or on top of a spinach purée. The newest recipe is oysters in aspic, as served in the restaurant *Apicius,* which Françoise Bernard remembers fondly. But they'd better be cooked properly, she says—a few seconds too long, and you end up with a guaranteed rubber effect, she assures. Great chefs tolerate oysters in their sauces now. Most consider oysters as an ingredient and not as a base for a recipe. Françoise Bernard has been won over by Alain Ducasse's recipe for oysters in their own juices and cream, but she admits to "very rarely cooking oysters."

Apart from these few "beautiful" dishes, our two cooks, like all true aficionados, favor raw oysters from an oyster-man's stand. There are so many varieties—strong-tasting high-sea oysters, *Fines de Claire et Spéciales de Claire*, green *Marennes d'Oléron* oysters, flat oysters with a strong iodine taste. Eat them simply with one twist of the pepper mill and a slice of bread spread with salted butter or, as in Arcachon and Monaco, with traditional sausages or *crépinettes* and some red Bordeaux wine. "There is something that is both magical and cruel about this food. After eating a dozen live oysters, I absolve myself," Françoise Bernard confesses.

Oysters with a Spicy Sauce

Huîtres sauce piquante

û ∞

Françoise Bernard

Serves 4 ✦ Preparation time : 10 minutes ✦ 1 tbsp. mayonnaise ✦ 2 tbsp. tomato ketchup ✦ 1 tbsp. chili sauce ✦ salt and pepper ✦ paprika, optional ✦ 1 tbsp. horseradish, optional ✦ ice cubes ✦ 24 oysters

Beat the mayonnaise, ketchup, chili sauce, salt, and pepper with the paprika and horseradish, if desired. The sauce should be a thin, almost liquid mayonnaise. Pour into 4 small, individual shallow glasses and place the glasses in the center of 4 dinner plates **C**rush the ice cubes by wrapping them in a kitchen towel and lb.ing with a rolling pin. Put some crushed ice around each glass. **O**pen the oysters and arrange 6 on each plate around the glasses. Your guests can spoon some of the mayonnaise on the oysters before eating them.

NOTE BY **ALAIN DUCASSE** Always choose top-quality oysters. I like Belons or the flat oysters from the Bassin d'Arcachon. In my restaurant, I present oysters on a bed of ice covered with a layer of seaweed (available at any good fish market). The seaweed helps keep the oysters from becoming too cold, which will kill the taste.

Oyster Casserole with Shallots

Cassolette d'huîtres chaudes aux échalotes

⬠ ⬠ ⬠ ◠◠◠

Alain Ducasse

Serves 4 ♦ Preparation time : 55 minutes ♦ Cooking time : 1 hour 10 minutes
6 oz. (160 g) butter ♦ 3 shallots, long bulbs, peeled and cut lengthwise into fine slices ♦ 1 lb.
(450 g) very small waxy potatoes, scrubbed clean ♦ coarse gray sea salt ♦ freshly ground black
pepper ♦ 7 oz. cup (200 g) duck fat ♦ ½ tsp. thyme ♦ 1 bay leaf ♦ 4 garlic cloves, unpeeled ♦
2 gray shallots (strong-flavored shallots with a tough outer skin), finely chopped ♦ 2½ cups
(50 cl) champagne ♦ 24 medium oysters ♦ 1¼ cups (25 cl) light cream or half-and-half ♦ 10
oz. (300 g) baby spinach leaves, washed ♦ slices of warm rye bread topped with salted butter
swirls

Melt the butter in a small saucepan over low heat. Skim the foam from the surface and strain, leaving the milky residue in the bottom of the pan. Sauté the sliced shallots in 1 tbsp. of the clarified butter and drain on paper towels. Set aside. **S**eason the potatoes, to taste, with coarse salt and ground pepper. Simmer over low heat in the duck fat with the thyme, bay leaf, and garlic for about 1 hour. **S**often the gray shallots in a little of the clarified butter over low heat, add the champagne, and reduce to one-quarter its volume. **O**pen the oysters, reserving the liquid. Add the juice to the reduced champagne sauce. Reduce the sauce again to one-quarter its volume and add the cream, one third at a time, beating after each addition. Strain. **C**ook the spinach, covered, in a little butter over low heat until tender. Check the potatoes with the point of a knife for doneness, drain, and pat dry with paper towels. Slice the potatoes, place them in individual baking dishes, and cover with a spoonful of spinach and 6 oysters. Pour the sauce on top and heat under the broiler until brown and crisp. Garnish each serving with a few slices of the sliced shallots. Serve with slices of warm rye bread with salted butter swirls.

Combining two types of shallots add a particular refinement to this dish, but I don't believe that it is absolutely necessary. To reduce the cost of this recipe, I would suggest replacing the champagne with a good dry sparkling wine.

NOTE BY **FRANÇOISE BERNARD**

Oysters as I Love Them

Les huîtres comme je les aime

⌂ ◌◌◌

Françoise Bernard

Serves 4 ✦ Preparation time : 10 minutes ✦ 2 shallots, minced ✦ ½ cup (10 cl) vinegar ✦ seaweed, to line the serving platter ✦ 24 to 36 oysters, opened ✦ thinly sliced rye bread or country bread ✦ salted butter ✦ 1 lemon, quartered ✦ freshly ground pepper, optional

Combine the shallots and vinegar and transfer into small individual sauce bowls. Make a bed of seaweed on a large serving platter and arrange the oysters on top. Serve with sliced rye bread, butter, lemon wedges, and the bowls of shallot vinaigrette. Invite those guests who love pepper to give one twist of the mill to each of their oysters.

NOTE BY **ALAIN DUCASSE** There are many ways to enjoy oysters. Some connoisseurs eat them with vinegar, lemon, lightly salted butter, and pepper. Personally, I favor the twist of the pepper mill.

Oysters with Cream Sauce and Grilled Sausages

Huîtres au jus crémé, crépinette grillée

⌂ ⌂ ∞

Alain Ducasse

Serves 4 ✦ Preparation time : 40 minutes ✦ Cooling time : 40 minutes ✦ Cooking time : 20 minutes ✦ 10 peppercorns ✦ zest of 1 orange, cut into thin strips ✦ 1 leek, white part only ✦ 1 medium carrot ✦ 2 scallions, trimmed ✦ 1½ (20 g) tbsp. butter ✦ ¼ cup (5 cl) white wine ✦ 20 medium Belon oysters ✦ 1 cup (20 cl) crème fraîche or sour cream ✦ juice of 1 lemon ✦ 4 pork, lamb, or veal *crépinettes* or sausage links ✦ 4 oz. (100 g) *mâche*, or lambs lettuce washed ✦ 2 tsp. chopped chervil ✦ 4 tbsp. caviar, optional

Tie the peppercorns and orange zest in a small cheesecloth pouch. Cut the leek into fine strips and the carrot and scallions into rounds. Sauté the vegetables in butter for about 2 minutes. Deglaze with the wine, boil, and add 1 cup of water and the cheesecloth pouch. Simmer for 15 minutes over low heat, remove, and let the bouillon cool. **O**pen the oysters, reserving the liquid. Heat the oysters and juice in a saucepan until the liquid starts to bubble. Immediately remove the pan from the heat and let the oysters cool for about 30 seconds. Remove the oysters from the pan with a skimmer and drain on a cloth. **A**dd an equal amount of the vegetable bouillon to the oyster broth in the saucepan. Reduce to one-half its volume. Add the crème fraîche, bring to a boil—this sauce must remain relatively liquid—and add the lemon juice. Remove from the heat and let cool, adjusting the seasoning if necessary. **G**rill the *crépinettes* until done, about 15 minutes, depending on their size. Arrange the mâche in a circle in 4 soup dishes. Place 5 oysters and a few vegetables in the middle of each circle, top with the cream sauce, sprinkle with chervil, and serve with the hot *crépinettes*. If you like, you can replace the *crépinettes* with a tbsp. of caviar, placed in the center of each serving.

It would be a pity to change anything in this succulent recipe. To keep it simple, I would not replace the *crépinettes* with caviar.

NOTE BY
FRANÇOISE BERNARD

Scallops

When the season for scallops begins in October, Françoise Bernard begins to looks forward to the fragrant fricassee she will cook. It's so good with chopped parsley and garlic! Or she will bake scallops, covered in cream. Or maybe grill them on a skewer. No, she has made up her mind—she will slice the scallops thin and leave them under the broiler for a short time. How delightful, with some *mâche*, a twist of the pepper mill, and a drizzle of olive oil. Françoise Bernard is open to anything new. She is crazy about hot and cold contrasts. She enjoys the scallop salad with Parmesan cheese pancakes created by Alain Ducasse—a perfect match of boldness and balance. She loves the uncooked white meat of the scallops as an appetizer, sliced very thin and topped with a delicate marinade. She even enjoys them en tartare, that is, raw.

"In the past, the scallop was always served cooked, even overcooked," she says. "Today's cooking methods are much more respectful of its delicate taste." Scallops cooked in an aromatic court bouillon must never be boiled, but only barely simmered for three minutes. Cooking them too aggressively or for too long will toughen them.

When she has a little time, Françoise Bernard steams scallops and serves them with a shallot *beurre blanc*. This recipe respects the refined character of the seafood. Alain Ducasse feels the same way about scallops. He is always trying to preserve the natural taste—so he prefers to serve scallops very simply, with some grated white truffle, for example, or a lettuce coulis.

Our two specialists are adamant on this point. When choosing scallops, buy them in the shell, large and alive. This is the only way to be sure that the white meat will not expel water while cooking and that the flavor of the sea will linger in your mouth.

Scallops with Cream

Coquilles Saint-Jacques à la crème

⇧ ⇧ ⇧   ◌◌◌

Françoise Bernard

Serves 4 ✦ **Preparation time : 35 minutes** ✦ **Cooking time : 20 minutes**
2 shallots, chopped ✦ **1 bouquet garni** ✦ **1 garlic clove** ✦ **salt and pepper** ✦ **2 cups (40 cl) dry**
white wine ✦ **16 scallops, shelled** ✦ **1 tbsp. (30 g) butter** ✦ **1 tbsp. (10 g) flour** ✦ **2 egg yolks** ✦
2 tbsp. crème fraîche or sour cream

To make a court bouillon, boil the shallots, bouquet garni, garlic, salt, pepper, wine, and 2 cups (40 cl) of water for 5 minutes. Remove from the heat and let cool in the pot. Carefully clean the scallops. Bring the court bouillon almost to a boil and poach the scallops for 3 minutes. Strain 2 cups (40 cl) of the court bouillon. Set the pot aside, keeping it warm. Melt the butter in a small saucepan over low heat and blend in the flour. When the mixture starts to bubble, add the strained bouillon. Stir with a wooden spoon over low heat until the mixture thickens slightly—the finished sauce should be somewhat liquid. Simmer over low heat for a few minutes. Lightly beat the egg yolks and the crème fraîche. Mix in a little of the warm sauce to temper the yolks, and then pour the egg-yolk mixture into the saucepan. Strain the rest of the court bouillon, reserving the scallops. Warm the court bouillon over low heat for a short time, stirring constantly. Remove from the heat just before it comes to a boil; the sauce should be somewhat thickened. Pour some of the sauce into a deep serving dish, add the warm scallops, smother them with the rest of the sauce, and serve.

NOTE BY **ALAIN DUCASSE** You can fry the scallops instead of poaching them. The current trend is to cook them very little. Some people even dare to eat them almost raw inside and only warm on the outside.

Grilled Scallops with Parmesan Galettes

Coquilles Saint-Jacques grillées et galettes de parmesan

⇧ ⇧ ◌◌◌

Alain Ducasse

Serves 4 ◆ Preparation time : 50 minutes ◆ Cooking time : 10 minutes
24 large scallops, shelled ◆ 8 tbsp. (250 g) butter ◆ 1½ cups (100 g) mesclun greens ◆ 1½ cups (100 g) red oak leaf lettuce ◆ 1 small head radicchio ◆ ½ cup (10 cl) olive oil ◆ ¼ cup (5 cl) sherry vinegar ◆ ¼ cup (5 cl) balsamic vinegar ◆ sea salt and freshly ground pepper ◆ ½ cup (60 g) grated Parmesan cheese ◆ 1 tbsp. (10 g) flour ◆ about 1½ cups (100 g) *mâche* or lambs lettuce ◆ 12 sprigs of fresh chervil, leaves only ◆ ¼ cup chopped chives

Preheat the oven to 450°F (240°C) **C**lean and rinse the scallops well, removing as much sand as possible. Place in a large bowl, seal with plastic wrap, and refrigerate. Heat the butter in a pan until it stops foaming and turns hazelnut gold, then strain. **W**ash and dry the mesclun, oak leaf lettuce, and radicchio. Reserve 1 tbsp. of the olive oil and mix the rest with half of each of the vinegars. Season with salt and pepper to taste. Mix the salad greens with the vinaigrette. **T**o make the galettes, combine the Parmesan cheese and flour. Spread small clumps of the mixture in a very hot nonstick pan and sauté over low heat. **B**rush the scallops with the reserved oil. Sauté quickly in a frying pan over high heat and set aside on a greased baking dish. Whisk together the browned butter and the remaining vinegar. **D**ecorate the plates with a fan of *mâche* and neat, loose bunches of salad greens. Bake the scallops for 1 minute. Arrange the scallops around the greens, adding a pinch of salt to each. Cover the scallops with the browned butter sauce and arrange the Parmesan galettes. Sprinkle the whole plate with chervil leaves and chopped chives, and serve immediately.

These small Parmesan galettes have been very much in style in recent years. Their texture and salty flavor mix well with scallops. The thinner they are, the crunchier and crispier they will be. To give them a pretty, round form, Alain Ducasse shapes them with a mold.

NOTE BY **FRANÇOISE BERNARD**

Scallops in the Style of Nantes

Coquilles Saint-Jacques nantaises

⇧ ⇧ ◌◌◌

Françoise Bernard

Serves 4 ✦ **Soaking time : 1 hour** ✦ **Preparation time : 35 minutes** ✦
Cooking time : 30 minutes ✦ **8 scallops** ✦ **4 oz. (100 g) mushrooms** ✦ **1 shallot** ✦ **5 tbsp.**
(70 g) butter ✦ **1 cup (20 cl) dry white muscadet wine** ✦ **salt and pepper** ✦ **¾ cup (100 g) white**
bread crumbs ✦ **4 tbsp. minced parsley, chervil, and chives**

Ask the fishmonger to open the scallops, leaving on the beards. Cut off the beards
and soak the scallops for 1 hour, changing the water regularly. Rinse the white meat
and the pink coral tails. Wash the 4 best-looking shell halves and set aside. **C**lean the
mushrooms, removing the ends of the stems. Peel the shallot. Chop the mushrooms,
shallot, and scallop beards and sauté in 2 tbsp. of butter over low heat. Add the wine
and salt and pepper to taste. Simmer for 20 minutes. **D**ice the white part of the scallops
(not the coral). Add to the mushroom mixture and simmer lightly for 3 minutes. Add
just enough bread crumbs to absorb the liquid, making sure that the mixture does not
become too dry. Add the minced herbs. Spoon the mixture into the 4 reserved half-
shells. Place raw coral on each serving, sprinkle with the remaining bread crumbs, and
dot with the remaining butter. Brown the filled shells under the broiler for about 2
minutes.

NOTE BY **ALAIN DUCASSE** The scallop does not like prolonged cooking or temperatures that are too high. Don't
cut the scallops into too small pieces. Protect them with the stuffing so that they don't
burn under the broiler.

Sautéed Scallops with Cream of Lettuce

Coquilles Saint-Jacques poêlées à la crème de laitue

⏶ ⏶ ⦵⦵

Alain Ducasse

Serves 4 ✦ **Preparation time : 35 minutes** ✦ **Cooking time : 10 minutes**
20 firm scallops, shelled ✦ **2 heads Boston lettuce** ✦ **1 cup (20 cl) chicken stock (page 322)** ✦
10 peppercorns ✦ **1 tbsp. cornstarch** ✦ **6 tbsp. (80 g) butter** ✦ **sea salt**

Remove the beards from the scallops. Rinse the scallops well, making sure to remove the sand, and set aside on a clean cloth in a cool place. Clean the lettuce, keeping only the outer green leaves. **B**oil the chicken stock. Add the lettuce leaves and cook for 1 minute. Remove the leaves and refresh under running cold water to keep their color. Drain, purée in a food processor, then strain through a sieve. **A**dd the peppercorns to the stock and bring to a simmering boil. Stir the cornstarch into 1 tbsp. of water and add to the stock. Boil for 2 minutes and strain. Heat 2 tbsp. of butter in a frying pan until it turns hazelnut gold, then remove from heat. Blend the warm lettuce purée and the butter into the stock and whip to a creamy mayonnaise texture with an electric stick blender or a whisk. **H**eat the remaining butter in a frying pan. When it starts to foam, sauté the scallops for 4 minutes, then drain on paper towels. Pour the warm lettuce cream on the plates and arrange the scallops on top. Sprinkle each scallop with a pinch of salt and serve immediately.

Buy live scallops, in their shells, and have the fishmonger open them for you. I cut the scallops in half, widthwise, so they brown more quickly in the butter. When you cook them for only a short time, any coral attached to the scallops is less likely to burst open.   NOTE BY **FRANÇOISE BERNARD**

Shrimp

There are more than 162 species of shrimp, but only 5 of them are really familiar to Europeans: the brown shrimp; the sword shrimp (pink in color and 5 in. [13 cm] long at most), which the French call bouquet; the pink prawn, netted in deep ocean waters; the Nordic red prawn (6.5 in. [16 cm] at most); and the tropical pink prawn (a giant, which can be 11 in. [28 cm] long). *Gamba* is a term that applies to a medium-to-large shrimp or prawn, reserved for the broiler or the frying pan.

Françoise Bernard's preferences are the brown shrimp and the bouquet shrimp—but, of course, you will have to use what you can find, especially if you don't live on a seacoast. That is the difference between the home cook and the master chef: Chefs can more easily contact fishermen to get the best of what they need. Whatever kind of shrimp you choose, it must not smell of ammonia. It's best to buy live shrimps, but this is often not possible when you live far from the sea.

Alain Ducasse also likes bouquet shrimp, which he serves in a soup in his restaurant in Paris. His preference is for the large shrimp called *gamberoni* in Italian. He puts them in a salad, a very tasteful and rich cocktail with rock octopus, *supions* (small cuttlefish from the Mediterranean), clams, fresh vegetables, beans, and other ingredients. Françoise Bernard thinks that this recipe should be awarded three stars. This is, she says, "a famous chef's recipe for amateur chefs, who will have to follow the whole process step by step and stick to its every detail." More modestly, she serves her shrimp cold with a spicy cocktail sauce or fried crisp in the Italian fashion.

Mediterranean aromas mix well with shrimp, but a little exotic touch doesn't hurt either, as Alain Ducasse knows well. He has adapted a well-known Thai soup recipe, in which the characteristic scents of fresh lemongrass and lime enhance the iodine taste of the shrimp. Alain Ducasse and Françoise Bernard have different ideas about shrimp, but both insist on utilizing every bit of it. Both of them crush the heads and the shells (which amount to about 50 percent of the total weight) to bring out all the "perfume" of the shrimp and give body to the sauce.

Shrimp Fritters

Beignets de crevette

⌂ ∞

Françoise Bernard

Serves 4 ♦ Preparation time : 15 minutes ♦ Cooking time : 5 minutes
20 large shrimp, fresh or frozen, peeled and deveined ♦ milk, or oil and lemon juice marinade,
optional ♦ 2 egg whites ♦ salt ♦ 1 tsp. lemon juice ♦ 2 tbsp. cornstarch ♦ 2 quarts (2 l) vegetable
oil, for frying

If the shrimp are frozen, defrost them in the refrigerator—preferably, in milk or the marinade. Beat the egg whites, 2 pinches of salt, and a few drops of lemon juice to form stiff peaks. Sprinkle the cornstarch on top of the beaten egg whites and gradually fold in with a wooden spoon. Heat the oil in a large, deep pan until very hot but not smoking. Dip the shrimps into the egg white batter and drop 4 or 5 into the oil at a time, depending on their size. When they are golden brown, lift them out with a slotted spoon, drain on paper towels, and serve hot.

NOTE BY **ALAIN DUCASSE**   I am especially fond of light batters. I would opt for a Japanese tempura batter, made with rice flour and ice water.

Jumbo Shrimp and Italian Vegetable Salad

Grosses crevettes à l'italienne

♔ ♔ ♔ ∞

Alain Ducasse

Serves 4 ♦ Preparation time : 2 hours ♦ Marinating time : 3 hours ♦ Cooking time : 4 hours ♦ 1¾ lbs. (800 g) littleneck or cherrystone clams ♦ 2 small octopus ♦ 8 oz. (200 g) bulb fennel ♦ 4 Roma or plum tomatoes ♦ 4 shallots ♦ ½ cup (10 cl) olive oil ♦ 1½ cups (30 cl) white wine ♦ 3 lemons, individually juiced ♦ 12 large shrimps or prawns ♦ 8 ounces (200 g) fresh white beans or dried white beans, soaked overnight ♦ 2 garlic cloves ♦ 1 sprig fresh thyme ♦ 15 peppercorns ♦ 1 lb. (400 g) cleaned small cuttlefish ♦ ¼ cup chopped flat-leaf parsley ♦ 8 oven-dried tomatoes (page 231), cut into strips ♦ salt and pepper ♦ 1 head romaine ♦ 1 bunch arugula ♦ 1 cup chopped fresh basil ♦ olive oil, for drizzling

Place the clams in cold water for 3 to 4 hours to clean out the sand. Rinse and boil the octopus. Dice the fennel, 2 Roma tomatoes, and 2 shallots. Sauté in 1 tbsp. of olive oil, then add octopus and ½ cup (10 cl) wine. Add water to cover and simmer for 2 to 3 hours. Remove from the heat and let cool. Remove and discard the outer skins of the octopus. Marinate the octopus for 3 hours in ¼ cup (5 cl) oil and the juice of 1 lemon. Thinly slice the 2 remaining Roma tomatoes and shallots. Sauté the heads of the shrimps in 1 tbsp. of olive oil over high heat. Crush them and mix in the sliced shallots and tomatoes. Cook over low heat until thickened into a coulis, about 10 minutes. Add ½ cup (10 cl) wine and reduce for 5 minutes. Add water to cover and cook 15 minutes more. Purée the coulis in a food processor, strain, return to heat, and boil. Add 1 tbsp. lemon juice and 1 tbsp. olive oil and purée again in the food processor. Cook the beans with the garlic, thyme, peppercorns, and 1 tbsp. of olive oil until done (less than 1 hour for fresh beans, longer for dried beans). Remove the garlic, thyme, and peppercorns. Sauté the cuttlefish in 2 tbsp. of olive oil for 5 minutes, then remove from heat. Fry the shrimps in the remaining olive oil 5 minutes. Put the clams in a large pot, add ½ cup (10 cl) of the wine, cover, and cook 10 minutes. Strain the cooking juice and reduce for 10 minutes. Add the parsley and remaining lemon juice. Combine the shrimp, cuttlefish, clams, beans and oven-dried tomatoes. Season with salt and pepper. Mix the romaine and arugula and top with the shrimp-bean-tomato mixture. Sprinkle with chopped basil and the shrimp sauce. Drizzle a little olive oil on top and serve.

If you place small octopus and cuttlefish in the freezer for about 1 hour, it will be easier to remove their ink pouches. Leave large octopus in the freezer all night, and they will be easier to peel.

NOTE BY
**FRANÇOISE
BERNARD**

Kiwi Shrimp Cocktail

Cocktail de crevettes au kiwi

⌂ ∞

Françoise Bernard

Serves 4 ◆ Marinating time : 30 minutes ◆ Preparation time : 20 minutes
12 oz. (300 g) cooked large shrimp or prawns ◆ 1 tbsp. rum ◆ 1 egg yolk ◆ ½ tsp. mustard ◆
¾ cup (15 cl) safflower oil ◆ ½ tsp. vinegar or lemon juice ◆ 1 tbsp. crème fraîche or sour
cream ◆ 10 chives, snipped ◆ 2 pinches of cayenne or a few drops of Tabasco ◆ salt and pepper
◆ 4 lettuce leaves, cut into chiffonade ◆ 2 kiwis

Set aside 4 large shrimps then peel and devein the others. Place the peeled shrimps
in a large bowl and marinate in the rum for 30 minutes. Make a mayonnaise with the
egg yolk, mustard, and oil. Whisk together the egg yolk and mustard. Gradually drizzle
in the oil, whisking constantly until smooth. Whisk in the vinegar, crème fraîche, chives,
cayenne, and salt and pepper to taste. Spoon the mayonnaise over the shrimp and
mix gently. Layer the lettuce chiffonade alternately with the shrimp mixture in four
wide shallow glasses. Peel the kiwis, slice into thin rounds, and arrange in a circle on
top of the lettuce and shrimp. Perch 1 unshelled shrimp on the rim of each glass and
refrigerate until serving.

NOTE BY **ALAIN DUCASSE** You can replace the kiwi and mayonnaise with a marmalade made from the peels and
pulp of citrus fruits (orange, grapefruit, and lemon). Spice up the sauce with a mixture
of ground aromatic peppercorns, a shellfish coulis (made with the heads of the shrimp),
and some vinegar.

Shrimp in Thai Broth

Crevettes au bouillon thaïlandais

⌂ ○

Alain Ducasse

Serves 4 ⋆ **Preparation time : 35 minutes** ⋆ **Cooking time : 15 minutes**
1 small piece (15 g) galangal or ginger, available in Asian markets ⋆ 2 pieces lemongrass ⋆ 2½
cups (50 cl) chicken stock (page 322) ⋆ 2 bergamot leaves ⋆ 2 tbsp. sugar ⋆ 4 tbsp. fish sauce,
such as *nuoc-nam* ⋆ 10 oyster mushrooms, cleaned and cut into large pieces ⋆ 20 raw large
shrimps or prawns, peeled and deveined ⋆ ½ cup chopped chives ⋆ ½ cup chopped cilantro
leaves ⋆ juice of 1 lime ⋆ 2 tsp. red curry oil or 4 pinches of red curry powder, available in
Asian markets

Peel the galangal and lemongrass with a knife and cut into slivers. Heat the stock in
a wok or frying pan. Add the galangal, lemongrass, bergamot, sugar, fish sauce, and
mushrooms. Bring to a boil. Poach the shrimp for 5 minutes in the broth, then add
the chives and cilantro. Portion the lime juice into 4 soup bowls. Pour in the hot soup
and place 5 shrimp in each bowl. Add a few drops of the red curry oil or a pinch of
red curry powder to each serving. Serve immediately.

This soup is exotic and delicious, even without the galangal, which tastes like ginger
but is more difficult to find.

NOTE BY
**FRANÇOISE
BERNARD**

Dogfish

No fish is more preposterous than the dogfish. This cartilaginous fish belongs to the shark family, and it is sold skinned. It has a single spine down the center of its long body, which is very easy to remove. By comparison, one-third of a whiting has to be discarded.

Dogfish is popular because of its low price and because it doesn't have any bones. It is perfect for everyday cooking. Its meat is firm, and its salmon pink color is very attractive. It glistens like jelly on ice. The pink color also allows you to cheat a little—you can cook this fish in place of salmon. "You may sometimes run across recipes for dogfish with sorrel or *à l'Américaine*. This is too much of an honor for such a simple fish," Françoise Bernard says. She prefers cooking it as a cassoulet with beans or boiled with a Provençal sauce. These are simple and affordable recipes. They are well suited to the dogfish, which is not only inexpensive, but also quite economical—almost nothing is wasted.

You can also cook dogfish as you would cook skate. Alain Ducasse serves it with a *grenobloise* sauce—small croutons, capers, and diced lemon pulp. Although he generally uses garlic sparingly, Ducasse sautés dogfish in garlic butter to give some spirit to the taste, which is a bit bland. A few grains of sea salt and some freshly ground pepper would also be welcome. Ducasse serves the fish with mashed potatoes that are also flavored with garlic.

Dogfish Casserole

Roussette en cassoulet

⇧ ⇧ ○

Françoise Bernard

Serves 4 ♦ Preparation time : 25 minutes ♦ Cooking time : 25 minutes
16 oz. (440 g) can cooked white beans, such as navy or Great Northern beans ♦ 4 tbsp. flour
♦ 2¼ lbs. (1 kg) dogfish, cut into 4 pieces ♦ 4 tbsp. (50 g) butter ♦ 2 garlic cloves, chopped ♦
4 onions, chopped ♦ 16 oz. (440 g) can whole peeled tomatoes, drained and diced ♦ ¾ cup
(15 cl) dry white wine ♦ pinch of sugar ♦ salt and pepper ♦ 3 tbsp. bread crumbs

Heat some water in a saucepan. Remove from heat, add the beans, and let soak for 5 minutes to rinse and warm them. Sprinkle the flour onto a plate. Season the fish with salt and pepper, then roll them quickly in the flour. Melt 2 tbsp. of the butter in a stew pot and sauté the fish on both sides. Add the garlic, onions, tomatoes, wine, sugar, and salt and pepper to taste. Cover and cook for 5 minutes. Remove the fish. Drain the beans and add to the pot. Season with salt and pepper and simmer for 10 minutes. Pour the mixture into a baking dish, add the fish, sprinkle with bread crumbs, and dot with the remaining butter. Brown the casserole under the broiler for 5 minutes.

NOTE BY **ALAIN DUCASSE**   I would cook the beans in some chicken stock or in water with a bouillon cube. Do not season the bouillon with salt because it tends to harden the skin of the beans.

Dogfish *Grenoblois*

Roussette à la grenobloise

⌂ ⌂ ○

Alain Ducasse

Serves 4 ✦ Preparation time : 40 minutes ✦ Cooking time : 30 minutes
4 slices of bread without the crust ✦ ¾ cup (15 cl) olive oil ✦ 4 garlic cloves ✦ 4 medium
potatoes, scrubbed ✦ 8 tbsp. (100 g.) butter ✦ Fine sea salt and freshly ground pepper ✦ 4
dogfish steaks, 12 oz. (350 g) each ✦ 3 tbsp. flour ✦ 4 tsp. small capers ✦ 3 lemons, skinned,
segmented and diced ✦ ½ cup (10 cl) milk ✦ 5 tbsp. chopped parsley ✦ coarse sea salt and
freshly ground pepper

Cut the bread into small squares and sauté in 2 to 3 tbsp. of the olive oil until golden brown. Heat ½ cup (10 cl) olive oil and 2 garlic cloves. Remove from heat and set aside to infuse. Cook the potatoes in boiling salted water for about 20 minutes. Heat 3 tbsp. butter and the remaining garlic in a frying pan over very low heat. Season the fish steaks with salt and pepper to taste, flour them, and cook in the foaming butter, basting often. Melt 2 tbsp. of butter over low heat. When it begins to turn a light hazelnut brown, add the capers, diced lemon, and, at the last minute, the croutons. Sauté for a few minutes and season with salt and pepper to taste. Peel the potatoes. Mash them lightly with a fork while adding the milk. Mix in the garlic-oil infusion and the chopped parsley, without mashing too much. Arrange the dogfish steaks on individual plates and place a mound of mashed potatoes on the side. Drizzle with the crouton mixture and sprinkle with a few grains of coarse sea salt and pepper. Serve immediately.

This should be one of your everyday recipes. It's not expensive to make, requires only readily available ingredients, and does not take long to prepare.

NOTE BY
FRANÇOISE
BERNARD

Traditional Dogfish in the Pot

Roussette en cocotte à l'ancienne

⌂ ○

Françoise Bernard

Serves 4 ✦ Preparation time : 30 minutes ✦ Cooking time : 25 minutes
4 onions, chopped ✦ 1 tbsp. oil ✦ 3 tbsp. butter ✦ 2 garlic cloves, chopped ✦ 4 tomatoes, seeded
and chopped ✦ salt and pepper ✦ 2¼ lbs. (1 kg) dogfish, cut into 4 steaks ✦ ¼ tsp. saffron ✦ 4
slices of bread without the crust

Lightly sauté the onions in a pot with the oil and half the butter. Add the garlic, tomatoes, salt, and pepper and cook for 5 minutes. Add the fish steaks, burying them under the vegetables. Sprinkle with the saffron and the rest of the butter cut in small pieces. Season with salt and pepper to taste. Cover and cook over low heat for 10 to 15 minutes. Toast the bread. Place 1 slice of toast on each plate and 1 fish steak on top. Arrange a bit of the vegetable garnish around each plate, and serve immediately.

NOTE BY **ALAIN DUCASSE** To preserve the tenderness of the fish, be sure not to overcook it. About 10 to 12 minutes should be enough. If you would like to make a vegetable compote, leave the vegetables on the stove for 5 to 10 minutes longer before adding the fish to the pot.

Baked Dogfish with Swiss Chard and Chicken Sauce

Roussette au four, blettes et jus du poulet

♔ ♔ ◯

Alain Ducasse

Serves 4 ◆ Preparation time : 1 hour ◆ Cooking time : 1 hour 15 minutes
10 garlic cloves, unpeeled ◆ 1 cup (20 cl) olive oil ◆ 4 dogfish steaks, 10 oz. (300 g) each ◆ 4½
lbs. (2 kg) Swiss chard ◆ 1 quart (1 l) chicken stock (page 322) ◆ 4 tbsp. (50 g) butter ◆ 2
ounces (50 g) slab bacon, blanched and diced ◆ 2 carrots, diced ◆ 1 cup (100 g) diced button
mushrooms ◆ 2 scallions, diced ◆ 1 small stalk celery, diced ◆ ½ cup (10 cl) chicken jus (page
323) ◆ 1 tbsp. sherry vinegar ◆ salt and freshly ground pepper

Preheat the oven to 175°F (80°C). Bake the garlic cloves in ½ cup (10 cl) olive oil for 1 hour. Peel and cut into quarters, discarding the inner germinating sprouts, if any. Make small slits in the fish steaks and insert the garlic pieces. Tie the steaks by wrapping kitchen string around them 3 or 4 times to hold their shape. Raise the oven temperature to 350°F (180°C). Wash the Swiss chard, separating the stalks from the leaves. Set aside the leaves. Cut the stalks into pieces 3 in. (8 cm) long. Cook, covered, over low heat in 2 tbsp. of the olive oil. Check for doneness with a fork. Add the stock and 3½ tbsp. of the butter. Reduce until it has almost completely evaporated. In a baking dish, layer the Swiss chard stalks alternately with layers of bacon. Sauté the carrots, mushrooms, scallions, and celery in 2 tbsp. of olive oil until translucent. Transfer to the baking dish. Season the dogfish with salt and pepper to taste and sauté over high heat in the remaining olive oil. Arrange the fish steaks on top of the vegetables, baste with chicken jus, and add the remaining butter and a few drops of olive oil. Bake for 10 minutes, basting often. Turn off the oven. Spoon out some cooking juice and mix with a few drops of olive oil to make a sauce, adding a dash of sherry vinegar. Sauté the Swiss chard leaves in a little olive oil. Place the baked vegetables on a serving plate and lay the dogfish steaks on top. Arrange the Swiss chard leaves around the edge of the plate. Drizzle with a little sauce and a few drops of olive oil.

Alain Ducasse's Dogfish *Grenoblois* (page 55) is very flavorful, whereas this recipe is very light and subtle. Chicken stock, which is unexpected with fish, rounds off the dish nicely.

NOTE BY
FRANÇOISE
BERNARD

Hake

Colin is the French name for hake, a variety of fresh cod. Françoise Bernard is very fond of round, white-meat fish, like fresh cod, pollack, and haddock, all of which are easy to prepare. She asks her fishmonger to cut the fish right in front of her. "If you buy it already sliced, be sure that the meat is white enough, firm, not slimy, and that it does not smell bad," she advises.

Françoise Bernard cooks hake very simply—under the broiler and lightly drizzled with lemon juice, seasoned with salt and pepper. She also likes it topped with a butter-lemon sauce, but, floured and pan-fried in butter, it's a real treat. "Flour the fish lightly to get it completely dry. The minute the flour comes in contact with a hot, greased surface, it will form a golden crust. This crust makes the fish look good, and it enriches its flavor." Irresistible! When she wants her fish tender rather than crisp, she braises it in the oven with parsley, shallots, white wine, lemon juice, and grated nutmeg.

Alain Ducasse also cooks hake simply—with a light sea-soning of mashed lemon and green vegetables, for example. His baked hake steak has a childlike simplicity. He arranges the fish in an earthenware baking dish, tops it with slices of lemon and tomato, bastes it in chicken stock, and bakes for a short time to cook off the juices. That's it! His trick: He drizzles a little lemon juice over the hake so that it remains firm while baking. Ducasse has one minor regret about this fish—its size, which he thinks is too small. Françoise Ber-nard regrets the price.

Oven-Baked Hake

Colin au four

⌂ ○

Françoise Bernard

Serves 4 ◆ Preparation time : 15 minutes ◆ Cooking time : 15 minutes
4 slices of hake ◆ 1 cup chopped parsley ◆ 1 shallot, chopped ◆ 1¼ cups (25 cl) white wine ◆
Juice of ½ lemon ◆ 2 pinches of grated nutmeg ◆ Salt and pepper ◆ 4 tbsp. (50 g) butter, cut
into small pieces ◆ 2 tbsp. bread crumbs

Preheat the oven to 425°F (220°C). Butter a baking dish that is large enough to hold
the 4 slices of hake. Reserve some of the chopped parsley and mix the rest with the
shallot. Sprinkle the bottom of the dish with the chopped herbs. Lay the slices of hake
on top, add the white wine, lemon juice, and grated nutmeg. Add salt and pepper to
taste. Dot with all but 1 tbsp. of the butter. Bake for about 15 minutes, basting the
fish a few times while baking. With a slotted spoon, gently remove the hake and place
each slice on a warmed dinner plate. Mix the bread crumbs, the reserved parsley, and
the rest of the butter with the cooking juice in the baking dish. Pour this sauce over
the fish and serve.

NOTE BY **ALAIN DUCASSE** If you have time, marinate the hake in lemon juice and salt for about 30 minutes. This
quick marinade will make the fish slices firm so that they hold together well while
baking.

Roasted Hake with Eggplant Caviar

Colin rôti et caviar d'aubergine

⚬ ⚬ ◯

Alain Ducasse

Serves 4 ✦ **Preparation time : 45 minutes** ✦ **Cooking time : 45 minutes**
10 small eggplants ✦ **10 garlic cloves, quartered** ✦ **20 anchovy fillets** ✦ **1¾ cups (200 g) bread**
crumbs ✦ **grated zest of 1 lemon** ✦ **10 sprigs parsley (about 5 tbsp. chopped)** ✦ **3 white onions,**
diced ✦ **1 tbsp. olive oil** ✦ **1 tsp. marjoram** ✦ **salt and freshly ground pepper** ✦ **4 tbsp. (50 g)**
butter ✦ **4 skinless hake steaks, about 6 oz. (160 g) each** ✦ **anchovy butter, for garnish, optional**

Preheat the oven to 350°F (180°C). **C**ut 4 slits in each eggplant and place a piece of
garlic in each slit. Wrap each eggplant in aluminum foil and bake for 35 minutes. Mash
the anchovies with a fork and mix with the bread crumbs, lemon zest, and chopped
parsley. Remove the eggplants from the oven, scoop out the pulp, and chop it well.
Brown the onions in the oil. Add the eggplant pulp, marjoram, and salt and pepper
to taste. Cover to keep warm and set aside. **M**elt the butter over low heat. First, roll
the pieces of hake in the butter, then dip them in the bread-crumb mixture. Roast the
hake for 8 minutes on a skewer or in a pan with melted butter. As soon as the fish is
done, season with salt and pepper to taste. **A**rrange a circle of the eggplant "caviar"
at the center of each of 4 plates and gently place 1 piece of hake on top. Top the fish
with a little anchovy butter before serving, if you wish.

What a good idea! Stuff the eggplant with garlic, then bake in aluminum foil. It's novel **NOTE BY**
and quite practical. Cooking in aluminum foil is also healthier than cooking in a frying **FRANÇOISE**
pan, where the vegetables will quickly soak up the oil. **BERNARD**

Sautéed Hake, *Meunière*-Style

Colin meunière

⌂ ⌂ ○

Françoise Bernard

Serves 4 ✦ **Preparation time : 10 minutes** ✦ **Cooking time : 15 minutes**
4 hake steaks, about 7 oz. (200 g) each ✦ **salt and pepper** ✦ **2 tbsp. flour** ✦ **5 tbsp. (70 g) butter**
✦ **2 lemons** ✦ **6 sprigs parsley, chopped**

Wash the fish, pat dry with paper towels, and season with salt and pepper to taste. Dredge the steaks in flour, gently shaking off the excess. Heat all but 1 tbsp. of the butter in a large frying pan. Sauté the steaks over medium heat for about 5 minutes, depending on thickness. Turn with a spatula and sauté the other side for 5 minutes. Arrange the fish on a warm platter. **Q**uarter 1½ lemons. Juice the remaining half. Melt the rest of the butter over low heat in the pan in which the fish was cooked. Mix in the lemon juice and pour over the steaks. Sprinkle with chopped parsley, decorate with lemon wedges, and serve immediately.

NOTE BY **ALAIN DUCASSE** How about tying a string around each hake steak? You'll surprise your guests because the fish will have the shape of a filet mignon, and the cooking will be much more even.

Baked Hake Steaks

Darne de colin au plat

⬠ ⬠ ◯

Alain Ducasse

Serves 4 ✦ Preparation time : 15 minutes ✦ Cooking time : 25 minutes
4 garlic cloves ✦ 4 hake steaks, about 7 oz. (200 g) each ✦ juice of 2 lemons ✦ 1 tomato, sliced
✦ 1 lemon, sliced ✦ 1 stalk of dried fennel ✦ 1 cup (20 cl) chicken stock (page 322) ✦ 2 tbsp.
olive oil ✦ fine sea salt and freshly ground pepper

Preheat the oven to 325°F (160°C). **C**rush the garlic cloves with the palm of your hand and set aside. Tie each of the hake steaks with kitchen string to hold their shape. Marinate in lemon juice for 5 minutes. Lay the fish in an earthenware baking dish and cover with the tomato and lemon slices, crushed garlic cloves, and fennel. Add some stock and 1 tbsp. of the olive oil. Season with salt and pepper to taste. Bake for 10 to 12 minutes. **R**emove the hake from the baking dish, place on a serving platter, and gently remove the string. Strain the cooking juice into a small saucepan and reduce over low heat for 5 to 10 minutes. Whisk in a little olive oil. Cover the hake steaks with this sauce. Serve the fish with a mound of mashed potatoes, drizzled with olive oil and topped with a little parsley.

Need I say how much I love this kind of recipe? It is simple, quick, and delicious. The same method can be applied to a number of different kinds of fish, depending on what you find at the market on any particular day. You can even cook a fragile fish, like grenadier, in this way because the method requires little handling. NOTE BY **FRANÇOISE BERNARD**

Mackerel

Fished from February to October, mackerel is pretty to look at, with its vivid colors and highlights of silver and gold. Françoise Bernard likes it only when it has just been pulled out of the water, wiggling and shiny. Be sure the highlights are still bright and the eyes are not dull. Mackerel can have a strong fishy smell. To mask it, Françoise Bernard bakes the fish on a bed of garlic purée—nothing can overpower that aroma. Her favorite recipe is *lisette*, or young mackerel, cooked in white wine. A *lisette* is cooked like a sardine. This fish should not be mistaken for the mackerel that is caught with a fishing rod or the mackerel caught with a net. A netted mackerel is less tasty, because it has remained on the trawler for several days before being sold.

Alain Ducasse has never put this small, popular fish on the menu in his restaurants. It would be possible to serve it in his Monaco restaurant, where people seek out his Southern cuisine, but it is out of the question in his Parisian restaurant, where he presents contemporary French cuisine. The mackerel is just not chic enough. Still, this chef enjoys the marked flavor and oily texture of mackerel, marinated in the *escabeche* style, with red or white currants, vinegar, mustard, capers, sorrel, and lemon.

Vinegary condiments and bitter sauces work very well with its rich meat. Gooseberries, *groseilles à maquereau* in French, take their name from a traditional sauce for the mackerel. If you dislike acidic flavors, try the soups and chowders, like *cotriades* from southern Brittany; the cream and Provençal sauces; the terrines and potted rillettes. Tipping his hat to Alain Chapel, Alain Ducasse also created a mackerel and piperade pie, quite an appropriate recipe for this fish.

Mackerel in White Wine

Maquereaux au vin blanc

⌂ ○

Françoise Bernard

Serves 4 ◆ Preparation time : 25 minutes ◆ Cooking time : 25 minutes
1 garlic clove ◆ 2 onions, sliced ◆ 1 carrot, sliced ◆ 1¼ cups (25 cl) dry white wine ◆ ½ cup
(10 cl) vinegar ◆ 12 coriander seeds ◆ 1 bouquet garni ◆ salt and pepper ◆ 8 to 12 young
mackerel

To make a court bouillon, combine the garlic, onions, carrot, wine, vinegar, coriander seeds, bouquet garni, salt, pepper, and ¾ cup (15 cl) of water. Boil for 15 minutes, remove from the heat, and cool. Slit open the stomach of the mackerels, cutting carefully. Do not remove the heads. Wash the fish and pat dry with paper towels. Lay the mackerels next to each other in wide pan. Pour the unstrained court bouillon over the fish. Cover with aluminum foil and bring to a boil over very low heat. Immediately remove from the heat and let the fish cool completely in the court bouillon before serving. The taste is even better the next day or two later.

NOTE BY **ALAIN DUCASSE** This recipe is simple, but the cooking is tricky. Be careful not to poach the mackerel too long, or it will crumble and lose its beautiful shape.

Mackerel and Piperade Pie

Tarte au maquereau et à la piperade

⬭ ⬭ ◯

Alain Ducasse

Serves 4 ✦ **Preparation time : 1 hour** ✦ **Cooking time : 45 minutes**
¼ **cup (5 cl) olive oil** ✦ **2 white onions, thinly sliced** ✦ **3 garlic cloves, crushed** ✦ **2 thick slices of cured ham, diced** ✦ **1 red pepper, thinly sliced** ✦ **1 yellow pepper, thinly sliced** ✦ **4 tomatoes, peeled, seeded, and chopped** ✦ **salt and pepper** ✦ **4 mackerel fillets** ✦ ⅓ **cup (30 g) flour** ✦ **9 oz. puff pastry crust (200 g)**

Preheat the oven to 425°F (220°C). **T**o prepare the piperade, heat 3 tbsp. of the olive oil. Add the onions, garlic, ham, and peppers. Cook over low heat for 10 minutes. Add the tomatoes and simmer for 15 to 20 minutes. **D**ebone the mackerel. Slice the fillets lengthwise and brush with olive oil. **F**lour a pastry board and roll out the puff-pastry crust to about ⅛ in. (2 mm) thick. Prick with a fork and lay it in a pie dish. Bake the crust until golden brown, remove from the oven, and cool at room temperature. Add the warm piperade, top with the mackerel fillets, and bake for 10 minutes. Serve this mackerel pie warm, accompanied by a mesclun salad.

The bold mixture of mackerel and ham gives this pie a very special flavor. This is no ordinary recipe. Your friends will remember it for a long time.

NOTE BY
**FRANÇOISE
BERNARD**

• 67

Mackerel with Garlic

Maquereaux à l'ail

⌂ ○

Françoise Bernard

Serves 4 ✦ **Preparation time : 25 minutes** ✦ **Cooking time : 20 minutes**
15 garlic cloves, unpeeled ✦ **8 small mackerel** ✦ **3 tbsp. (40 g) butter, cut into small pieces** ✦
1 lemon, sliced ✦ **salt and pepper**

Preheat the oven to 375°F (190°C). Heat some water to medium temperature and add
the garlic cloves. Boil for 2 to 3 minutes. Drain the garlic and arrange the cloves in the
bottom of a baking dish, crushing them slightly with a fork. Place the mackerel on top,
add salt and pepper to taste, then dot with butter. Bake for 15 minutes. Arrange the
lemon slices around the mackerel and serve from the baking dish.

NOTE BY   I would like to repeat the advice I gave earlier. People tend to overcook fish. It is better
ALAIN   to cook it for a short time and at a low temperature.
DUCASSE

Mackerel in White Wine and Braised Vegetables *à la Barigoule*

Maquereaux au vin blanc, légumes en barigoule

⌂ ⌂ ○

Alain Ducasse

Serves 4 ◆ Preparation time : 1 hour ◆ Cooking time : 1 hour 15 minutes
2 large onions ◆ 5 carrots, with tops ◆ 1 small celery stalk ◆ 4 garlic cloves ◆ ½ cup (10 cl)
olive oil ◆ 1 bouquet garni ◆ 1½ cups (30 cl) white wine ◆ 2 turnips, with tops ◆ 2 purple
artichokes ◆ 4 scallions ◆ 2 small fennel bulbs ◆ 2 radishes ◆ ½ cup (10 cl) white wine vinegar
◆ 1 sprig of thyme ◆ 2 bay leaves ◆ 12 small mackerel, cleaned and rinsed under cold water ◆
fine sea salt and freshly ground pepper ◆ 4 basil leaves, chopped

Preheat the oven to 350°F (180°C). **T**o make a *barigoule* sauce, peel and dice 1 onion, 1 carrot, the celery, and garlic. Sauté in a saucepan for 5 minutes with ¼ cup (5 cl) of the olive oil. Add the bouquet garni and 1 cup (20 cl) of the wine. Add water to cover and boil for 45 minutes. Set aside. **P**eel the turnips and 3 of the remaining carrots, leaving on a couple of inches of the tops. Cut off the tips of the artichoke leaves and remove the stems so as to keep only the hearts. Quarter the artichokes. Peel away the first white layer of the scallions and remove the outer green stems. Peel the outer skin and quarter the fennel. Clean the radishes. Fry all the vegetables in a little olive oil without browning—about 10 minutes—and then drizzle them with the sauce. With a slotted spoon, remove each type of vegetable as soon as it is cooked. Drain and cool. **S**lice the remaining onion and carrot. Combine ½ cup (10 cl) of the wine and the vinegar in a saucepan. Add the onion, carrot, thyme, and bay leaf. Bring to a boil, reduce heat, and simmer the marinade for 15 minutes. **S**eason the mackerel with salt and pepper and lay them in a baking dish. Cover the fish with the marinade and bake for 8 to 10 minutes. Remove from the oven and cool. Carefully remove the fish bones. Arrange the mackerel on a mound of vegetables, give the platter a twist of the pepper mill, and sprinkle a little olive oil and chopped basil on top.

So many ingredients! But I understand what Alain Ducasse is trying to do in this recipe. Like any Mediterranean cook, he is striving for a festival of vegetables. This cocktail of springtime flavors enhances the oily meat of the mackerel. Of course, your vegetable basket can differ, depending on what you find at the market.

NOTE BY **FRANÇOISE BERNARD**

Salmon

One need only look at their recipes to realize that our two cooks do not belong to the same school. For Françoise Bernard, salmon is cooked as a terrine or served whole in aspic. For Alain Ducasse, it is presented as a *pavé*, or slab—a very modern cut. The presentations differ, but both types of recipes are suited to special occasions. Whether the salmon is presented as a steak, a square chunk, or a fillet matters little to Françoise Bernard. She just wants the salmon to be fresh and not too fatty. She lets her fishmonger cut it as he sees fit, but she demands very fresh fish and refuses to pay too much for it.

Thanks to the fish farms, today it is possible to find great salmon at a more affordable price than ever before. "One can, of course, pay an exorbitant price for a fresh salmon from the Adour river," she tosses mischievously at Ducasse. "It is splendid! But is it worth the price?" Our chef answers right away. "The Adour is one of our last rivers with wild salmon, and you have to pay the price!" He is bold because he knows that he has won Françoise Bernard with his salmon served "lukewarm-warm," that is, pink at the bones.

Even though salmon has become more readily available, Françoise Bernard loves to use a "Sunday recipe," one of those recipes reserved for family parties when she was a child. Her cold salmon is still a popular classic, although she would present it today as a thick slice or a steak. But the arrival of a superb salmon in aspic at a table of eight to ten people is so spectacular! She likes the contrast between warm salmon and a mayonnaise, plain or seasoned with herbs and garlic. "The young are very fond of this particular dish," she adds. Contrasting temperatures are popular today.

Salmon is synonymous with Sunday dinners for Alain Ducasse too. With a touch of nostalgia—rare for this man who never looks back—he remembers the grilled Béarnaise salmon that was often served at a child's first communion dinner.

Salmon Loaf with Shrimp Sauce

Pain de saumon, sauce crevette

☗ ☗ ∞

Françoise Bernard

Serves 4 ◆ Preparation time : 1 hour ◆ Cooking time : 55 minutes
2½ cups (50 cl) court bouillon ◆ 1½ lbs. (700 g) salmon fillets, skinned ◆ 4 eggs, separated ◆
salt and pepper ◆ 1 cup (20 cl) milk ◆ 1¼ cups (100 g) fresh white bread crumbs ◆ 4 tbsp.
(50 g) butter ◆ ⅓ cup (30 g) flour ◆ 1 tsp. tomato paste ◆ pinch of cayenne ◆ ½ tsp. paprika
◆ 4 cooked large shrimps or prawns (50 g), peeled and deveined

Preheat the oven to 350°F (180°C). Bring the court bouillon to a boil, then reduce the heat to a simmer. Poach the salmon for 5 to 8 minutes, remove it with a slotted spoon, and drain, reserving the court bouillon. Strain the court bouillon and set aside. Mash the fish with a fork. Warm the milk and pour into a large bowl. Crumble the bread crumbs into the milk. Squeeze the bread into a ball, then press it in a sieve to remove excess milk. Reserve the liquid. Break the eggs, separate the whites and yolks. Combine the bread, fish, egg yolks, salt, and pepper. Mash it well with a fork to form a paste and refrigerate at least 30 minutes. Beat the egg whites with 1 pinch of salt until stiff. Mix gently with the cold fish paste. Butter a ring mold or a soufflé dish. Pour in the salmon mixture. Put a pan large enough to fit the mold in the oven and fill it with about 2 in. (5 cm) of water. Gently place the mold in the pan (the water level should be about halfway up the sides of the mold). Bake for about 45 minutes. Add enough court bouillon to the reserved milk to make ½ cup (10 cl) of liquid. Melt the remaining butter over low heat. Add the flour and stir over the heat just until the mixture foams. Immediately whisk in the court bouillon mixture. Then whisk in the tomato paste, cayenne, and paprika. Season with salt and pepper to taste. Stir with a wooden spoon until the sauce thickens, and simmer over low heat for 10 minutes. Unmold the salmon loaf onto a circular serving platter. Mix the shrimp into the sauce and pour into the center of the loaf or around the fish ring or "turban." Serve right away.

NOTE BY **ALAIN DUCASSE** I never cook this type of dish, in which the taste of the main ingredient disappears beneath a strong sauce—especially these days, when we are lucky enough to have very fresh products. I prefer serving salmon simply grilled or as a carpaccio.

Gravlax with Mustard Sauce

Gravlax sauce moutarde

⛉ ⛉ ∞

Alain Ducasse

Serves 6 ◆ Preparation time : 20 minutes ◆ Marinating time : 48 hours
4½ lbs. (2 kg) salmon fillet, with the skin ◆ 1 cup (150 g) coarse salt ◆ ¾ cup (170 g) sugar ◆
coarsely ground white pepper ◆ 2 bunches or 1 cup dill, chopped ◆ 3 tbsp. mild Dijon mustard
◆ 2 tbsp. cider vinegar ◆ 1 cup (20 cl) peanut oil ◆ fine salt and coarsely ground pepper

Place the salmon on a large serving platter. Cover with the coarse salt, 1 cup (150 g) of the sugar, some coarsely ground white pepper, and ¾ cup of the minced dill. Cover with aluminum foil, place a flat weight on top, and refrigerate for 48 hours. Remove the salt coating from the fish and carefully pat dry with paper towels. To make the mustard sauce, mix the mustard with the remaining sugar and the vinegar. Drizzle in the oil in a fine stream, whisking the mixture constantly to make a mayonnaise. Add the reserved dill. Season with salt and pepper to taste. Cut the salmon into very thin, angled slices. Serve cold with the sauce, and, perhaps, boiled red-skinned potatoes.

Here's a trick for cutting the marinated salmon easily. Leave the fish in the freezer for about 1 hour. It won't be difficult to cut very thin slices if you use a knife with a wide, well-sharpened blade.

NOTE BY
FRANÇOISE
BERNARD

Cold Salmon in Aspic

Saumon froid en gelée

☝ ☝ ☝   ∞

Françoise Bernard

Serves 10 ♦ Preparation time : 55 minutes ♦ Cooking time : 45 minutes ♦ Refrigeration time : 2 hours ♦ 2 onions, sliced ♦ 2 carrots, sliced ♦ 1 bouquet garni ♦ 2 quarts (2 l) water ♦ 3 cups (75 cl) dry white wine ♦ salt and pepper ♦ 6½ lbs. (3 kg) salmon, cleaned and scaled ♦ 2 packets powdered gelatin ♦ 1 leek, green part only ♦ 1 tomato, seeded ♦ 1 hard-boiled egg

Make a court bouillon by boiling the onions, carrots, bouquet garni, water, wine, salt, and pepper in a fish poacher for 30 minutes. Remove from the heat and let cool about 15 minutes. **P**lace the salmon in the poacher, simmer just below boiling, and poach for 10 minutes. Remove from the heat. Let the salmon cool in the court bouillon in the refrigerator. **P**repare the gelatin according to the instructions on the packet. Spread a thin layer on an oblong platter large enough to hold the fish and refrigerate until it sets—about 15 to 20 minutes. **W**ash the leek greens, plunge them in boiling water, and cook for 10 to 15 minutes. Refresh the greens in cold water and drain. Cut the tomato, the white of the hard-boiled egg, and the leek greens into decorative shapes. **C**arefully drain the salmon and pat dry with paper towels. Arrange the fish on the chilled gelatin. Remove a 2 in. (5 cm) wide strip of skin from the center of the fish, working from the head to the tail. Brush the salmon with gelatin and refrigerate for 15 minutes. **D**ip the decorative pieces of tomato, egg, and leek in the gelatin (if the gelatin thickens, warm it a little to melt it). Arrange the pieces around the salmon and along the skinned center section. Refrigerate for another 15 minutes. Brush another thin layer of gelatin on top and refrigerate for a few more minutes. Mash the remaining gelatin with a fork and arrange it around the salmon just before serving.

NOTE BY **ALAIN DUCASSE** We offer very few dishes in aspic at my restaurants, with the exception of *bœuf miroton*, which is served cold in its own jelly. You could also serve the gelatin on the side, broken into irregular-sized chunks. In this case, the gelatin should not have too much body—it should still quiver.

Grilled Salmon Béarnaise with Hazelnut Butter

Saumon grillé, béarnaise au beurre noisette

⬠ ∞

Alain Ducasse

Serves 4 ✦ Preparation time : 35 minutes ✦ Cooking time : 20 minutes
4 salmon steaks, 6 oz. (200 g) each, with the skin ✦ 1 tbsp. olive oil ✦ 2 shallots, chopped ✦ ¼
cup (5 cl) sherry vinegar ✦ ¼ cup (5 cl) white wine vinegar ✦ 2 sprigs fresh tarragon ✦ 1 sprig
parsley ✦ 1 tbsp. ground white pepper ✦ 4 tbsp. (50 g) butter ✦ salt

Preheat the oven to 350°F (180°C). **R**ub the salmon steaks with the olive oil and refrigerate. **B**oil the shallots with the two vinegars, 1 tarragon sprig, the parsley, and the pepper. Reduce the liquid completely. **M**elt the butter over low heat. It will foam up, and then the foam will disappear. When it foams a second time, remove the brown butter from the heat, strain into a bowl, and cool in the refrigerator. **R**apidly sear the salmon on both sides over high heat, then bake for about 5 minutes to cook the interior. As soon as the fish is cool enough to handle, remove the central backbone and skin from each steak. **M**ince the remaining tarragon. To make the béarnaise sauce, remove the parsley and tarragon sprigs from the reduced shallot vinegar. Pour the cooled brown butter into the vinegar and heat while whisking vigorously. Whisk in the minced tarragon and salt to taste. Place 1 heaping tbsp. of the béarnaise sauce on each plate, arrange a salmon steak on top, and serve the rest of the béarnaise in a sauceboat. Serve immediately, perhaps with Cooked and Raw Belgian Endives (page 175) or Fork-Mashed Potatoes (page 219).

Pay close attention to your brown butter. You must stop cooking before it burns. The originality of Alain Ducasse's recipe centers on the butter. This dish is inspired by the béarnaise sauce, which is made with a simple clarified butter—that is, melted over low heat, with its liquid residue discarded.

NOTE BY
FRANÇOISE
BERNARD

Sea Bream

Françoise Bernard has learned a lot about sea bream from her favorite fishmonger on Rue des Martyrs in Paris. She has learned the difference between the golden-head or gilt-head sea bream—the only one that can be truly called a *dorade*—and the other more modest sea breams, or *daurades*. The gray sea bream is more common and much cheaper. There is also the pink sea bream, with a golden skin and a black spot near the gills.

The golden-head sea bream has a yellow streak on its head. This fish preys on other fish, and its teeth protrude notice-ably. The golden-head sea bream is the only variety served at Alain Ducasse's restaurants. He loves the firmness of the meat and the thick fillets. This type of bream is more expen-sive than the others—but definitely worth it. With respect for its delicate taste, he cooks it as simply as he can. Fran-çoise Bernard is a fan of his salt-crusted sea bream, in part because you do not have to scale the fish—an operation that makes cooking fish an unpleasant task. Another advantage is that the salt crust reduces the strong cooking smell of the bream.

Françoise Bernard is not opposed to exotic flavors. People in the West Indies and Africa are especially fond of braised or grilled sea bream. Depending on her mood, she may prepare it Martinique style or marinate it with saffron and vinegar, then simmer it in an onion and tomato compote. When she is more tempted by tradition, she prepares sea bream with a mushroom stuffing, an excellent recipe that she received from her mother—a dish engraved in her memory forever.

Martinique-Style Sea Bream Steaks

Dorade martiniquaise en tronçons

⌂ ∞

Françoise Bernard

Serves 4 ◆ **Preparation time : 15 minutes** ◆ **Cooking time : 25 minutes**
1 onion, chopped ◆ **1 large sea bream, 2 to 2½ lbs. (1 to 1,2 kg), cleaned and scaled, cut into**
4 steaks ◆ **2 garlic cloves, chopped** ◆ **2 sprigs thyme leaves** ◆ **2 bay leaves, broken** ◆ **1 tbsp.**
curry powder ◆ **salt and pepper** ◆ **1 cup (20 cl) dry white wine** ◆ **3 tbsp. (40 g) butter** ◆ **2 tbsp.**
chopped parsley

Preheat the oven to 375°F (190°C). Spread the chopped onion evenly over the bottom
of a buttered baking dish. Place the sea bream steaks on the bed of onions, arranging
the steaks into the original shape of the fish. Sprinkle with the garlic, thyme, bay leaves,
and curry. Season with salt and pepper to taste. Pour the wine over the fish and dot
with the butter. Bake for 25 minutes. Remove from oven, sprinkle with chopped parsley, and serve directly from the baking dish.

NOTE BY **ALAIN DUCASSE** Instead of butter, I would pour a fine stream of olive oil in the bottom of the dish. The
oil would bind all the other flavors of the fish. At the end, you might want to add a
dash of lemon juice.

Baked Sea Bream

Dorade au Plat

⛑ ⛑ ∞

Alain Ducasse

Serves 4 ◆ Preparation time : 35 minutes ◆ Cooking time : 35 minutes
4 sprigs basil ◆ 2 golden-head sea bream, 1½ lbs. (700 g) each, cleaned and scaled ◆ 1 large
tomato, quartered ◆ 1 lemon, sliced ◆ 20 black Niçoise olives, pitted ◆ 4 stalks dried fennel ◆
salt and pepper ◆ 3 cups (60 cl) water or chicken stock (page 322) ◆ 1 bunch or ½ cup arugula,
shredded ◆ ½ cup (10 cl) olive oil ◆ 2 tbsp. (30 g) butter

Preheat the oven to 425°F (225°C). **R**inse 12 large basil leaves, pat dry on paper towels, and snip with scissors. Leave the other small leaves on the stems. Rinse and drain the sprigs. **A**rrange the sea breams next to each other in a heavy, oiled baking dish. Add the tomato, lemon slices, olives, fennel leaves, basil sprigs, and salt and pepper to taste. Sprinkle with water or stock and bring to a boil over high heat. Bake for 15 to 20 minutes, basting often. **P**lace the fish on a hot plate. Reduce the cooking juice to one-third its volume, strain it, and pour it back into a saucepan. Add the shredded arugula, half of the olive oil, and the butter—but don't mix in the oil and butter. The sauce should have drops of oil and butter floating in it. Pour the sauce over the fish and sprinkle with the remaining olive oil. You might wish to serve these sea breams with Fork-Mashed Potatoes (page 219).

Alain Ducasse includes dried fennel in many of his recipes, such as this one. I recommend drying a few stalks of this aromatic plant in the summer sun or on a rack in a dry area.

NOTE BY
FRANÇOISE
BERNARD

Sea Bream with Mushroom Stuffing

Dorade farcie aux champignons

⬠ ⬠ ⬠   ◯◯◯

Françoise Bernard

Serves 4 ♦ Preparation time : 45 minutes ♦ Cooking time : 50 minutes
1 sea bream, about 2½ lbs. (1,2 kg), scaled and cleaned ♦ 6 tbsp. milk ♦ ½ cup (60 g) white
bread crumbs ♦ 4 tbsp. (50 g) butter ♦ 7 oz. (200 g) button mushrooms, trimmed and sliced ♦
1 shallot, chopped ♦ 1 egg yolk ♦ 4 tbsp. chopped parsley ♦ salt and pepper ♦ strip of bacon,
optional ♦ ¾ cup (15 cl) dry white wine

Preheat the oven to 375°F (190°C). **A**sk the fishmonger to scale and clean the sea bream. If you are going to scale it yourself, boil it for 1 minute first, rinse well, and pat dry with paper towels. **H**eat the milk and add the bread crumbs. Sauté the mushrooms and shallot in half of the butter over medium-high heat. Squeeze the milk out of the bread crumbs. Mix the bread with the egg yolk, parsley, and mushroom mixture. Season with salt and pepper to taste. **S**tuff the sea bream and sew the slit with kitchen string—or simply wrap the string around the fish 3 or 4 times—to keep the stuffing in place. You may also cover the slit with a thin strip of bacon before tying to prevent any stuffing from falling out. **P**lace the sea bream in a baking dish, pour on the wine, and dot with the rest of the butter. Bake for 30 to 40 minutes, then serve directly from the baking dish.

NOTE BY **ALAIN DUCASSE** Cook this dish to perfection by choosing an earthenware baking dish and filling it with slices of button mushrooms. The mushrooms will add moisture, which will make the fish juicy. A few slices of lemon and tomato will add a little touch of acidity and fresh flavor to the cooking juice. Deglaze the dish with a bit of chicken stock, a few drops of olive oil for a smooth finish, and some arugula leaves for a tart, peppery flavor.

Salt-Crusted Sea Bream

Dorade en croûte de sel

⇧ ⇧ ∞

Alain Ducasse

Serves 4 ◆ Preparation time : 40 minutes ◆ Cooking time : 35 minutes
1 large golden-head sea bream, 3½ lbs. (1,4 kg) ◆ 2 stalks of dried fennel ◆ 2¼ lbs. (1 kg)
coarse sea salt ◆ 3 egg whites ◆ 12 small fennel bulbs ◆ 7 oz. (200 g) zucchini ◆ 3 tbsp. olive
oil ◆ 1 cup (20 cl) chicken stock (page 322) ◆ 12 Niçoise olives, pitted ◆ 4 oven-dried tomatoes
(page 231) ◆ 4 zucchini blossoms, pistils removed ◆ fine sea salt and pepper ◆ extra-virgin olive
oil

Preheat the oven to 400°F (210°C). Ask the fishmonger to clean the fish without removing the fins or scales. Scrape the backbone of the fish with a knife to remove all the blood. Rinse the fish and pat dry. Insert the fennel stalks into the stomach cavity. Mix the coarse salt and egg whites. Place some of the mixture in a baking dish, lay the fish on top, and envelop it with the rest of the mixture. Bake for about 35 minutes. Boil the fennel bulbs just until tender and a little crunchy, about 20 minutes, depending on their size. Refresh under cold running water and pat dry with paper towels. Halve the zucchinis lengthwise, then slice the halves into 2 in. (5 cm) pieces. Sauté in olive oil. Add enough stock to cover and boil gently for 10 to 15 minutes. Add the fennel bulbs, olives, oven-dried tomatoes, and zucchini blossoms. Season with salt and pepper to taste. Sprinkle with extra-virgin olive oil, which will blend the flavors. Take the fish from the oven and remove the salt crust with a knife. Arrange the bream on a serving dish, surrounded by vegetables.

Baking in a salt crust is very practical, because the dish needs little surveillance. The thick crust will protect the fish, even if you forget it in the oven for a little too long. Be sure to use a good knife to remove the salt crust.

NOTE BY
FRANÇOISE
BERNARD

Trout

Trout is a freshwater fish that swims in moving waters. It is a member of the prestigious salmon family. Françoise Bernard and Alain Ducasse both associate trout with almonds. Françoise Bernard sautés her almonds lightly in warm butter, which she pours over the trout just before serving, with slices of lemon. Alain Ducasse roasts his almonds in the oven. He drizzles brown butter over the fish, then bastes with lemon juice, and finally sprinkles the almonds on top. Beyond the subtleties, the basic idea is the same: Clean the trout, dip it in milk and flour, then sauté in butter. If you don't flour the trout, it will stick to the frying pan, or its skin will break apart. The flour protects the fish by forming a crust. The milk is not absolutely necessary, but is strongly recommended by our two cooks. There's another trick for keeping the trout from breaking apart while cooking—always clean the fish through its gills, instead of slitting it open.

Some recipes are no longer in style—for example, *truite au bleu*, in which the trout was knocked senseless just before it was cooked so it would turn a beautiful shade of blue in the court bouillon. Today, the most popular method of cooking trout is frying. Once in a while, when she is in a hurry, Françoise Bernard will cook trout in the microwave oven, placing the fish side by side in a dish and lightly bathing them in court bouillon.

Trout with almonds, trout with sorrel—the recipes for this small river fish are still very traditional, in everyday cuisine and in restaurants, too.

Trout with Almonds

Truite aux amandes

⭓ ⭓ ○

Françoise Bernard

Serves 4 ◆ **Preparation time : 15 minutes** ◆ **Cooking time : 15 minutes**
1 cup (20 cl) milk ◆ **salt and pepper** ◆ **½ cup (50 g) flour** ◆ **4 whole trout, cleaned** ◆ **4 tbsp.**
(50 g) butter ◆ **¼ cup (50 g) slivered almonds** ◆ **1 lemon, thinly sliced and cut in half**

Pour the milk into a bowl and season with salt and pepper. Sprinkle the flour on a plate. Rinse the fish and pat dry with paper towels. Dip each trout in milk and roll in the flour, gently shaking off the excess. Heat 3 tbsp. of the butter in a large frying pan over medium heat. Sauté the fish for 7 to 8 minutes on each side. With a slotted spoon or a spatula—don't use a fork—turn the fish carefully. If your frying pan is too small, cook the trout two at a time, adding a little butter each time. **S**auté the almonds in the remaining butter, stirring constantly so they don't burn. Just before serving, sprinkle the trout with almonds and decorate the plate with a few half circles of lemon.

NOTE BY **ALAIN DUCASSE** You must clean the inside of the trout very thoroughly to eliminate all the blood. I prefer to remove the skin before serving to make the dish more elegant. Rather than serving the lemon on the side, you can deglaze the almonds in the sauté pan with some lemon juice.

Trout with Sorrel

Truite à l'oseille

⌂ ⌂ ○

Alain Ducasse

Serves 4 ◆ Preparation time : 25 minutes ◆ Cooking time : 20 minutes
4 salmon trout (lake trout) steaks, about 7 oz. (200 g) each ◆ salt and pepper ◆ 1 lemon ◆ 4
tbsp. (50 g) butter ◆ 2 shallots, thinly sliced ◆ ½ cup (10 cl) white wine ◆ ½ cup (10 cl) chicken
stock (page 322) ◆ 3 sprigs parsley ◆ ½ cup (10 cl) light cream ◆ 1 bunch or 2 cups of sorrel,
cut into chiffonade

Preheat the oven to 350°F (180°C). Season the trout steaks with salt and pepper. Peel the lemon, removing the skin and white membrane. Cut the pulp into quarters and then dice. Line the bottom of a buttered, earthenware baking dish with the shallots and diced lemon. Place the fish on top and add the wine, stock, and parsley. Bake for 10 minutes. Remove the trout from the dish and set aside in a warm place. Pour the cooking juice into a saucepan and reduce to half its volume over high heat. In another saucepan, reduce the cream to half its volume. Combine the cooking juice and cream, then strain. Add the sorrel to the cream sauce, which should still be very warm. Whisk in the rest of the butter, cut in small pieces. Season with salt and pepper. Place the trout steaks on individual plates and top with sauce. You might like to serve this dish with Fork-Mashed Potatoes (page 219).

Large trout, which are easy to find at the fish market, can be cooked in the same way. As far as I am concerned, it is much more interesting to cook small trout with almonds. NOTE BY **FRANÇOISE BERNARD**

Trout with Chives

Truite à la ciboulette

⇧ ⇧ ◯

Françoise Bernard

Serves 4 ◆ Preparation time : 30 minutes ◆ Cooking time : 15 minutes
4 trout, cleaned ◆ 1 tbsp. butter ◆ 1 shallot, chopped ◆ ½ cup chives, snipped ◆ 1½ cups
(30 cl) white wine ◆ juice of ½ lemon ◆ salt and pepper ◆ 4 tbsp. (50 g) crème fraîche

Preheat the oven to 425°F (220°C). Rinse the trout and pat dry with paper towels. Butter a baking dish that is large enough to hold the fish, line the bottom with the shallot, and lay the trout on top. Add 1 tbsp. of the chives, the wine, and lemon juice. Season with salt and pepper to taste. Bake for 10 minutes. Remove the trout with a spatula, drain the cooking juice, and keep the fish warm on a serving platter. Heat the cooking juice in a small pot and whisk in the crème fraîche. Boil for 2 to 3 minutes to thicken, then pour the sauce over the trout. Sprinkle the remaining chives over the fish and serve immediately. This dish can be served with steamed potatoes, lightly sprinkled with parsley.

NOTE BY **ALAIN DUCASSE** For more precise cooking, you might want to cook large trout steaks, which you can prepare somewhat like Trout with Sorrel (page 85). The larger cut is quite appropriate for fish served with a sauce, because it frees your guests from having to separate the meat from the central bone.

Pan-Fried Trout with Almonds

Truite poêlée aux amandes

⌂ ○

Alain Ducasse

Serves 4 ◆ Preparation time : 25 minutes ◆ Cooking time : 20 minutes
4 trout, 10 oz. (300 g) each, cleaned ◆ Salt and freshly ground pepper ◆ 2½ cups (50 cl) milk
◆ ¾ cup (80 g) flour ◆ juice of 1 lemon ◆ 7 oz. (200 g) butter ◆ 1 cup (100 g) slivered almonds
◆ ½ cup parsley, chopped

Preheat the oven to 425°F (220°C). Clean the trout and pat dry with paper towels. Season the inside of the fish with salt and pepper. Dip the pieces in the milk, roll in flour, and gently shake off the excess. In a large frying pan, melt 5 oz. (150 g) of the butter over low heat, do not brown. Carefully place the trout in the pan and sauté for 6 to 8 minutes. Turn the pieces, baste with the butter, and sprinkle with half of the lemon juice. Sauté for 6 to 8 minutes more, depending on the size. In the meantime, roast the almonds in a hot oven, watching them closely so that they do not burn. Melt the remaining butter over low heat. Stir in the other half of the lemon juice, the roasted almonds, and parsley. Sprinkle the trout with this almond butter and serve immediately.

In my opinion, the best vegetable to serve for trout with almonds is steamed potatoes. I mash them a little with a fork to mix in the flavored butter. They're just great.

NOTE BY **FRANÇOISE BERNARD**

Tuna

Different times, different tastes. Fried, overcooked tuna is a thing of the past. Long live the *pavé* of California tuna—a slab of fish cooked pink on the inside, almost rare. Our famous French chef approves of the American method of cooking tuna. He only tolerates half-cooked tuna, and he positively loathes over cooked tuna. Is there anything drier than fried tuna? If feels like a piece of parched cardboard in your mouth—and it's even worse when cut into thin slices.

Tuna is being liberated. Traditionally combined with Mediterranean aromas, it has recently been associated with Asian spices. At Spoon, Alain Ducasse's newest restaurant, where you'll discover the most recent trends in French cuisine, you can enjoy tuna as a steak or skewered and marinated in a *saté* sauce. Tuna has definitely forsaken its Provençal origins—it now associates with coconut milk and lemongrass. Whether a simple slice or an entire fillet, our chef demands that the pieces be cut from a 44 lb. (20 kg) tuna. This is the right weight for ensuring meaty tuna steaks. The *nec plus ultra* ("ultimate") for him, however, is the heart of the fillet. Alain Ducasse loves to roast it, then let it melt in a warm sauce inspired by the *pissaladière*, the famous onion tart of Nice. It is even better cold. "But the best way to cook this fish is to cook it very slowly in olive oil. In Monaco, I serve it with crayfish and cucumber."

Tuna and oil—olive oil, of course—is a great love story. Olive oil is the best oil for canned tuna. Françoise Bernard is crazy about white tuna in olive oil. She has just discovered the thin strips taken from the back of the fish. They have great finesse and show a little of the tuna's aristocratic side. New flavors, new cuts. Tuna "ain't what it used to be!"

Fresh Provençale Tuna

Thon frais à la provençale

⇧ ⇧ ∞

Françoise Bernard

Serves 4 or 5 ✦ **Marinating time : 2 hours** ✦ **Preparation time : 20 minutes** ✦ **Cooking time : 40 minutes** ✦ **juice of 1 lemon** ✦ **3 tbsp. olive oil** ✦ **1 sprig thyme, leaves only** ✦ **2 bay leaves, broken** ✦ **1 sprig rosemary** ✦ **8 peppercorns** ✦ **1¾ lbs. (800 g) tuna** ✦ **8 anchovy fillets** ✦ **2 onions, chopped** ✦ **3 garlic cloves, chopped** ✦ **1½ lbs. (750 g) tomatoes, peeled, seeded, and chopped** ✦ **2½ cups (50 cl) dry white wine** ✦ **salt and freshly ground pepper** ✦ **1 tbsp. capers** ✦ **5 tbsp. chopped parsley** ✦ **3 tbsp. (40 g) butter**

The day before serving, make a marinade by combining the lemon juice, 2 tbsp. olive oil, the thyme leaves, bay leaves, rosemary, and peppercorns. Make slits in the tuna and insert the anchovy fillets. Marinate the fish, covered, in the refrigerator for about 12 hours. Turn the pieces several times while marinating. Carefully drain the tuna. In a sauté or stew pan, sauté the fish on both sides in the remaining tbsp. of olive oil. Add the onions, garlic, tomatoes, white wine, and ½ cup (10 cl) of water. Season with salt and pepper to taste. Cover and simmer for 30 minutes. Remove the tuna with a slotted spoon. Drain, place on a serving dish, and set aside in a warm place. If necessary, reduce the sauce over high heat. Add the capers, chopped parsley, and butter to the sauce, pour over the tuna, and serve immediately. This dish is also very tasty when served as a cold first course.

NOTE BY **ALAIN DUCASSE**

I love tuna that is rare in the center. In my restaurant, Spoon, we marinate tuna as we would a thick chunk of meat, then we roast and slice it. We also serve tuna *a la plancha* (seared on a griddle) with a saté sauce. For this recipe, however, I would suggest a Provençal garnish made with three types of tomatoes (oven-dried, sun-dried, and fresh), some basil, and a few capers.

Cooked Tuna with Cucumbers

Thon confit aux concombres

⚜ ⚜ ∞

Alain Ducasse

Serves 4 ✦ **Preparation time : 1 hour** ✦ **Cooking time : 1 hour**
1 heart of tuna fillet, 1¾ lbs. (800 g) ✦ 1½ cups (1½ l) olive oil, for frying ✦ crushed ice ✦ 12
langoustines, peeled ✦ 10 lemons ✦ sea salt and freshly ground pepper ✦ 2 shallots, sliced ✦ ¼
cup (5 cl) extra-virgin olive oil, for the sauce ✦ 2 tomatoes, peeled, seeded, and chopped ✦ 1
cup (20 cl) chicken stock (page 322) ✦ 2 medium cucumbers ✦ 1½ tbsp. sugar ✦ 2 tbsp. basil
leaves ✦ coarsely ground pepper

Preheat the oven to 450°F (240°C). Slowly deep-fry the tuna in a deep-sided pot or
deep fryer for 1 hour. Be sure the tuna is completed covered with oil that has reached
140°F (60°C)—check the temperature with a cooking thermometer. Remove the tuna
and cool on a bed of crushed ice. Make a sauce by marinating the langoustines in the
juice of 2 of the lemons and salt for 15 minutes. Sauté the heads and shallots in a few
drops of extra-virgin olive oil. Add the tomatoes and reduce to a thick purée over low
heat for 15 minutes. Add the stock and cook for 15 more minutes. Purée the mixture,
including the heads, in a food processor. Strain, then purée to a more uniform consistency with an electric stick blender or food processor. Cool on a bed of ice. Peel
and seed the cucumbers. Slice them lengthwise into strips, salt lightly, and drain in a
colander. Peel 2 of the lemons and cut the zest into very thin slices. Cook the zest in
the sugar and the juice of 5 lemons over low heat for 20 minutes. Arrange the langoustines in a baking dish with the sauce, the juice of the remaining lemon, and salt
and pepper to taste. Bake for 5 minutes. Flake the tuna and mix with the cucumbers
and 2 tbsp. of extra-virgin olive oil. Arrange the tuna mixture on individual plates, top
with sauce, and add the langoustines. Decorate each serving with strips of lemon zest.
Quickly dip the basil leaves in the remaining extra-virgin olive oil and then in coarsely
ground pepper. Garnish the dishes with the leaves.

Cooking tuna at a relatively low temperature, completely immersed in olive oil, will
make it very tender. This recipe is very demanding, but the result is very gratifying.

NOTE BY
**FRANÇOISE
BERNARD**

Tuna Simmered with Tomatoes

Thon mijoté à la tomate

⌂ ∞

Françoise Bernard

Serves 4 ✦ **Preparation time : 25 minutes** ✦ **Cooking time : 30 minutes**
1 piece fresh tuna, 1¾ lbs. (800 g) ✦ **4 tbsp. (50 g) butter** ✦ **2 tbsp. olive oil** ✦ **5 onions, sliced**
✦ **1 tbsp. flour** ✦ **4 tomatoes, chopped** ✦ **2 cups (40 cl) dry white wine** ✦ **1 bouquet garni** ✦ **salt**
and pepper ✦ **4 *cornichons* (sour gherkins), diced** ✦ **5 tbsp. chopped parsley**

Sauté the tuna on both sides in a pan with 1½ tbsp. of the butter and the oil. Remove the fish and set aside. **P**ut the onions and remaining butter in the pot. Simmer over low heat for 2 minutes, just until the onions become translucent. Sprinkle with the flour and stir. **A**dd the tomatoes, wine, bouquet garni, salt, pepper, 2 cups (40 cl) of water, and the tuna. Cover and simmer for 20 minutes. Serve the tuna in the sauce, sprinkled with cornichons and parsley, and accompany with a dish of boiled potatoes.

NOTE BY **ALAIN DUCASSE** For this dish, I would suggest using *la ventrèche* (the belly of the tuna), browned in a sauté pan as indicated in the recipe. When tuna is not rare in the center, I prefer to eat it cold. In this case, I would simply put the fish in an earthenware terrine dish with the tomato sauce, cover it with a sheet of aluminum foil, and let it cool.

Asian Saté Tuna

Saté de thon à l'asiatique

⌂ ⌂ ∞

Alain Ducasse

Serves 4 ✦ **Preparation time : 45 minutes** ✦ **Cooking time : 30 minutes**
⅔ cup (150 g) jasmine rice ✦ 1 lb. (450 g) bluefin tuna ✦ Marinade : (2 tbsp. peanut butter ✦
1 tsp. sugar ✦ 1 tbsp. oil ✦ 1 tbsp. water ✦ ¼ tsp. each of ground coriander, cumin, cinnamon,
and turmeric ✦ 2 shallots, chopped ✦ salt) ✦ 1 tsp. red curry ✦ ½ cup (10 cl) olive oil ✦ 5 tbsp.
saté powder, available in Asian markets ✦ 1 can, 13 oz. (400 ml), coconut milk ✦ 2 tbsp. sugar
✦ 4 tbsp. fish sauce, such as *nuoc-nam*, available in Asian markets ✦ 3 tbsp. white vinegar ✦ 1
tbsp. peanut oil ✦ 1 egg ✦ 2 scallions, minced ✦ 1 small fresh hot pepper, seeded and minced,
optional ✦ 1 tbsp. soy sauce

Cook the rice for 20 minutes in boiling salted water and drain. Combine all the ingredients for the marinade. Cut the tuna into 20 chunks, thread the chunks onto skewers,
and coat with the marinade. Refrigerate. To make the saté sauce, rapidly heat the red
curry in a wok or large frying pan. Add the olive oil and stir with a flat wooden spoon.
Add the saté powder, coconut milk, sugar, fish sauce, and vinegar. Let the mixture
thicken for 10 minutes over medium heat. As soon as the oil begins to rise to the
surface, remove from the heat. Heat the peanut oil in a frying pan. Break the egg into
the oil and cook, stirring with a flat wooden spoon. Add the rice, scallions, and hot
pepper, if desired. Sauté for 5 minutes. Add the soy sauce. To sear the tuna skewers,
place them in a hot, lightly oiled frying pan. Sauté for 5 minutes, turning so that each
side is seared. Place the rice in the center of 4 dishes and arrange tuna skewers around
it. Serve with the saté sauce in a sauceboat.

The saté sauce harmoniously balances sweet and sour flavors. I love the combination,
which is popular in the north of France, where my family comes from.

NOTE BY
FRANÇOISE
BERNARD

Whiting

Whiting fries rapidly. Choose large, fresh pieces and flour it well. This fish is simply delicious cooked over low heat, with lemon and butter. "For a simple fish, choose a simple recipe," Françoise Bernard says.

Alain Ducasse imagines something else. Whiting is most frequently filleted rather than served whole. He coats the fillets with mushroom butter, bakes them, and serves them with a button mushroom sauce. He strongly advises his readers against frying whiting fillets. The crumbly meat is ideal for a terrine, because it is rich in collagen, but it is very likely to fall apart in a frying pan. Be sure not to bread it, he says. Our illustrious chef does not care much for masking foods in that way. Fans of light cuisine can always opt for simply steaming or wrapping the fish "en papillote."

One of Alain Ducasse's gourmet friends once amazed him with a new technique for cooking whiting—he cooked the fish between two plates with a bit of olive oil and a few crushed cloves of garlic. The friend had received the recipe from his own father, who was a fishing fanatic. The result is perfect, because the cooking method does not modify the taste of the fish. For those who wish to astonish their guests with an unusual presentation, there is always the so-called angry fried whiting, a classic preparation. Tie the fish with string so that it appears to be biting its tail, then drop it into a bath of boiling oil. Whole whiting is often floured and fried. This explains why, in the days when France had kings, the hairdressers—who were always covered in wig powder—were nicknamed *merlans*, or whitings.

Stuffed Whiting with Cream

Paupiette de merlan à la crème

♤ ♤ ○

Françoise Bernard

Serves 4 ✦ Preparation time : 20 minutes ✦ Cooking time : 20 minutes
5 whiting fillets ✦ 3 tbsp. crème fraîche or sour cream ✦ 1 small egg white ✦ salt and pepper ✦
2 sprigs tarragon, leaves only ✦ 1½ cups (25 cl) court bouillon ✦ 1 tsp. vinegar ✦ 1 bouquet
garni ✦ 2 tbsp. butter ✦ 1 heaping tbsp. flour

Purée 1 whiting fillet in a food processor. Add 1 tbsp. of the crème fraîche, the egg white, salt, and pepper. Set aside. Flatten the other fillets with the side of a large knife. Season with salt and pepper. Spread the whiting mixture on top, and place a few leaves of tarragon in the center. Roll the fillets into paupiettes. Secure each with a toothpick or string. Place the rolled fillets side by side in a heavy saucepan. Cover with court bouillon and add a dash of vinegar and the bouquet garni. Simmer over low heat. Remove from heat before it comes to a boil. Remove the whiting with a slotted spoon, drain, and set aside in a warm place. Reserve the cooking juice. Melt the butter over low heat and slowly mix in the flour. When the mixture begins to bubble, add the cooking juice and thicken over high heat, whisking constantly. Lower the heat, simmer for 10 minutes, and stir in the remaining crème fraîche. Remove the toothpicks or strings. Arrange the whiting on a dish, top with the sauce, and serve immediately with plain rice or steamed potatoes.

NOTE BY **ALAIN DUCASSE** I would strongly advise you to sprinkle some lemon on the fish, but I admit I am very partial to acidic flavors. Also, be generous with the pepper. It is an often-neglected condiment.

Whiting between Two Plates

Merlan entre deux assiettes

⌂ ○

Alain Ducasse

Serves 2 ✦ **Preparation time : 20 minutes** ✦ **Cooking time : 15 minutes**
2 garlic cloves ✦ **3 tbsp. olive oil** ✦ **4 whiting fillets, skinned and deboned** ✦ **sea salt and pepper**
✦ **2 sprigs of thyme** ✦ **juice of 1 lemon** ✦ **1 thin baguette** ✦ **1 lb. (500 g) spinach leaves** ✦ **3 tbsp.**
whole grain mustard vinaigrette

Preheat the oven to 300°F (130°C). Rub a plate with one of the garlic cloves and pour
on a little olive oil. Fold each whiting fillet into thirds and place on the plate. Season
with salt and pepper to taste. Add a few drops of oil, the thyme sprigs, and lemon
juice. Cover with a second plate. Rest the plates on the rim of a pot of boiling water—
be sure that the pot is smaller in diameter than the plates. Cook the fish until it flakes
when you press it with your finger—about 15 minutes. Remove the thyme sprigs. Cut
the baguette into thin rounds, arrange on a baking sheet, and dry in the oven. Rub
the bread with the remaining garlic clove. Toss the spinach with the vinaigrette, add
the croutons, and serve with the fish.

Many people—myself among them—are convinced that the simpler, the better. It
would be difficult to find anything simpler than this recipe. Remember, the quality of
the whiting must be perfect.

NOTE BY
FRANÇOISE
BERNARD

Whiting with Hazelnut Butter

Merlan au beurre noisette

⇧ ⇧ ◯

Françoise Bernard

Serves 4 ✦ **Preparation time : 15 minutes** ✦ **Cooking time : 15 minutes**
1 cup (20 cl) milk ✦ **salt and pepper** ✦ **2 tbsp. flour** ✦ **4 whitings, cleaned** ✦ **3½ tbsp. butter** ✦
1 lemon ✦ **4 sprigs of chervil, leaves only, chopped** ✦ **3 sprigs of parsley, leaves only, chopped**

Pour the milk into a bowl and season with salt and pepper to taste. Sprinkle the flour on a plate. Rinse the fish and pat dry. Dip each whiting in the milk, then in the flour, gently shaking off the excess. Sauté the fish in 2 tbsp. of butter over medium heat—about 7 minutes on each side, depending on the size. Peel the lemon, removing the skin and white membrane, and dice the pulp. Arrange the whiting on a warm serving dish. Heat the remaining butter in a saucepan. When the butter turns a golden hazelnut color, immediately remove from the heat and pour over the fish. Sprinkle the whiting with chervil, parsley, and diced lemon. Serve immediately. You might also like to serve white rice or Provençal tomatoes.

NOTE BY **ALAIN DUCASSE** If you add a few capers and some chopped flat-leaf parsley to this dish, you will have whiting *grenobloise*. As you can see, you can modify any recipe by changing just one or two ingredients. It's a game I never grow tired of playing!

Whiting with Mushroom Butter

Merlan au beurre de champignon

⛉ ⛉ ○

Alain Ducasse

**Serves 4 ◆ Preparation time : 45 minutes ◆ Cooking time : 30 minutes
1 lb. (500 g) medium button mushrooms ◆ 4 lemons ◆ ½ lb. (226 g) softened butter ◆ 1 tsp.
confectioners' sugar ◆ 1 tsp. fine salt ◆ ½ cup (50 g) brioche bread crumbs ◆ 1 tbsp. coarsely
ground pepper ◆ 1 lb. (500 g) small button mushrooms ◆ ½ cup (10 cl) light cream ◆ 4 whiting
fillets, skinned**

Preheat the oven to 350°F (180°C). Clean the medium button mushrooms, separating
the caps from the stems. Reserve the stems for the cream sauce. Dice the caps and
place in a saucepan with the juice of ½ lemon, 2 tbsp. butter, ½ tsp. confectioners'
sugar, and ½ tsp. salt. Add water to cover and cook for 10 to 15 minutes. Remove
from the heat and cool. Peel 2 lemons, removing the skin and white membrane, and
dice the pulp. Combine 10 tbsp. butter, the diced lemon, bread crumbs, coarsely
ground pepper and the cooked mushrooms. Clean the small button mushrooms. Place
in a saucepan with the juice of ½ lemon, 2 tbsp. butter, ¼ tsp. salt, and ¼ tsp. sugar.
Add enough water to cover and cook for 15 minutes. To make a cream sauce, dice
the reserved mushroom stems. Place in a saucepan with the juice of ½ lemon, 2 tbsp.
butter, the remaining salt and sugar. Add enough water to cover and cook for 15
minutes. Mix in the cream. Fold the whiting fillets in thirds and secure with a toothpick.
Coat with the mushroom butter and bake until the top turns golden. Mix the small
mushrooms into the cream sauce and place some in the center of each plate. Add the
whiting and serve with lemon wedges.

I have only one thing to say about this apparently simple dish. It is so rich that very
few gourmets, even those on a diet, will be able to resist it.

NOTE BY
**FRANÇOISE
BERNARD**

Chicken

Is there anyone who cannot recall the succulent aroma of a superbly roasted chicken? Alain Ducasse is no exception. When he was a child, a chicken was roasted in the fireplace every Sunday. Since then, and on all the menus of his restaurants, he has always served chicken roasted on the spit. His favorite chicken—besides the superb AOC Bresse chicken—is the farm-raised yellow chicken from the Landes region, which he likes for its texture. This beautiful plump bird, with a large breast, is best when roasted. The white-meat Bresse chicken, on the other hand, should be poached in an aromatic broth.

For a chicken with a good balance of meat and not too much fat, choose one that is 3¼ to 4½ lbs. (1½ to 2 kg). The best pieces are, of course, the breasts (nobody can resist a yellow Landes chicken breast with morel mushrooms!), the drumsticks, and—above all—the thighs.

The many quality labels that are found on chickens in the

markets of France somewhat bewilder Françoise Bernard. She does not consider the label the main criterion for purchasing a bird. She looks at the price, and the rest is obvious. A bird that is too cheap cannot be a good chicken. Of course, it's best to buy the chicken at the farm where it was raised, but this is not always possible. She usually chooses a black-leg chicken from Loué or a yellow chicken. She likes her chickens large, even if it means having to freeze part of it on those days when she has no dinner guests.

This smart woman always has a jar of chicken stock, made with chicken giblets, in her freezer. Stock is so much better than bouillon cubes. Because her stock is ready to use, she does not waste time when she cooks chicken fricassees. She just loves chicken with a sauce, especially sautéed chicken in the style of the Auge Valley in Normandy.

Chicken *à la Diable*

Poulet à la diable

⑂ ⑂ ◯

Françoise Bernard

Serves 4 ✦ **Preparation time : 40 minutes** ✦ **Cooking time : 1 hour**
1 chicken, 4 to 5 lbs. (2.5kg.) ✦ **2 tbsp. oil** ✦ **2 shallots** ✦ **3 tbsp. (40 g) butter** ✦ **¼ cup (5 cl)**
vinegar ✦ **½ cup (10 cl) dry white wine** ✦ **½ cup (10 cl) chicken stock (page 322)** ✦ **salt and**
pepper ✦ **4 oz. (100 g) stale sandwich bread** ✦ **5 tbsp. strong Dijon mustard**

Ask your butcher to butterfly the chicken by removing the backbone and leaving the carcass in one piece. Brush with oil. Broil or cook on an outdoor grill for 15 to 20 minutes, turning once halfway through the cooking. **T**o make the sauce, sauté the shallots in the butter. Add the vinegar, wine, and stock. Season with salt and pepper to taste. Simmer, uncovered, for 10 minutes, uncovered. Pulverize the bread in a blender and place on a large plate. **I**f you are using the broiler, turn it off. Preheat the oven to 325°F (150°C). **R**emove the chicken from the broiler or grill. Brush the chicken with mustard and roll it in bread crumbs. Bake for 30 minutes, making sure that the bread crumbs don't brown too quickly. Serve with watercress, sautéed potatoes, and grilled tomatoes. Serve the sauce on the side in a sauceboat.

NOTE BY **ALAIN DUCASSE** A chicken that is deboned this way is called *en crapaudine* in French ("butterflied" in English). You must pay attention to how you cook the thighs and the white meat. The thighs require a much longer cooking time, so remember to protect the breast with aluminum foil.

Chicken Fricassee with Morel Mushrooms

Fricassée de poulet aux morilles

⇑ ⇑ ∞

Alain Ducasse

Serves 4 ♦ Preparation time : 45 minutes ♦ Cooking time : 45 minutes
4 chicken breasts, drumsticks and thighs of free-range chicken ♦ 2 tbsp. olive oil ♦ 8 tbsp. (100 g) butter ♦ 2 cloves garlic, crushed ♦ 1 cup (20 cl) chicken stock (page 322) ♦ 2 cups (40 cl) chicken jus (page 323) ♦ fine sea salt and freshly ground pepper ♦ 2 shallots, finely chopped ♦ 2¼ lbs. (1 kg) fresh morel mushrooms ♦ 1½ cups (30 cl) heavy cream ♦ 1 lemon ♦ 4 tbsp. whipped cream, optional

Preheat the oven to 350°F (180°C). Lightly sauté the chicken pieces in a baking pan in the oil and 4 tbsp. of the butter. Add the garlic and bake—10 minutes for the breasts and 15 minutes for the drumsticks. Transfer to a wire rack and let rest for 10 minutes. Discard the grease from the pan, deglaze with the stock, and add the chicken juice. Reduce to a quarter of its volume—about 20 minutes. Strain. Carefully wash the morels and drain. Cook the shallots in the rest of the butter in a covered pot over low heat. Add the morels and salt and pepper to taste. Cook 20 more minutes. Remove the morels with a slotted spoon and set aside. Reduce their cooking juice to half its volume—about 10 minutes. Add the heavy cream and reduce the sauce until thick. Return the morels to the pot, add the juice of the lemon, and the whipped cream, if desired. Reheat the chicken. Arrange the chicken pieces and creamed morels on warm plates, top with the reduced chicken jus, and serve.

Personally, I would use "Jura yellow" wine instead of chicken stock. It goes very well with the morels and will turn the fricassee into a classic regional dish. Plan to make this recipe for a holiday meal—the yellow wine and morels are rather costly. NOTE BY **FRANÇOISE BERNARD**

Sautéed Chicken from the Auge River Valley

Poulet sauté vallée d'Auge

⌂ ⌂ ○

Françoise Bernard

Serves 4 ✦ Preparation time : 20 minutes ✦ Cooking time : 40 minutes
1 chicken, 4 to 5 lbs. (25 kg), cut in pieces ✦ 2 tbsp. (30 g) butter ✦ salt and pepper ✦ ½ cup
(10 cl) calvados liqueur ✦ 2 egg yolks ✦ ¾ cup (15 cl) crème fraîche or sour cream

Rapidly brown the chicken pieces with the butter, making sure that they do not get too brown. Season with salt and pepper. Cover and simmer over low heat for about 30 minutes. Baste the chicken with the calvados and flambé it, being careful that the flame doesn't get too high. Immediately transfer the chicken pieces to a warm dish. With a spoon, carefully skim off most of the grease that rises to the surface of the sauce. **S**tir the egg yolks into the crème fraîche. Vigorously whisk the egg mixture into the sauce. Do not let it boil. Stir continuously with a wooden spoon, to thicken the sauce. Pour some sauce over the chicken and the rest into a warm sauceboat. Rice, boiled potatoes, or sautéed apples make the best side dishes.

NOTE BY **ALAIN DUCASSE** Generally speaking, plan on 10 minutes for cooking the wings, and 15 to 20 minutes for cooking the thighs. It depends, of course, on the size of the pieces. To play it safe, I prefer making the cream sauce in its own pan so that it will not separate.

Chicken with Herb Butter

Poulet au beurre d'herbes

⛑ ⛑ ⛑ ∞

Alain Ducasse

Serves 4 ✦ **Preparation time : 1 hour** ✦ **Cooking time : 1 hour** ✦ **Refrigeration time : 20 minutes** ✦ 8 oz. (226 g) butter, softened ✦ 1 cup parsley, chopped ✦ 1 cup chervil, chopped ✦ 1 tsp. tarragon ✦ 1 cup chives, snipped ✦ sea salt and freshly ground pepper ✦ 2 cups (200 g) cubed white sandwich bread ✦ 3 chicken livers (100 g) ✦ 5 oz. (150 g) slab bacon, diced ✦ 7 oz. (200 g) duck foie gras, diced ✦ 1 chicken, 3 lbs. (1,3 kg), cleaned ✦ 1½ lbs. (600 g) new potatoes, peeled ✦ 2 tbsp. (30 g) goose or duck fat ✦ 7 oz. (200 g) pearl onions, peeled ✦ 2 tbsp. sugar ✦ 1½ lbs. (600 g) chanterelle mushrooms, cleaned and trimmed ✦ 2 tbsp. olive oil ✦ 1 shallot, chopped

Preheat the oven to 425°F (220°C). **M**ix 11 tbsp. (150 g) of the butter with the parsley, chervil, tarragon, chives, salt, and pepper. Spread a very thin layer of this herb butter between 2 sheets of wax paper. Refrigerate for 20 minutes. **S**auté the bread in a skillet with 3 tbsp. butter. Remove and set aside. In the same pan, sauté the chicken livers and diced bacon. Fry the foie gras without adding any fat. Combine the bread, liver, bacon, and foie gras. Stuff the chicken with the mixture. **M**ake slits under the skin of the chicken. Insert small slices of the chilled herb butter between the meat and skin. Truss the chicken, season with salt and pepper, and bake for 50 minutes, basting often. Let rest on a wire rack for 10 minutes. Reserve some of the juice. **P**an-roast the potatoes in the goose or duck fat. Sauté the pearl onions in the sugar, salt, pepper, and about 2 tbsp. of butter. Add enough water to cover. Fry the mushrooms in the olive oil and add the remaining butter and the shallot. Season with salt and pepper. Remove the string from the chicken. Place the chicken on a platter, arrange the vegetables around it, and serve hot.

This herb butter inserted under the skin obviously makes the meat of the chicken even more tender. It will give it a delicious flavor, too. You must try this recipe—even without the foie gras.

NOTE BY
FRANÇOISE
BERNARD

Duck

How could Alain Ducasse not love duck? What other meat better lends itself to the acidic flavors that he likes so much? Citrus fruits go especially well with the duck's strong tasting meat.

For Françoise Bernard, duck is most beautiful when cooked whole and perfectly golden brown. In the old days, people bought the whole bird rather than have butchers cut it into pieces. Food habits have changed, however, and eating duck today means eating *magret*, the boneless breast served with the skin and layer of fat still attached; *aiguillette*, the breast meat from either side of the breastbone; or the leg and thigh. Françoise Bernard does not care for the leg and thigh, which is all right because, with duck, a lot of this meat is wasted. Actually, the best piece is the breast, but— as she says with her usual solid common sense—there are only two *magrets* per bird; what can we do with the other cuts? Alain Ducasse does not have the same concerns. A restaurant chef is expected to serve only the best portions.

There is still one recipe in which a whole bird must be used, a recipe that is always a success, regardless of trends— duck *à l'orange*. "This dish can be pure bliss or sheer hell," Françoise Bernard exclaims. Both chefs have offered their own versions. The two recipes have some aspects in common, although Alain Ducasse's orange sauce may be slightly more caramelized. They differ as to the recommended cooking time, because Françoise Bernard does not approve of today's tendency to serve duck that is pink. At any rate, no recipe can truly reveal the secret of what happens between the duck and the orange. Success is in the right balance of flavors. Duck *à l'orange* is one of those dishes for which you have to forget the recipe and listen only to your own feelings.

Of course, there are thousands of ways to prepare duck. Françoise Bernard mentions a good friend from Poland who simmers duck, as if it were goose, until the meat is thoroughly tender. You can imagine duck with turnips, figs, or gingerbread . . . but you always return to duck *à l'orange*.

Duck *à l'Orange* I

Canard à l'orange I

⚬ ⚬ ⚬   ⚬⚬⚬

Françoise Bernard

Serves 4 ✦ **Preparation time : 1 hour** ✦ **Cooking time : 2 hours**
1 onion, diced ✦ **1 carrot, diced** ✦ **1 tbsp. oil** ✦ **duck liver, heart, and gizzard, chopped** ✦ **2 cups**
(40 cl) dry white wine ✦ **1 bouquet garni** ✦ **pepper** ✦ **1 duck, 4 to 4½ lbs. (1,8 to 2 kg), or 2**
ducklings ✦ **2 tbsp. (30 g) butter** ✦ **salt and pepper** ✦ **3 oranges** ✦ **1 tbsp. vinegar** ✦ **2 sugar**
lumps ✦ **1 tbsp. curaçao** ✦ **juice of ½ lemon** ✦ **1 tsp. cornstarch**

To make a duck stock, sauté the onion and carrot in the oil with the duck liver, heart, and gizzard. Add the wine, the bouquet garni, 2 cups (40 cl) of water, and pepper to taste. Bring to a boil, skim off the foam, and simmer for 40 minutes. Strain and set aside. In a roasting pan, sauté the duck in the butter. Season with salt and pepper, cook 45 to 50 minutes over medium heat. Wash the oranges and rub the sugar lumps over the skin of 1 orange. Boil the vinegar and sugar to obtain a very syrupy juice. Add the duck stock, simmer for 15 minutes, and set aside. Carefully remove the zest of 1 orange and cut into thin strips. Drop the strips into a small saucepan of cold water, bring to a boil, and drain. Marinate the zest in the curaçao. Peel the remaining 3 oranges and slice the pulp into rounds. When the duck is cooked, add the lemon juice, marinated orange zest, and duck stock. Cook for 5 more minutes. Place the duck in a deep, warm serving dish. Stir the cornstarch into 1 tbsp. cold water, stir into the sauce, and boil as the sauce thickens—about 5 minutes. Add the orange slices. Pour the sauce over the duck and serve immediately.

NOTE BY **ALAIN DUCASSE** You can vary the flavor of the sauce by adding aromatic pepper to the vinegar (Szechwan pepper, for example), and a few spices that go well with the orange—such as nutmeg, cinnamon, or anise.

Duck *à l'Orange* II

Canard à l'orange II

⌂ ⌂ ◯◯◯

Alain Ducasse

Serves 4 ✦ **Preparation time : 50 minutes** ✦ **Cooking time : 50 minutes**
4 to 6 orange leaves, optional ✦ **salt and pepper** ✦ **2 cleaned and trussed ducklings** ✦ **4½ tbsp.**
(55 g) butter ✦ **4 large oranges** ✦ **3 tbsp. sugar** ✦ **3 tbsp. sherry vinegar** ✦ **1¾ cups (35 cl) duck**
jus (page 323) ✦ **juice of ½ lemon, optional**

Preheat the oven to 425°F (220°C). If available, place 2 or 3 orange leaves inside the stomach cavity of each duckling. Season the cavity with salt and pepper. Truss and roast the ducks on a spit or rotisserie. You may, instead, brown them in about 2 tbsp. butter, then roast in the oven for 25 to 30 minutes, basting often. Carefully remove the zest of 1 orange, slice into thin strips, and place in a saucepan. Add enough cold water to cover. Boil, remove from the heat, and let cool. Drain the zest, return it to the saucepan with cold water to cover, and repeat the boiling and draining process two more times. Juice the peeled orange and 1 additional orange. Caramelize the sugar with 1 tbsp. of water, then deglaze it with the vinegar and orange juice. Reduce slightly, add the duck jus, cook to reduce for about 15 minutes. Remove the ducklings, let rest for 15 minutes in a warm place, then untie them. When the sauce is syrupy, whisk in 1 tbsp. of the butter to create a glossy texture. Add the lemon juice, if desired. Stir the orange zest into the sauce. Cut the skin from the 2 remaining oranges, removing the white membranes. Cut the pulp into quarters and sauté in the remaining butter. Carve the ducklings. Arrange one breast in the center of each individual plate, and surround with the oranges. Top with a little sauce and serve the rest in a sauceboat. Save the thighs for another meal.

I have rarely tasted an excellent duck *à l'orange* in a restaurant—but Jean Bertrand, who taught me the trade, used to make a great one. He also slipped orange leaves inside the ducks.

NOTE BY
FRANÇOISE
BERNARD

Braised Duck with Turnips

Canard braisé aux navets

⬦ ⬦ ○○○

Françoise Bernard

Serves 4 ⬦ Preparation time : 1 hour ⬦ Cooking time : 1 hour 45 minutes
1 large onion, sliced ⬦ 1 small carrot, sliced ⬦ duck liver, heart, and gizzard, chopped ⬦ 4 tbsp.
(50 g) butter ⬦ 1 tbsp. flour ⬦ 1½ cups (30 cl) dry white wine ⬦ 1 bouquet garni ⬦ salt and
pepper ⬦ 1 duck, 4 to 4½ lbs. (1,8 to 2 kg) ⬦ 6 scallions, peeled and cut into pieces ⬦ 2¼ lbs.
(1 kg) round baby turnips, peeled and cut

To make the sauce base, sauté the onion, carrot, liver, heart, and gizzard in 2 tbsp. of butter. Sprinkle and stir in the flour. Add the white wine and 1½ cups (30 cl) water. Add the bouquet garni and salt and pepper to taste. Stir, bring to a boil, then simmer, uncovered, for 30 minutes. Strain. Brown the duck in a roasting pan with the remaining butter. When brown on all sides, season with salt and pepper. Pour the fat from the pan, if the duck has rendered a lot of fat. Add the sauce base to the roasting pan, cover, and simmer for 10 minutes over low heat. Add the scallions and turnips to the roasting pan. Cook for 40 to 50 minutes, covered. Baste the duck with the sauce frequently during the last 15 minutes of cooking. Serve immediately.

NOTE BY **ALAIN DUCASSE** In place of small baby turnips, substitute large, long turnips. They cook easily and will absorb the cooking juice well, which will make them very tender. Cook the turnips at a low temperature to give them time to soak up all the flavor of the sauce.

Grilled Boneless Duckling and Polenta au Gratin

Caneton en crapaudine et polenta gratinée

☖ ☖ ☖   ∽∞

Alain Ducasse

**Serves 4 ✦ Preparation time : 50 minutes ✦ Cooking time : 2 hours
1 quart (1 l) chicken stock (page 322) ✦ 1 cup (200 g) polenta ✦ 3 tbsp. olive oil ✦ salt and
pepper ✦ 3 lemons ✦ duck liver, heart, and gizzard ✦ 3 tbsp. (40 g) butter ✦ 1½ cups (30 cl)
duck jus (page 323) ✦ ⅔ cup (60 g) Parmesan cheese, grated ✦ 1 lb. (500 g) turnips, with
greens ✦ 2 cleaned ducklings, butterflied**

Reserve ½ cup (10 cl) of the chicken stock and bring the rest to a boil. Add the polenta
gradually, in a stream, while stirring with a spatula. Add 2 tbsp. oil and season with
salt and pepper to taste. Cook, covered, for about 1 hour. **C**ut the skin from 1 lemon,
removing the white membrane, and dice the pulp. Sauté the liver, heart, and gizzard
in 1 tbsp. butter and the remaining oil. Add the diced lemon pulp and the stock.
Simmer for 25 minutes. Strain. Salt and pepper to taste. **S**poon the polenta onto a
large platter and let cool. Cut into triangles, sprinkle with Parmesan cheese, and broil
for 3 minutes. **S**auté the turnips and some of the turnip greens in the remaining butter.
Color them lightly, then deglaze with the reserved chicken stock. Cook until fork-
tender—about 20 minutes. **R**emove the thighs of the ducklings and save for another
recipe. **J**uice the remaining 2 lemons. Brush the ducklings with the lemon juice and
broil for 15 minutes. The meat should be pink. Arrange the ducklings on a serving dish
with the turnips and polenta triangles. Serve with the sauce—which must be hot—on
the side.

It's a good idea not to serve anything but breast of duck. The thighs are always a little
tough, but can be prepared as a stew or braised with turnips, as in my recipe on page
110.

NOTE BY
**FRANÇOISE
BERNARD**

Guinea Hen

Is the guinea hen considered poultry or game? It is a farm animal, so it is actually poultry—but the flavor is very similar to game. Its wild taste may derive from the guinea hen's African origins. The bird was originally named after Numidia, an ancient country in north Africa. Because it prefers to roost in trees and argue with its relatives rather than abide by the rules of the chicken coop. The guinea hen used to cause quite a few problems for farmers. (This independent spirit also made it the symbol of Haiti.) For a long time, guinea hens were a luxury item—but since the 1970s, breeding, artificial insemination, and new farm designs have made it much easier to raise them.

In his two recipes, Alain Ducasse calls for young guinea hens (called *pintadeau* in French) because he prefers tender meat. These recipes are newly created, because Ducasse has never served guinea hen in his restaurants. There is no label of origin for guinea hen, and top quality is a must for him.

The only recognized guinea hen is the "red label," a free-range bird, which lives and eats outside under a net—but that is not good enough for Alain Ducasse.

The guinea hen may not be very popular in the world of *grande cuisine*, but this does not seem to bother Françoise Bernard. She finds the bird especially easy to cook. She chooses it rather lean, with a flexible wishbone and a transparent skin—basically, she selects guinea hens as if they were chickens. The comparison does not stop there. Guinea hen slips easily into chicken recipes. It can be fried with mushrooms, stewed, or grilled *en crapaudine*. Because the meat is lean, however, it's best when braised, stewed, cooked in the pressure cooker, or *en papillote*.

Here's an age-old trick for making sure the meat stays tender: Stuff the guinea hen with a grated apple mixed into some cream cheese.

Guinea Hen with Onions, Potatoes, and Mushrooms

Pintade bonne femme

⌂ ⌂ ∞

Françoise Bernard

**Serves 4 ♦ Preparation time : 30 minutes ♦ Cooking time : 1 hour 15 minutes
8 oz. (250 g) pearl onions, peeled ♦ 1½ lbs. (750 g) potatoes, peeled and cut into medium
cubes ♦ 2 guinea hens ♦ salt and pepper ♦ 6 tbsp. (80 g) butter ♦ 8 oz. (250 g) mushrooms,
cleaned, trimmed, and sliced ♦ 5 sprigs parsley, minced**

Drop the onions and potatoes into a large pot of boiling water. Cook for 5 minutes,
drain, and set aside. **S**eason the insides of the hens with salt and pepper. Melt 4 tbsp.
of the butter in a large casserole and brown the guinea hens on all sides over low
heat. Remove the hens from the pot. Sauté the onions and potatoes in the pan drippings. When the vegetables are well browned, season with salt and pepper. Return
the hens to the pot and cook, covered, over medium heat for 40 to 50 minutes. **Q**uickly
sauté the mushrooms in the remaining butter. Season with salt and pepper, add to
the hens, and simmer for 5 minutes. Just before serving, sprinkle the dish with parsley.
Serve hot.

NOTE BY **ALAIN DUCASSE** Be sure to let the birds sit a while after cooking. Ideally, position them on their backs,
with their thighs in the air. This will force the meat to relax and the juice to spread
into it.

Young Guinea Hen with Lemon, Couscous, and Raisins

Pintadeau au citron, semoule de blé aux raisins

⌂ ⌂ ∞

Alain Ducasse

Serves 4 ✦ Preparation time : 1 hour 30 minutes ✦ Cooking time : 1 hour 30 minutes ✦ 4 lemons ✦ 4 tbsp. sugar ✦ salt and pepper ✦ 12 pearl onions ✦ 4 tbsp. (50 g) butter ✦ 1 tbsp. sherry vinegar ✦ 3 celery stalks, thinly sliced ✦ 1¼ cups (25 cl) olive oil ✦ 2 young guinea hens, or butterflied ✦ 1 cup (200 g) couscous ✦ 1¼ cups (25 cl) chicken stock (page 322) ✦ ½ cup (10 cl) chicken jus (page 323) ✦ 12 blanched almonds ✦ ¼ cup (40 g) raisins ✦ ¼ cup (30 g) capers ✦ 6 chives, minced ✦ 8 oven-dried tomatoes (page 231)

Cook zests of 2 of the lemons for 1 hour in ¾ cup (15 cl) water, 2 tbsp. sugar, and a pinch of salt, first bringing to a boil, then simmering over low heat. Cool completely in the juice, then drain on paper towels. Caramelize the pearl onions in 1½ tbsp. butter, the vinegar, 1 tbsp. sugar, and a pinch of salt, adding a little water as needed to keep the onions from burning. Set aside. Cook the celery, covered, in 1 tbsp. of the olive oil over low heat for 15 minutes. Set aside. Peel 1 of the remaining lemons. Reserve the rind and chop the pulp. Juice the remaining lemon, reserving the rind. Combine the chopped lemon pulp, lemon juice, 1 cup (20 cl) olive oil, 2 tbsp. water, and 1 tbsp. sugar. Marinate the guinea hen in the mixture. Sprinkle 3 tbsp. of warm water into the couscous. Roll a handful of the grains between your palms to break up the clumps. Repeat until all of the couscous is moistened. Add more water as needed. Sift through a large-holed colander and mix in 1 tbsp. olive oil. Place in a steamer lined with cheese cloth. Steam, covered, for 15 to 25 minutes. Preheat the oven to 350°F (180°C). Pour the steamed couscous into large bowl and add remaining butter. Repeat the hand-rolling process to break up clumps. As you work, toss grains slightly to lighten the mixture. Brown the guinea hens in olive oil in a large skillet. Place in a casserole, finish in the oven for 20 minutes. Remove and set aside for 10 minutes. To make the sauce, pour baking juices into the skillet and deglaze with ¼ cup (5 cl) chicken stock. Add remaining stock, reduce for 5 minutes, and add the chicken jus and uncooked lemon rinds. Strain. Sauté the celery, onions, almonds, and raisins in 1 tbsp. olive oil. Add the capers, chives, tomatoes, cooked lemon rinds, and 1 tbsp. of the sauce. Mix well. Serve the almond-raisin mixture with the guinea hen and couscous.

Almonds, lemons, raisins—this Middle Eastern-inspired dish makes your mouth water. The flavors are intense and caramelized. The dish is very tasty and slightly spicy for couscous.

NOTE BY **FRANÇOISE BERNARD**

Stewed Guinea Hen with Mushrooms and Fried Bread

Pintade compotée aux champignons et pain doré

⌂ ⌂ ⌂   ∞

Françoise Bernard

Serves 4 ✦ **Preparation time : 1 hour** ✦ **Cooking time : 1 hour 50 minutes**
1 guinea hen 3 lbs. (1.2 kg) ✦ **8 tbsp. (100 g) butter, softened** ✦ **1 guinea hen liver and giblets,**
chopped ✦ **1 chicken or poultry giblets** ✦ **2 cups (40 cl) dry white wine** ✦ **1 onion, diced** ✦ **1**
carrot, diced ✦ **1 bouquet garni** ✦ **salt and pepper** ✦ **4 oz. (100 g) button mushrooms, cleaned**
and trimmed ✦ **½ lemon** ✦ **2 slices white sandwich bread, each cut into 4 triangles** ✦ **2 oz.**
(50 g) slab bacon, diced

Preheat the oven to 400°F (210°C). Place the guinea hen in a baking dish and brush
with about 1½ tbsp. of the butter. Bake for 20 minutes. Cool, cut the meat from the
bones. Reserve the cooking juice in a separate bowl. Sauté the carcass, guinea hen
giblets, and chicken giblets in 1½ tbsp. butter. Add the wine, cooking juice from the
hen, onion, carrot, bouquet garni, and about 1½ cups (30 cl) of water. Season with
salt and pepper. Simmer, uncovered, for 1 hour. Strain. Put the reserved meat in a
saucepan, pour the sauce on top, cover, and cook over low heat for 20 minutes. Rub
the mushroom caps with lemon and sauté in 1 tbsp. of butter for 5 minutes. Cut the
bacon and chop the liver finely. Sauté the bacon with the mushrooms. Add the liver,
season with salt and pepper. Cook for 3 to 5 minutes. Place the mixture on a plate
and mash well with a fork. In a separate pan sauté the bread triangles in 2 tbsp. of
hot butter, then drain on paper towels. Place the hen in the center of a warm serving
dish. Stir the bacon mixture into the sauce. Pour sauce over the guinea hen and arrange
the mushrooms and fried bread triangles around it. Serve immediately.

NOTE BY **ALAIN DUCASSE**   There is an old-fashioned garnish for this dish; "grandmother's casserole," a few caramelized small onions, some sautéed bacon cooked with mushrooms, and new potatoes.

Winter Salad
with Roast Guinea Hen

Salade d'hiver au pintadeau rôti

⌂ ∞

Alain Ducasse

Serves 4 ◆ Preparation time : 1 hour ◆ Cooking time : 1 hour 30 minutes
1 guinea hen, 3 lbs. (1.2 kg), cleaned and trussed ◆ ½ cup (10 cl) olive oil ◆ 3 garlic cloves,
peeled ◆ 1 small baguette, sliced ◆ olive oil, for sautéing the bread ◆ 1 cup (20 cl) chicken
stock (page 322) ◆ 1 guinea hen liver, chopped ◆ ¼ cup (5 cl) sherry vinegar ◆ 3 oz. (80 g)
mesclun ◆ 2 oz. (50 g) purslane ◆ 2 oz. (50 g) oak leaf lettuce ◆ 1 oz. (30 g) dandelion ◆ ½
head frisée lettuce ◆ 5 sprigs flat-leaf parsley ◆ 2 sprigs marjoram ◆ 5 chives ◆ 7 oz. (200 g)
porcini mushrooms in oil ◆ salt and pepper

Preheat the oven to 350°F (180°C). Brush the guinea hen with 1 tbsp. of the olive oil.
Bake for 40 minutes. Set aside to cool. Rub the garlic cloves on the baguette slices
and fry the bread in a little olive oil. Remove the guinea hen's legs and separate the
thighs and drumsticks. Debone the entire bird, including the breast. Dice the meat of
the thighs and drumsticks but leave the breasts whole. Fry the diced meat in olive oil
until crisp. Transfer the cooking juice to a baking dish and lay the breasts on top. Break
the carcass with a mallet or cleaver. Sauté in olive oil, then add the chicken stock.
Cook for 30 minutes. Strain. To make the vinaigrette, sauté the liver in olive oil. Mix
in the strained stock and reduce for 15 minutes. Add the vinegar, ¼ cup (5 cl) olive
oil, salt, and pepper. Set aside. Wash the salad greens and herbs. Separate the parsley
and marjoram leaves from the stems, discarding the stems. Mince the chives. Toss the
salad greens, herbs, and one third of the vinaigrette in a large bowl. Roast the guinea
hen breasts to reheat, then cut the meat into thin slices. Arrange the white-meat slices,
mushrooms, fried bread, and diced meat on top of the salad. Drizzle the rest of the
vinaigrette on top and serve.

There is no longer a special season of the year for salads. Now that you can buy NOTE BY
packaged salad greens everywhere, you can make a nice mixed salad at any time. **FRANÇOISE**
Don't deprive your roasted guinea hen of a salad. It's simple to make and quite nice. **BERNARD**

Pigeon

Pigeon with peas is a traditional dish of good fortune, heralding the coming of beautiful days. In the seventeenth century, during the reign of King Louis XIV, young pigeons were cooked with peas that were just as young and tender as the meat of the bird. By the 1970s, pigeon was considered a delicacy in family cookbooks, as was woodcock, which is often replaced with pigeon today.

Alain Ducasse always has pigeon on the menu in his restaurants. It is almost always cooked in a salmis sauce, made with the heart and liver of the bird. In Monaco, the salmis is flavored with herbs. As for his young pigeon with grilled potatoes and herbs, it has been brought back to the menu by popular request time and again.

Ducasse's pigeons come from the town of Saint-Brevin-les-Pins in the Côte de Jade on the Atlantic coast. These young pigeons weigh about 1.2 lbs. (500 g) each. Most pigeons have white meat, but the meat of the pigeons from the

Côte de Jade is red. These birds are extremely tender because they are caught while they are still in their nests, before they learn to fly. Pigeon must be eaten young or not at all.

It's not enough to know how to choose a pigeon. You have to know how to prepare it, too—and it's not as easy as it looks. Of course, old pigeons can just be stewed. Or, their meat can be sliced thin and baked in Françoise Bernard's delicious pigeon pie with olives—but this will not do for young birds. Alain Ducasse always cuts his pigeons before cooking, because not all the pieces cook in the same way. It's impossible to cook thighs correctly if you cook the whole pigeon. Françoise Bernard has found her own way to avoid this problem. She finishes her young pigeon halves by roasting them in aluminum-foil papillotes to keep the birds tender and tasty. Alain Ducasse has solved the problem by suggesting one recipe for legs only, and another for breasts only. By creating two recipes for one pigeon, Alain Ducasse has developed a truly original concept.

Pigeon in Papillotes

Pigeonneau en papillote

⇧ ⇧   ∞

Françoise Bernard

Serves 4 ◆ **Preparation time : 45 minutes** ◆ **Cooking time : 45 minutes**
2 young pigeons, 1.2 lbs. (500 g) each ◆ **4 tbsp. (60 g) butter** ◆ **salt and pepper** ◆ **2 shallots,**
chopped ◆ **1 cup (20 cl) dry white wine** ◆ **7 oz. (200 g) mushrooms, cleaned, trimmed, and**
chopped ◆ **1 tbsp. tomato paste** ◆ **5 sprigs parsley, chopped** ◆ **2 slices boiled ham, cut into 4**
pieces each

Preheat the oven to 425°F (220°C). **S**plit the pigeons in half lengthwise with a knife
or a cleaver. Sear them in a frying pan with 2 tbsp. of butter. Season with salt and
pepper, set aside. **T**o make the stuffing, simmer the shallots in wine, uncovered. Add
the mushrooms, tomato paste, and parsley, season with salt and pepper to taste.
Reduce until the liquid has almost completely evaporated. **M**easure out 4 squares of
aluminum foil, large enough to wrap half a pigeon. On one-half of each square, layer
1 piece of ham, 1 tbsp. of stuffing, a sautéed pigeon half, 1 tbsp. of stuffing, 1 piece
of ham, and 2 dabs of butter. Fold the aluminum foil, then pleat and twist the opening
to seal the package. Bake the papillotes for about 25 minutes. Serve the pigeons still
wrapped in the foil, setting the papillotes on individual plates for your guests to open
themselves.

NOTE BY **ALAIN DUCASSE** Cooking in an aluminium-foil papillote produces excellent results. It concentrates the
flavors without drying out the meat, which is why it is a particularly good method for
cooking pigeon.

Pigeon Breast with Grilled Potatoes and Herbs

Poitrine de pigeonneau et pommes de terre grillées

☝ ☝ ☝   ◯◯◯

Alain Ducasse

Serves 4 ✦ **Preparation time : 1 hour** ✦ **Cooking time : 1 hour 30 minutes**
4 medium red-skinned potatoes, about 4 oz. (100 g) each, scrubbed and dried ✦ **2¼ lbs. (1 kg)**
duck fat ✦ **2 sprigs sage** ✦ **1 sprig thyme** ✦ **1 sprig rosemary** ✦ **1 bay leaf** ✦ **3 garlic cloves, peeled**
✦ **1 shallot, peeled** ✦ **4 pigeons, about 1.2 lbs. (500 g) each** ✦ **sea salt and freshly ground pepper**
✦ **2 tbsp. olive oil** ✦ **½ tsp. thyme flowers** ✦ **1 cup (20 cl) pigeon jus (page 323)** ✦ **6 tbsp.**
(80 g) butter, cut into small pieces ✦ **1 tbsp. sherry vinegar, optional** ✦ **2 oz. (50 g) fresh herb**
leaves, such as basil, chervil, parsley, and chives ✦ **4 pigeon livers and hearts, chopped**

In a covered skillet, cook the potatoes in duck fat with a sprig of the sage, the thyme, rosemary, bay leaf, garlic, and shallot over low heat for 1 hour. Let the potatoes cool in the fat. Preheat the broiler or preheat the oven to 350°F (180°C). Split the pigeons lengthwise with a knife or cleaver. Remove the legs and thighs, reserve for another recipe. Season the 4 split breasts with salt and pepper and rub with oil. Grill or bake for 10 minutes. Remove from oven and set aside for 10 minutes. In a saucepan, combine the thyme flowers and pigeon jus and reduce for 10 minutes. Remove from heat and whisk in the butter. If you wish, enhance the sauce by adding a dash of vinegar. Cut the potatoes into ½ in. (1 cm) rounds, brush with oil, and grill for 5 minutes. Mince the fresh herb leaves and the remaining sage leaves. Detach the breasts from the breastbones. Coat the potatoes with the sauce to give them a glossy appearance. Bring the rest of the sauce to a boil. Add the chopped livers, hearts, minced herbs, salt and pepper to taste. Cook over low heat for 1 to 2 minutes, careful not to boil. Arrange the pigeon breasts on top of the potatoes and serve the herb sauce on the side.

I would never have thought of preparing one dish with two methods—broil the breasts and sauté the thighs. These pieces do require different cooking times. What an intelligent and refined recipe.

NOTE BY
FRANÇOISE
BERNARD

Pigeon Pie with Olives

Tourte de pigeon aux olives

⬠ ◠◠◠

Françoise Bernard

Serves 4 ✦ Preparation time : 50 minutes ✦ Cooking time : 1 hour 15 minutes
2 cups (280 g) flour ✦ 2 pinches of salt ✦ 9 tbsp. (125 g) butter, softened ✦ 1 large or 2 small
pigeons, split ✦ 2 tbsp. (30 g) butter ✦ 4 oz. (100 g) slab bacon, diced ✦ 4 oz. (125 g) pearl
onions ✦ 1 tbsp. flour ✦ 1¼ lb. (500 g) tomatoes, seeded and diced ✦ 7 oz. (200 g) green olives,
pitted ✦ 1 bouquet garni ✦ salt and pepper ✦ 1 egg

In a large bowl, work the flour, salt, and softened butter with your fingertips. When
the mixture has a grainy texture, add 2 to 3 tbsp. of cold water. Knead to form a
dough. Refrigerate for at least 30 minutes. Sauté both sides of the pigeon halves in
the butter. Add the bacon and pearl onions, sauté until brown—about 5 minutes.
Gradually add and mix in the flour. Add the tomatoes, olives, bouquet garni, salt and
pepper to taste. Cover and simmer for about 30 minutes to reduce to a light syrup.
Preheat the oven to 425°F (220°C). Beat the egg. Roll out the dough to fit over the
pie, and prick with a fork. Spoon the pigeon and sauce into a buttered pie pan. Moisten
the rim of the plate with water and cover the mixture with the dough. Press and pinch
the dough around the rim to seal it. Brush the top of the pie with the beaten egg.
Bake for 10 minutes, reduce the temperature to 375°F (190°C), and bake for 20 more
minutes.

NOTE BY **ALAIN DUCASSE** This is a sample of good country-style cuisine. I can almost hear the crackling of the
wood as I sit by the fireplace on a fall evening, eating pigeon pie and a fresh crunchy
salad from my garden.

Sautéed Pigeon Drumsticks in Pastry

Cuisses de pigeonneau en rissoles

☝ ☝ ◌◌◌

Alain Ducasse

Serves 4 ✦ **Preparation time : 1 hour 15 minutes** ✦ **Cooking time : 30 minutes**
8 pigeon legs ✦ 1 quart (1 l) vegetable oil, for frying ✦ salt and pepper ✦ 1¾ cups (35 cl) olive oil ✦ 4 oz. (100 g) fresh foie gras of duck, diced ✦ 8 pigeon or chicken livers and hearts, diced ✦ 1½ oz. (40 g) unsmoked slab bacon, ✦ 1 white onion, thinly sliced ✦ 1 small celery stalk, diced ✦ 4 oz. (100 g) button mushrooms, cleaned, trimmed, and diced ✦ 1½ cups (30 cl) chicken stock (page 322) ✦ 1 cup (100 g) fresh bread crumbs ✦ 10 sprigs chives, minced ✦ 5 sprigs chervil, minced ✦ 3½ cups (530 g) flour ✦ 1 egg yolk

Immerse the pigeon legs in a deep fryer of hot oil. Take them out quickly and remove the skin. Season with salt and pepper. Sauté with 2 tbsp. of the olive oil over high heat for 5 minutes. Remove the bones, leaving on the drumstick. Sauté the foie gras for 1 minute in a hot frying pan without adding any fat. Remove, reserve on the side. In the same pan add the livers and hearts. Sauté the bacon and onion in 1 tbsp. of olive oil. Add the celery and mushrooms and sauté for 5 minutes. Add ¼ cup (5 cl) chicken stock and reduce to a syrupy consistency. Add the foie gras, livers, hearts, bread crumbs, chives, and chervil. Mix well and season to taste. Spoon some stuffing into the boneless part of the drumsticks. Mix the flour with about ¾ cup (15 cl) water, egg yolk, 1½ cups (30 cl) olive oil, and salt to taste. Knead for 5 to 10 minutes to form a smooth dough. Thinly roll out the dough and cut into 8 squares, 3 in. (8 cm) wide. Wrap a drumstick with stuffing in each square, leaving the bone sticking out. Pinch the edges of the squares together and seal in the juices. Refrigerate on a floured dish until ready to cook. Sauté the stuffed pastries in the remaining olive oil. Serve with a warm lettuce salad embellished with cooked bacon bits and fresh baby fava beans.

To save time, you can use a pre-made pastry crust. Be sure to pinch the edges of the pastry squares tight and seal them with a beaten egg or water. It might be wise to prepare this recipe in a trial run before attempting to prepare it for guests. — NOTE BY **FRANÇOISE BERNARD**

Rabbit

Do you still consider Rabbit with Mustard a classic dish—or has it become ordinary? Just imagine the rabbit cooked on a spit, served on a bed of young vegetables, covered with sauce, and sprinkled with a few cloves of garlic gently sautéed in olive oil. This is how Alain Ducasse cooks *Rabbit à la Moutarde* for his friends. Françoise Bernard thinks that Alain Ducasse's term for the rabbit bottom, *cul de lapin* ("rabbit butt"), is very cute—but what exactly is rabbit bottom? It is the solid piece of rabbit saddle and the hind legs, what the French call *le baron*. "Chefs are very good at naming their recipes, and you must admit that Alain Ducasse's names, which are both witty and explanatory, have influenced many a modern chef," says Françoise Bernard.

Rabbit, for Bernard, means rabbit terrine that she ate as a child, when the little Parisian girl was on vacation in the north with her relatives. A rustic dish, in keeping with the mining communities there. Rabbit bones give the pâté its strong flavor and jellied texture. The terrine is eaten quite simply: with just a fork. When young Françoise would return home to the capital city, she would long for the rustic dishes of the north—although her mother preferred that she embrace more elegant flavors.

Let's admit it, the rabbit is not a citified creature. Alain Ducasse, who still fondly remembers the rabbits that his Landes grandmother bred, has never put it on the menu in his Paris restaurant. "I mostly cook rabbit in Monaco or in Moustiers," he says. "It is very successful in the south, but it has few fans in Paris." In Bastide de Moustiers, the only restaurant in which the Michelin star-studded chef cooks family dishes, Ducasse serves small tender morsels of rabbit—*bocconcini*, he calls them, in the Italian style. For both of these chefs, the only acceptable rabbit is an organic, free-range rabbit. This type is fleshier than its factory-farm brother and has a pink skin and a plump baron. But the piece that Alain Ducasse is crazy about is the shoulder. "Nothing is more tender than the front legs," he says.

Whether in a sauce or a terrine, the rabbit requires wholesome and mild-flavored recipes, dishes that evoke the countryside and wide expanses of land. This small animal is not easy to classify and is often banished from the chapter on poultry—but it has its place on our tables.

Sautéed Rabbit with Prunes

Sauté de lapin aux pruneaux

⌂ ⌂ ∽

Françoise Bernard

Serves 4 ◆ Marinating time : 12 hours ◆ Preparation time : 45 minutes ◆ Cooking time : 1 hour 40 minutes ◆ 2 carrots ◆ 3 onions ◆ 1 shallot ◆ 2 cloves garlic ◆ 1 celery stalk ◆ 1½ cups (30 cl) dry white or red wine ◆ 6 tbsp. vinegar ◆ 1 tbsp. oil ◆ 2 garlic cloves ◆ 1 sprig thyme, leaves only ◆ 1 bay leaf, broken ◆ 1 rabbit, cut into pieces ◆ 1 tbsp. flour ◆ 2 tbsp. (30 g) butter ◆ 1.2 lbs. (500 g) prunes ◆ 1 tbsp. red currant or blueberry jelly ◆ salt and pepper

The day before serving, peel and coarsely chop the carrots, celery, onions, shallot, and garlic. Combine the wine, vinegar, oil, cloves, thyme leaves, and bay leaf in a deep dish. Stir in the chopped vegetables. Marinate the rabbit pieces in the mixture overnight in the refrigerator. The next day, remove the rabbit from the marinade with a slotted spoon. Drain and pat dry with paper towels. Sprinkle the pieces lightly with flour and sauté in butter in a large skillet. While the meat is cooking, transfer the marinade to a saucepan large enough to hold the rabbit, and boil over high heat for 5 minutes. Strain, return to the pan with the rabbit pieces. Cover, simmer for 1 hour. Add the prunes halfway through the cooking. Arrange the rabbit pieces in a deep serving dish and keep warm. Reduce the cooking juice until it thickens slightly, lower the heat, stir in the jelly with a wooden spoon. Serve the rabbit hot with the sauce on the side. A few boiled potatoes go very well with this savory sauce.

NOTE BY **ALAIN DUCASSE** Instead of red currant jelly, I suggest binding the sauce with a fine prune purée. Soften some prunes in warm tea, pit them, and blend in a food processor.

Rabbit with Mustard and Early Vegetables

Lapin à la moutarde et jeunes légumes

⇧ ⇧ ∞

Alain Ducasse

Serves 4 ✦ **Preparation time : 55 minutes** ✦ **Cooking time : 30 minutes**
about ⅔ cup (150 g) whole grain mustard ✦ ¼ cup (5 cl) crème fraîche or sour cream ✦ salt
and pepper ✦ 1 rabbit baron, saddle and hind legs, 2¼ lbs. (1 kg) ✦ 2 carrots ✦ 12 scallions ✦
6 pearl onions ✦ 3 medium potatoes, about 10 oz. (300 g) ✦ ¾ cup (15 cl) olive oil ✦ 3 cups
(60 cl) rabbit jus (page 323) ✦ 4 tbsp. (50 g) butter ✦ 10 cloves garlic, unpeeled ✦ ½ cup (60
g) Parmesan cheese

Mix the mustard, crème fraîche, and salt and pepper to taste. Brush the rabbit with
the mixture. Spit rotisserie or roast in an oven preheated to 350°F (180°C) about 25
minutes. Let rest for 10 minutes. **P**eel the vegetables. Thinly slice the carrots, 4 of the
scallions, the pearl onions, and the potatoes. Sauté in ½ cup (10 cl) of the oil until
they are translucent but not brown. Season to taste, add 1 cup (20 cl) of rabbit jus,
and simmer 10 to 15 minutes. Transfer to a baking dish and set aside. **S**auté the
remaining scallions in the butter until translucent. Add the rest of the rabbit jus. In a
small, covered saucepan, sauté the garlic in ¼ cup (5 cl) oil over low heat until soft.
Mix with the scallions. **S**prinkle the vegetables with Parmesan cheese and place the
baking dish under the broiler to brown. Reheat the rabbit in the oven and arrange the
pieces on a serving platter with the vegetables and the garlic and scallions. Top with
a bit of the jus. Pour the rest of the jus into a sauceboat and serve immediately.

The flavorful rabbit jus and the vegetables with Parmesan cheese add a new twist to
the traditional recipe of *lapin à la moutarde*. Don't forget to carry a cutting board to
the table so you can carve the meat in front of your guests.

NOTE BY
FRANÇOISE
BERNARD

Country-Style Rabbit Terrine

Terrine paysanne de lapin à l'os

⌂ ○

Françoise Bernard

Serves 4 ◆ Marinating time : 12 hours ◆ Preparation time : 45 minutes ◆ Cooking time : 1 hour 30 minutes ◆ 1 onion, diced ◆ 1 carrot, diced ◆ 1 clove garlic, chopped ◆ 1 tbsp. oil ◆ 1 bouquet garni ◆ 1½ cups (30 cl) white wine ◆ ¼ cup (5 cl) Madeira wine, optional ◆ salt and pepper ◆ 2 saddles of rabbit, cut into pieces ◆ 2 lbs. (900 g) ground pork shoulder ◆ 8 thin slices fresh pork fatback

The day before serving, combine the onion, carrot, garlic, oil, bouquet garni, white wine and Madeira, if using. Season with pepper, add the rabbit pieces, mix well, and marinate in the refrigerator overnight. **T**he next day, preheat the oven to 300°F (180°C). **R**emove the rabbit with a slotted spoon and strain the marinade. Mix the ground pork with salt, pepper, and enough marinade to form a soft, but not mushy, mixture. **L**ine the bottom of an earthenware terrine dish with the slices of fatback. Add a layer of ground pork then a layer of rabbit (with the bones), packing the pieces close together. Cover the rabbit pieces with another layer of ground pork. Cover the terrine mixture with the remaining fatback. Bake in a hot water bath about 1 hour 30 minutes. Remove from the oven and water bath, let cool completely. This terrine cannot be sliced because of the rabbit bones. Serve it directly from the dish with a large serving spoon.

NOTE BY **ALAIN DUCASSE** Because the taste of rabbit meat is very delicate, it is important not to smother it with too many strong spices. This is also why you do not chop the meat too finely. Rather, cut it in large pieces. Rabbit bones are very brittle and are unpleasant to chew if broken. The success of such a dish depends on a correct cooking temperature. The terrine should be cooked in a medium oven in a *bain-marie* (pan of water).

Rabbit *Bocconcini* with Olives and Polenta

Bocconcini de lapin aux olives et polenta

♔ ♔ ∝

Alain Ducasse

Serves 4 ✦ Preparation time : 50 minutes ✦ Cooking time : 1 hour 30 minutes
½ cup (10 cl) olive oil ✦ 1 quart (1 l) chicken stock (page 322) ✦ 1 cup (200 g) cornmeal, medium or coarse ✦ 1 deboned rabbit, preferably organic ✦ salt and white pepper ✦ 1 yellow onion, thinly sliced ✦ 1 carrot, thinly sliced ✦ 2 leeks, white parts only, thinly sliced ✦ 1 celery stalk, thinly sliced ✦ 2 cloves garlic, unpeeled ✦ 5 sprigs flat-leaf parsley, chopped ✦ 1½ cups (30 cl) red wine ✦ 5 scallions ✦ 1 sprig thyme, leaves only ✦ 1 cup (100 g) olives, pitted ✦ ½ cup (100 g) pine nuts ✦ ⅓ cup (40 g) Parmesan cheese

Grease a saucepan with 1 tbsp. of the oil. Add the chicken stock, bring to a boil, and remove from the heat. Sprinkle in the cornmeal, to make polenta, a little at a time, stirring constantly with a wooden spoon or whisk. When all the cornmeal has been added, continue to stir until the mixture is smooth—about 5 minutes. Stir in 4 tbsp. of oil. Cover the pan with a sheet of parchment paper and simmer an hour over very low heat, stirring often. **C**ut the rabbit into bite-size pieces, season with salt, and mix well. Sauté the onion, carrot, leeks, and celery in 2 tbsp. oil in a large skillet over medium heat. Add the garlic and chopped parsley. Season with salt and pepper to taste. Sauté another 3 minutes. Place the rabbit pieces on the vegetables and cook 10 minutes, stirring often. Add the wine and simmer over low heat 10 to 15 minutes. Remove the meat, strain the sauce, and reduce over medium heat to two-thirds its volume. **L**ightly sauté the scallions in a little oil. Add the rabbit, thyme leaves, olives, salt, and pepper. Arrange the meat on warmed individual plates, cover with sauce, and sprinkle with pine nuts. Serve with the polenta (cooked cornmeal) sprinkled with Parmesan cheese.

Alain Ducasse's rabbit *bocconcini* (the Italian word for "bite-size pieces") is an ideal dish for a Sunday meal with your family. If you can't find whole rabbit, buy pieces.　NOTE BY **FRANÇOISE BERNARD**

Turkey

When it comes to buying turkey, first of all, do not choose a big one. Françoise Bernard is adamant on this point. "I know that they cook huge turkeys for Thanksgiving Day in the United States, but they also have enormous ovens." In France, a 6½ lb. (3 kg) turkey, 8 lbs. (4 kg) maximum, is fine. Alain Ducasse agrees. "The bird must be young if you want it tender and tasty. Besides, a smaller bird will dry out less while cooking. A turkey of more than 6 lbs. (2,7 kg) is likely to be tough and dry. It would have to roast much longer in a medium oven and would need to be basted very often. In any case, the prerequisites for tender meat are long, low-temperature cooking, and frequent basting. Choose your turkey as you would any other fowl—do not be impressed by its size. The signs of a good turkey are about the same as those of a good chicken: shiny, black legs; a flexible wishbone, meat that feels firm and elastic if you press on it with your finger; a soft, transparent skin. To be avoided: red legs or scaly legs, a warning of dry meat."

Neither of our chefs is inspired by sautéed turkey pieces. To Françoise Bernard, they look as if they were cut from some old, hard bird—although she admits that she might be biased. She concedes that a turkey thigh cooked like a *coq au vin* produces good results.

Actually, both of our chefs think about turkey only as a whole bird, roasted or braised. Alain Ducasse does not cook it often. Turkey is hardly eaten in the south of France— except, perhaps, for Christmas dinner—and he is a child of the south.

Turkey Stuffed with Chestnuts

Dindonneau farci aux marrons

⇧ ⇧ ∞

Françoise Bernard

Serves 4 ♦ **Preparation time : 50 minutes** ♦ **Cooking time : 3 hours**
3 lbs. (1,5 kg) chestnuts or 2¼ lbs. (1 kg) canned chestnuts ♦ **1 turkey liver and heart** ♦ **1 lb.**
(500 g) ground pork ♦ **2 sprigs thyme, leaves only** ♦ **salt and pepper** ♦ **1 turkey, about 1½ lbs.**
(3 kg) ♦ **4 tbsp. (50 g) butter, softened**

Preheat the oven to 400°F (210°C). Boil salted water in a large pot. Remove the hard skin of the chestnuts and drop the nut meat into the water. Boil for 30 minutes, remove the chestnuts, and peel off the second skin with a small, sharp knife. Purée the chestnuts with a food mill or processor. Chop the turkey liver and heart. Combine with the puréed chestnuts and ground pork. Season with the thyme leaves, salt and pepper, and mix well. Firmly pack this stuffing inside the turkey cavity. Sew closed or stuff a crumpled sheet of aluminum foil into the opening as a stopper. Rub the bird with butter and season with salt and pepper. Oven-roast the turkey in a turkey roaster, a large deep baking dish. When nicely browned—after about 45 minutes—reduce the oven temperature to 350°F (160°C). Roast for another 1 hour 45 minutes, basting frequently.

NOTE BY **ALAIN DUCASSE** This is a traditional Christmas dish. You can make the same chestnut stuffing for a capon, a bird I am particularly fond of.

Stewed Turkey Stuffed with Truffles

Dinde truffée au pot

⌂ ⌂ ⌂   ∞

Alain Ducasse

Serves 8 ◆ Preparation time : 1 hour 15 minutes ◆ Cooking time : 2 hours 40 minutes ◆ 1 medium turkey, cleaned ◆ sea salt and freshly ground pepper ◆ 3½ oz. (100 g) truffles, sliced ◆ 1½ tbsp. (20 g) butter ◆ 2 shallots, finely chopped ◆ 3½ oz. (100 g) beef marrow, chopped ◆ ⅓ cup (50 g) chopped truffles ◆ 1 turkey liver and heart, chopped ◆ ⅓ cup (8 cl) truffle juice ◆ ⅓ cup (8 cl) cognac ◆ ⅓ cup (8 cl) port wine ◆ ⅓ cup (8 cl) Madeira wine ◆ 1 cow bladder ◆ 1 cup (20 cl) chicken bouillon ◆ 4 cups (80 cl) heavy cream ◆ 5 oz. (150 g) foie gras of duck

Season the inside of the turkey with salt. Make slits in the skin and carefully insert the slices of truffle between the skin and the meat. Place the bird in a stockpot, add cold water to cover, season with salt, and bring to low boil. Skim and simmer at just under boiling—200°F (80°C)—for 1 hour 45 minutes to 2 hours. To test for doneness, pull on the wing—if the meat starts to come apart, the turkey is done. Remove from pot and let rest for 10 minutes. **M**elt the butter with the shallots over low heat. Mix with the marrow, chopped truffles, liver, and heart. Season with salt and pepper to taste. Stuff the turkey with this mixture and sew the opening. **P**our half of the truffle juice, cognac, port, and Madeira into the cow bladder. Slide the turkey inside the bladder and tie it tightly. Cook in the stockpot for 30 minutes at just below 200°F (80°C). In a saucepan, reduce the rest of the cognac, port, and Madeira to one-half its volume. Add the chicken bouillon and the rest of the truffle juice and reduce to half again. Gradually add the cream, in 3 parts, stirring after each addition. Just before serving, pass the foie gras through a sieve and whisk it into the sauce to bind it. Remove and discard the bladder and carve the turkey. Serve with the vegetables that you want to cook in the bouillon, such as turnips, celery and carrots.

You'll need a very large stockpot to hold a turkey of about 1½ lbs. (3 kg). Adding the cream gradually, in 3 steps, seems to me very judicious indeed. The cream cools the sauce, and adding it gradually will keep the hot bouillon from separating.   NOTE BY **FRANÇOISE BERNARD**

Turkey Kebabs

Brochettes de dinde en crépine

⌂ ∞

Françoise Bernard

Serves 4 ✦ Marinating time : 1 hour ✦ Preparation time : 30 minutes ✦ Cooking time : 15 minutes ✦ juice of 1 lemon ✦ 3 tbsp. oil ✦ 2 sprigs thyme, leaves only ✦ salt and pepper ✦ 1½ lbs. (700 g) boneless turkey breast ✦ 7 oz. (200 g) fresh lean bacon ✦ 1 large piece of caul, available from your butcher, cut into small pieces

Mix the lemon juice, oil, thyme leaves, salt and pepper to taste. Cut the turkey breast into large cubes, add them to the marinade, and toss to coat them well. Refrigerate for 1 hour. Preheat the oven to 450°F (240°C). Cut the bacon into pieces of the same size as the turkey cubes. Remove the turkey with a slotted spoon and reserve the marinade. Thread pieces of bacon and cubes of turkey, alternately, on skewers. Wrap each kebab with a piece of the caul. Grill 15 minutes or roast for 10 minutes, turn and baste each time with the marinade. Let stand 5 minutes, covered, in a warm place. Serve with corn and petite peas cooked in butter.

NOTE BY **ALAIN DUCASSE** I would love to try these kebabs with a peanut saté sauce. You can buy prepared saté sauces in Asian stores, which will save a lot of time.

Turkey Saltimbocca with Ham and Sage

Saltimbocca de dinde et de jambon à la sauge

⭑ ⭑ ∞

Alain Ducasse

Serves 4 ⁕ Preparation time : 45 minutes ⁕ Cooking time : 55 minutes
1 white onion ⁕ 3 carrots ⁕ 2 celery stalks ⁕ 1 cup (20 cl) veal or chicken jus (page 323) ⁕ 1
turkey breast, 1½ lbs. (700 g) ⁕ 4 slices prosciutto, preferably San Daniele ⁕ 16 sage leaves ⁕
1 cup (100 g) flour ⁕ 1 egg ⁕ ¾ cup (100 g) bread crumbs ⁕ 2 green asparagus spears ⁕ 3
artichokes ⁕ 2 zucchini, violin variety if available ⁕ 2 large tomatoes, peeled, seeded, and
coarsely chopped ⁕ 3 tbsp. olive oil ⁕ salt and pepper ⁕ 3 porcini mushrooms, cleaned, trimmed,
and diced ⁕ 4 tbsp. (50 g) butter

Peel and dice the onion, 1 carrot, and 1 celery stalk. Cook in their own juices, covered, over low heat until tender—about 4 to 5 minutes. Add 1 tbsp. of veal or chicken jus. Cut the turkey breast into 8 slices, ½ in. (1 cm) thick. Cut the prosciutto slices in half to fit on the turkey slices. Spread the onion, carrot, and celery over the turkey slices. Place 2 sage leaves on each slice and cover with a piece of prosciutto. Bread the prosciutto side of these piccatas, dipping first in flour, then in egg, and last in bread crumbs. **W**ash and peel the remaining celery and carrots, the asparagus, artichokes, and zucchini. Cut the vegetables into slices ⅛ in. (1 mm) thick. Cook the tomatoes for 20 minutes in a saucepan with a few drops of oil, season to taste with salt and pepper. **S**auté the mushrooms in 1 tbsp. of oil. Add the remaining veal or chicken jus, tomatoes, and a pinch of salt and pepper. **S**auté the piccatas in the butter, breaded side first, browning well before turning. Sauté the vegetables quickly over high heat in the remaining oil—they must be crunchy. Arrange the piccatas and the vegetables on individual plates, top with the sauce, and serve immediately.

This refined recipe adds elegance to simple turkey scallopini. To save time, ask your butcher to slice the turkey for you. You can prepare the saltimboccas in advance and keep them in a warm oven.

NOTE BY
FRANÇOISE
BERNARD

Beef

"Beef was sovereign when people spoke not of gastronomy but of food," Françoise Bernard remembers. Beef's image has suffered in the past few years, but you just cannot do without it if you want to cook all those tasty stews, hearty dishes, and country style specialties that our grandmothers were so good at preparing: beef bourguignon; the mellow daube casseroles that simmer for hours; the braised beef estouffades in heavy cast-iron pots whose lids were sealed with a ribbon of flour and water that made a clear gravy. Françoise Bernard has a weakness for meat sauces—women who are pressed for time can make them in a pressure cooker now—but she is not against a steak kebab on a wood fire or a good roast beef. She often chooses to cook beef ribs, because she is very fond of the meat that is close to the bone—they are so tasty, she says. She is also tempted by boneless rib steak, provided the meat is marbled, which guarantees that it will be flavorful.

There is always a beef rib on Alain Ducasse's menu. One day, you find it at the Restaurant Alain Ducasse, another day at *Le Louis XV*. It will always be on the menu somewhere, most often cooked *à la Rossini*—that is, with a piece of foie gras roasted separately in the oven. This dish employs one of chef Ducasse's favorite principles—different cooking processes in one recipe to meet the special needs of each food. Just mentioning beef leads him quite naturally to talk about pepper, "an exceptional condiment as in a simple *pavé de bœuf au poivre* [steak with peppercorns]. This is a simple dish, but it's worth serving in any three-star restaurant if you are willing to apply a little talent." Talent is, above all, knowing how to choose your ingredients. First, you need a boneless sirloin steak. The "mad cow" crisis drove many of us back to the quality Limousin or Charolais beef. "An exceptional meat," Alain Ducasse says, "provided it is marbled, that is, that its deep red meat is coated in a very pale yellow fat." The meat must hang in the cooler for at least three weeks if you want it to be tender. As for the peppercorns, Alain Ducasse uses a mixture of Java and Indonesian pepper, which gives off a long-lasting floral and spicy aroma. Meat from Limousin and pepper from the islands—there are no limits to good cuisine.

Rib Steak with Shallots

Côte de bœuf à l'échalote

⌂ ∞

Françoise Bernard

**Serves 4 ✦ Marinating time : 2 hours ✦ Preparation time : 20 minutes ✦ Cooking
time : 30 minutes ✦ 1 thick 3½ lb. (1,5 kg) rib steak, tied with string ✦ 3 tbsp. oil ✦ 2 sprigs
thyme, leaves only ✦ 2 bay leaves, crushed ✦ salt and coarsely ground pepper ✦ 2 shallots,
chopped ✦ 8 tbsp. (100 g) butter, softened**

Brush the steak with oil and sprinkle with thyme, bay leaf, and coarsely ground pepper.
Wrap in aluminum foil and refrigerate for at least 2 hours. **P**reheat the broiler or oven
to 425°F (230°C). **P**lace the steak on an oven rack and slide into the hot oven or under
the broiler. Place a baking dish underneath to collect the cooking juices. Roast or broil
30 minutes, turn after 15 minutes (average 9 minutes per lb.). **W**hile the meat is in
the oven, lightly sauté the shallots in 1 tbsp. butter until translucent but not brown.
Remove from the heat, cool, and mix in the remaining butter with a fork. **T**urn off the
heat and let the meat rest in the oven for 10 minutes. Just before serving, season with
salt and pepper. **C**arve with the grain of the meat and serve the steak slices on warm,
individual plates, topped with a dab of the shallot butter.

NOTE BY
**ALAIN
DUCASSE** It is difficult to broil meat in the oven because the heat source is at the top, not the
bottom. The meat loses blood and does not broil properly. Grilling is preferable—or
you could sauté the rib steak in a skillet. As for the marinade, I use grapeseed oil,
because it does not gel when the meat is cold.

Braised Beef with Marrow

Etouffée de bœuf à la moelle

☝ ☝ ☝ ∞

Alain Ducasse

Serves 4 ✦ Preparation time : 45 minutes ✦ Marinating time : 48 hours ✦ Cooking time : 2 hours 30 minutes ✦ 1¾ lbs. (800 g) boneless chuck, cut into 8 pieces ✦ 1¾ lbs. (800 g) boneless short-rib meat, cut into 8 pieces ✦ 1 tbsp. dried porcini mushrooms ✦ salt and pepper ✦ 6 cups (1,5 l) red wine ✦ 4 tbsp. olive oil ✦ 3 shallots, diced ✦ 2 carrots, diced ✦ 2 quarts (2 l) veal jus (page 323), heated ✦ about ¾ lb. (350 g) beef marrow ✦ 4½ cups (50 cl) chicken stock (page 322) ✦ 3 tbsp. good wine vinegar ✦ 2 sprigs flat-leaf parsley ✦ 5 oz. (150 g) calf brains, washed and blanched, chopped ✦ truffle slices and truffle juice, for garnish, optional

Place the meat, mushrooms, pepper, and red wine in a bowl. Marinate in refrigerator for 48 hours. In a large, heavy saucepan, sear the meat in 3 tbsp. of hot olive oil. Add the shallots, carrots, and marinade and boil for 20 minutes to reduce the liquid. Add the veal jus and cook, covered, until the meat is tender enough to pull apart—about 1½ to 2 hours. As soon as the meat is done, mix in the marrow. Remove the meat with a slotted spoon and set aside. Drain the sauce, season with salt and pepper to taste. Finely cut the 3 shallots. Sauté in a tbsp. of olive oil over low heat until translucent but not brown. Add the stock and sauce. Boil for 25 minutes to reduce. Add the vinegar, parsley, and calf brains. Season generously with pepper, pour the sauce over the braised beef, and serve immediately. As an extra finishing touch, add a few slices of truffle and some truffle juice.

Because this dish takes a long time to prepare, I would suggest cooking a large quantity. It is easily reheated. Be sure that you add the marrow at just the last minute—it must not boil or cook a long time.

NOTE BY **FRANÇOISE BERNARD**

Beef Stew, Nice-Style

Daube niçoise

♙ ♙ ∞

Françoise Bernard

Serves 8 ♦ Marinating time : 12 hours ♦ Preparation time : 40 minutes ♦ Cooking time : 4 hours ♦ 6 garlic cloves ♦ 10 peppercorns ♦ 3¾ cups (75 cl) dry white wine ♦ 2 tbsp. cognac ♦ 2 tbsp. olive oil ♦ 1 small fresh hot pepper, optional ♦ 1½ lbs. (2,5 kg) boneless rump or bottom round, cut into 2 to 3 in. (5 to 8 cm) cubes and larded, if possible ♦ 1 piece of fatback, thinly sliced ♦ 2 carrots, sliced ♦ 6 onions, sliced ♦ 7 oz. (200 g) slab bacon, diced ♦ 1 calf's foot, halved by the butcher ♦ 1 bouquet garni ♦ zest of 1 orange ♦ salt and freshly ground pepper ♦ 4 tomatoes, peeled, seeded, and diced ♦ 1 cup (200 g) black olives, pitted ♦ 6 sprigs parsley, chopped

The day before cooking, peel and chop 3 of the garlic cloves. In a large bowl, mix the chop garlic, peppercorns, wine, cognac, olive oil, and hot pepper, if using. Add the cubed meat and marinate for 12 hours in the refrigerator. **O**n the day of cooking, peel and chop the remaining garlic cloves. Drain the meat and strain the marinade, reserving the hot pepper. Line the bottom of a casserole with the fatback. Add the last 3 cloves of chopped garlic, carrots, onions, bacon, calf's foot, cubed meat, and marinade. Add enough water to cover. Add the bouquet garni and orange zest. Season with pepper and a little salt. Cover and cook over very low heat for 3 to 4 hours. About one hour before the stew has finished cooking, add the tomatoes, olives, and reserved hot pepper. Before serving, remove and discard the bouquet garni. Sprinkle with parsley and serve hot.

NOTE BY **ALAIN DUCASSE**   If you prefer your meat larded, choose a neck cut. It is especially good for simmering, and will produce a very flavorful stew.

Steak au Poivre with Old-Style French Fries

Pavé au poivre, grosses frites d'antan

⬦ ⬦ ∞

Alain Ducasse

Serves 4 ◆ Preparation time : 50 minutes ◆ Cooking time : 30 minutes
4½ lbs. (2 kg) large potatoes, such as Yukon Gold ◆ 3 tbsp. (50 g) black peppercorns ◆ 4
boneless sirloin steaks, 6 oz. (180 g) each ◆ 3 tbsp. (40 g) butter ◆ 2 quarts (2 l) vegetable oil,
for deep-frying ◆ 2 tbsp. cognac ◆ 4 tbsp. veal jus (page 323) ◆ 1 tbsp. crème fraîche or sour
cream ◆ fine salt

Peel the potatoes, rinse under cold water, and cut into large, fat french fries. Crush the peppercorns in a mortar and sift out the pepper dust. Coat the steaks with the crushed pepper, pressing the grains into the meat with a spatula so that they stick. **M**elt the butter in a frying pan over high heat and sear the steaks quickly on both sides. When they are just rare, transfer onto a wire rack set over a large plate or baking sheet to drain slowly. Reserve the fat in the pan. **P**reheat the oven to 325°F (150°C). **H**eat the oil in a deep fryer to 325°F (160°C). Deep-fry the potatoes for 10 minutes, drain in the wire basket, and cool on paper towels. Raise the temperature of the oil to 350°F (180°C). **P**our the reserved fat into a saucepan, heat and deglaze with the cognac. Gradually add the veal jus and crème fraîche. Mix well. Simmer the sauce over low heat until it thickens and correct the seasoning. **I**n the meantime, put the steaks in the oven for 5 minutes. Drop the french fries back into the hot oil and deep-fry them until golden brown. Drain in the basket. **A**rrange the steaks on a dish, cover with the sauce, and serve immediately. Sprinkle the hot french fries with salt and place in a large bowl (more practical for serving). If you wish, serve with a salad dressed with balsamic vinaigrette.

When I cook french fries, I never check the time—I simply wait for them to rise to the surface, golden in color. I drain them and let them cool. At the last minute, I drop them back into very hot oil to top them off. **NOTE BY FRANÇOISE BERNARD**

Lamb

For Françoise Bernard—and for most French people—the choicest piece of meat is roast leg of lamb. She loves lamb because it rarely disappoints and is much easier to select than beef. A beautiful pink color with a visible white rim of fat is bound to attract the eye of an experienced cook like her. Her favorite dish, even more than leg of lamb, is mixed grill. Just hearing her talk about it, you can almost smell the irresistible aroma of grilled lamb. The combination of lamb chops, kidneys, liver, sausages, button mushroom caps, and tomatoes—grilled medium rare—is pure heaven to her. Mixed grill was very popular in France in the 1960s. Bernard knows that fads come and go, so she is serenely waiting for restaurant chefs to put this dish back on their menus.

Alain Ducasse has his own expectations. He only buys lamb from Pauillac in southwest France. When the ewes are lactating, he buys young lamb from the Basque region or from the region around Sisteron in the Provençal Alps. At his restaurant *Le Louis XV,* he serves lamb with *panisse* (chickpea flour pancakes) or with braised lettuce, a classic garnish still popular in Monaco. In his Paris restaurant, where people want to sample the latest flavors in fashion, the lamb is sprinkled with small pieces of dried fruit.

Each part of the animal is unique. The shoulder is cooked a long time in oil. The loin is best roasted on the grill— although you do not roast a loin of lamb as if it were some plain old roast beef. This cut calls for elegance and precision. The loin must be roasted between 350 and 375°F (180 and 200°C), so as not to "attack" the meat. If you plan to open the oven door often to baste the lamb, best to roast it at 375°F (200°C).

Françoise Bernard has her own tricks. Her main concern is how to serve the meat hot at the table, because, unfortunately, lamb tends to cool quickly. And what could be worse than cold lamb? Her godchild, Renaud, a culinary-school graduate, had often heard her talk about this problem. One day, he served her a saddle of lamb on plates that he had previously heated in the oven. She was thrilled. It was just a detail, but aren't details what count in the world of cuisine?

Loin of Lamb with Parsley and Garlic

Carré d'agneau en persillade

⇧ ⇧ ∽∽

Françoise Bernard

Serves 4 ⋄ **Preparation time : 15 minutes** ⋄ **Cooking time : 25 minutes**
1 lamb rack, with 8 chops, chine bone removed, chopped at the base ⋄ **5 tbsp. (70 g) butter** ⋄
salt and pepper ⋄ **3 cloves garlic** ⋄ **5 sprigs parsley** ⋄ **½ cup (50 g) bread crumbs**

Preheat the oven to 400°F (210°C). **B**rown the lamb on both sides in 2 tbsp. of butter over high heat. Transfer to a baking dish and roast for 15 minutes. After 8 minutes, season with salt and pepper. Remove from oven and let rest for 10 minutes on a wire rack set over a dish or baking sheet. Raise the oven temperature to 500°F (260°C). **P**eel the garlic cloves, wash the parsley, and mince together. Mix in the bread crumbs seasoned with salt and pepper. Spread this mixture on the fat side of the meat, pressing with a spatula to make it adhere. Place the meat, crumb side up, in the baking dish and dot with the remaining butter cut into pieces. Bake for a few minutes. Serve hot, right out of the oven.

NOTE BY **ALAIN DUCASSE** A recipe is like a game. You can sometimes increase your pleasure by combining ingredients differently. Here, for example, why not start by mixing the butter with the bread crumbs, garlic, and parsley? You could spread the paste in a thin layer between two sheets of paper, refrigerate it, and then cut it to size to cover the meat. The butter will melt as the lamb cooks, and soon there will be nothing left of the hardened paste but buttery, herbed bread crumbs.

Loin of Lamb in a Thin Citrus Crust

Filet d'agneau en fine croûte d'agrumes

⇧ ⇧ ∞

Alain Ducasse

Serves 4 ✦ **Preparation time : 1 hour** ✦ **Cooking time : 30 minutes**
2 oranges, zested and juiced ✦ ½ grapefruit, zested and juiced ✦ 1 lemon, zested and juiced ✦
11 tbsp. (150 g) butter, softened ✦ ¾ cup (80 g) bread crumbs ✦ salt and pepper ✦ 1 tbsp. olive
oil ✦ 2¼ lbs. (1 kg) boneless loin of lamb, cut into 4 pieces ✦ 1½ oz. (40 g) green beans ✦ 1
oz. (30 g) chanterelle mushrooms ✦ 2 tbsp. olive oil ✦ 2 oz. (60 g) pearl onions ✦ 1 medium
carrot, sliced ✦ 6 scallions, cut diagonally ✦ 2 oz. (60 g) asparagus ✦ 15 tbsp. (200 g) butter ✦
Salt and pepper ✦ 1½ oz. (40 g) shelled peas ✦ 1¼ cups (25 cl) lamb jus (page 323)

To make citrus butter, finely chop 1½ tbsp. of the orange zest, 1 tbsp. of grapefruit zest, and 1 tbsp. of lemon zest. Mix 11 tbsp. butter with the bread crumbs. Add the chopped zest, ½ cup (10 cl) orange juice, ¼ cup (5 cl) grapefruit juice, ¼ cup (5 cl) lemon juice, salt, pepper, and 1 tbsp. olive oil. **P**reheat the oven to 400°F (210°C). **R**oast the meat on a spit, if you have one, for 15 minutes. Or sauté it in a frying pan, then roast in the oven for 12 minutes. Let rest for 10 minutes. **B**oil the green beans for 15 to 20 minutes in salted water, drain, cool and set aside. Sauté the mushrooms in 1 tbsp. of olive oil, set aside. Sauté the pearl onions, carrot, scallions, and asparagus in 1 tbsp. each of olive oil and butter. Season with salt and pepper, simmer. Add the peas, green beans, mushrooms, and 1 tbsp. butter. Reserve 1 tbsp. of butter and spread the rest on the meat. Brown the lamb under the broiler. **C**ombine 1 tbsp. of each of the three citrus juices and reduce with the cooking jus. Add the reserved butter. Reheat the lamb in the oven, arrange on the vegetables, top with jus. Serve immediately.

This recipe is very original. Although it's possible to combine citrus fruits with some meats, it's unusual to find them with lamb—but very tempting. This recipe reminds me of some North African dishes.

NOTE BY
FRANÇOISE
BERNARD

Indian Lamb Curry

Curry d'agneau à l'indienne

⇧ ⇧ ◯◯◯

Françoise Bernard

Serves 4 ♦ Preparation time : 45 minutes ♦ Cooking time : 1 hour
2¼ lbs. (1 kg) boned lamb shoulder, bones reserved ♦ 2 tbsp. oil ♦ 1 tbsp. curry powder ♦ ¼
tsp. ground cinnamon ♦ pinch of cayenne ♦ 1 tsp. turmeric ♦ 2 tsp. ground coriander ♦ 3
tomatoes, peeled, seeded, and chopped ♦ 3 cloves garlic, chopped ♦ 2 onions, chopped ♦ 4
cloves ♦ 2 tbsp. coarse salt ♦ 1 cup (200 g) long-grain rice ♦ 3 pinches of saffron ♦ 3 tomatoes,
quartered

Cut the lamb into 1 in. (2,5 cm) cubes. Heat the oil in a casserole, sear the bones and meat. When the lamb is brown on all sides, drain the fat, and add 1 cup (20 cl) hot water. Cover the casserole and boil over high heat for 5 minutes. Add the curry powder, cinnamon, cayenne, turmeric, and coriander. Stir over high heat for 5 minutes. Add the chopped tomatoes, garlic, onion, clove, salt, and 2 cups (40 cl) hot water. Cover and simmer for 45 minutes. Boil salted water in a saucepan. Rinse and drain the rice and pour into the boiling water. Boil gently for 20 minutes. Drain the rice and pour into a bowl. Sprinkle with the saffron and mix with a fork so that the spice colors the rice evenly. Transfer the rice into a large deep serving dish and pour the meat and sauce on top. Garnish with quartered tomatoes.

NOTE BY **ALAIN DUCASSE** I would roast the meat and prepare the sauce separately so that the meat remains firm. I believe that food should give us the satisfaction of chewing, provide the palate with something firm. In short, I prefer that my food resists when I chew.

Roasted Lamb Rib Roasts with Early Vegetables

Carré d'agneau rôti, primeurs en jus

⋔ ⋔ ◌◌◌

Alain Ducasse

Serves 4 ◆ **Preparation time : 35 minutes** ◆ **Cooking time : 25 minutes**
4 small racks of lamb, 3 ribs each ◆ **6 sprigs savory or thyme** ◆ **12 large carrots, with tops** ◆ **6 purple artichokes, trimmed and quartered, chokes removed** ◆ **20 small pearl onions, peeled** ◆ **sea salt and freshly ground pepper** ◆ **1 lb. (500 g) small new potatoes, scrubbed** ◆ **4 tbsp. (50 g) butter, softened** ◆ **1 head of garlic, cloves peeled** ◆ **¼ cup (5 cl) olive oil**

Preheat the oven to 375°F (190°C). **W**ith the tip of a knife, cut a crisscross design into the fat of the lamb. Insert sprigs of savory into the cuts. Peel the carrots and cut diagonally into ½ in. (1 cm) slices. Clean the artichokes and place in a bowl of water with lemon juice, to keep them from turning brown. **P**our a few drops of oil into a heavy casserole. Add the carrots, artichokes, and pearl onions. Season with salt, cook covered, for 20 minutes. **S**auté the potatoes and garlic cloves in butter. Season with salt. **R**ub the lamb roasts with salt. Sear in oil over high heat, then place in the oven for 12 to 14 minutes. Season with pepper and let rest about 10 minutes. Heat the cooking jus in a saucepan and sprinkle with the remaining savory. Transfer ¼ cup (5 cl) of the jus to a shallow bowl and roll the vegetables in it to caramelize them. Arrange the lamb roasts and vegetables on individual plates. Serve the remaining jus in a sauceboat.

Alain Ducasse's suggestion to ask your butcher to prepare the lamb—in 4 pieces with 3 bones each—is an excellent idea. Cutting lamb ribs is no easy task, sometimes requiring us to hide in the kitchen while we struggle with the bony chunk of meat on a heavy wood cutting board.

NOTE BY **FRANÇOISE BERNARD**

Pork

For Françoise Bernard, pork evokes the tasty dishes that she ate as a child. "On Sundays, my mother would make a pork roast with whole potatoes in a Dutch oven. It cooked for a long time. The potatoes were crisp on the outside and tasty, and the meat was so tender," she recalls. Curiously enough, Alain Ducasse, without knowing it, revived these memories for her by serving her a pork roast cooked in a Dutch oven. This recipe is apparently simple, but his roast cooked at a very low temperature for about 20 hours, as is usual today, and Françoise Bernard's mother's cooked for a little more than three hours. It was a great success for Alain Ducasse.

In his celebrated Parisian restaurant, Alain Ducasse offers a salad of pig snout and lean bacon, cooked with potatoes. Pork is always surprisingly good with prunes or pineapple. His pork loin with milk, which the chef created one day almost by accident, was popular beyond anything he had ever hoped for—which is why he has decided to reveal the recipe.

Ducasse favors bacon over pork. He is especially fond of the Italian, country-style pancetta. Pancetta is a piece of unsmoked, salted, lean bacon, which is dried and cooked (the cooking helps get rid of the salt) and then rolled into a sausage. It adds great flavor to vegetables, simmered peas, and stews with young vegetables. You can replace pancetta with lean, salted slab bacon, provided that you blanch it first.

Bacon is more than a just an animal fat. It is also a condiment. Françoise Bernard loves salads made with bacon, served with poached eggs or deviled potatoes. As for Alain Ducasse, he uses the Italian Colonna bacon, which is cured in brine. It is almost impossible to find this type of bacon, but you can substitute salted slab bacon. Sometimes, he cuts it into large cubes, which he sautés to use a vegetable garnish. Most often, he thinly slices the bacon on a meat slicer and sprinkles the bacon swirls on his vegetables to salt them. This is how he seasoned the porcini mushrooms in a special meal he prepared in Singapore, which greatly intrigued the chefs there.

Alsatian Sauerkraut

Choucroute alsacienne

⬆ ⬆ ◠◠◠

Françoise Bernard

Serves 8 ⬩ Preparation time : 45 minutes ⬩ Cooking time : 2 hours
4½ lbs. (2 kg) sauerkraut ⬩ 1 lb. (500 g) smoked bacon ⬩ 10 oz. (300 g) fatback ⬩ 1 clove ⬩ 1
onion, peeled ⬩ 1 lb. (500 g) smoked pork shoulder or picnic ham ⬩ 1 lb. (500 g) smoked
Boston butt ⬩ 1 garlic sausage ⬩ 1 carrot, sliced ⬩ 1 bouquet garni ⬩ 20 juniper berries ⬩ 20
peppercorns ⬩ 4 oz. (100 g) lard ⬩ salt ⬩ 2½ cups (50 cl) dry white wine ⬩ 1 lb. (500 g) potatoes,
peeled ⬩ 8 frankfurters or wieners

Put the sauerkraut in a large bowl and rinse with a lot of water. If the sauerkraut still smells strong, let it soak for a few hours. Change the water, squeeze the sauerkraut well with your hands, and loosen with a fork. **B**oil the bacon and fatback and drain. Stick the clove into the onion. **L**ine the bottom of a large casserole with the fatback. Spoon half of the sauerkraut on top. Add the bacon, pork shoulder, Boston butt, garlic sausage, onion, carrot, bouquet garni, juniper berries, peppercorns, lard, and salt to taste. Cover with the remaining sauerkraut. Add the wine enough hot water to cover. Cover the casserole and simmer for 2 hours. **A**fter 30 minutes, remove the sausage and add the potatoes. At the end of the cooking time, there should be little liquid left. **B**oil water in a large saucepan, add the frankfurters, and poach for 5 minutes. Drain. **T**o serve, reheat the frankfurters, garlic sausage, and sauerkraut mixture for 5 minutes. Remove the clove and serve hot.

NOTE BY **ALAIN DUCASSE** Make your sauerkraut even more Alsatian by cooking with good smoked pork and an Alsatian white wine. This hearty dish would cheer anybody, even on the coldest of days.

Vegetables with Bacon

Cocotte de légumes au lard

⌂ ○

Alain Ducasse

Serves 4 ✦ Preparation time : 45 minutes ✦ Cooking time : 30 minutes
8 carrots, with tops ✦ 8 small turnips, with greens ✦ 8 scallions, white and green parts ✦ 1 head
romaine lettuce ✦ 8 asparagus tips ✦ 3 tbsp. olive oil ✦ 2½ cups (50 cl) chicken stock (page
322) ✦ sea salt and freshly ground pepper ✦ 7 oz. (200 g) tiny round new potatoes, scrubbed
✦ 2 tbsp. (30 g) butter ✦ 1 clove garlic ✦ 2 oz. (50 g) salted slab bacon or pancetta ✦ 2¼ lbs.
(1 kg) peas in the pod, shelled ✦ 14 oz. (400 g) baby fava beans

Preheat the oven to 375°F (200°C). Peel the carrots and turnips, reserving the tops
and greens. Clean and trim the scallions, keeping 1 in. (2,5 cm) of the green stalk.
Remove the outer leafy part of the lettuce leaves, leaving about 1 in. (2,5 cm) around
the rib on each side. Save the lettuce ribs. Separately blanch the carrots, turnips,
scallions, and asparagus tips for about 10 minutes, then drain. In a large saucepan,
sauté the vegetables, carrot tops, and turnip greens in 1 tbsp. olive oil. Add 1 cup (20
cl) hot chicken stock, season with a little salt, and cook over low heat for 10 minutes.
Bake the potatoes topped with the butter, garlic, and 1 tbsp. olive oil for 15 minutes.
Cut the bacon into 6 pieces. Blanch and then sauté in a heavy casserole with 1 tsp.
olive oil. Add the peas and ½ cup (10 cl) stock. Cook, covered, for 15 minutes. Halfway
through the cooking, add the lettuce ribs and mixed vegetables. Add more stock if
necessary. Add the fava beans, 2 tsp. olive oil, salt and pepper to taste. Just before
serving, add the roasted potatoes. If desired, serve with grapes, a few roasted apple
or pear slices, and a garnish of raw grated apple or pear.

This extraordinary vegetable dish is an appropriate accompaniment for a veal roast or
a nice bird. It can also serve as the main course in a Sunday menu, with pan-fried
scallops to start and a fruit tart for dessert. **NOTE BY FRANÇOISE BERNARD**

Lentils with Smoked Pork

Petit salé aux lentilles

⏚ ∞

Françoise Bernard

Serves 4 ◆ Preparation time : 30 minutes ◆ Cooking time : 1 hour 15 minutes
2¼ lbs. (1 kg) smoked pork loin or shoulder ◆ 2 bouquets garnis ◆ 13 oz. (400 g) lentils ◆ 1
onion ◆ 1 clove ◆ 1 garlic clove ◆ 1 small carrot ◆ 1 small fresh hot pepper, optional ◆ salt and
pepper

Boil water in a large pot, add the meat, and boil 5 minutes. In the meantime, boil more water in separate pot. Drain the meat, return it to the pot with 1 bouquet garni, and cover with boiling water. Return to boil and simmer for about 1 hour. Remove the bouquet garni and drain the meat. **P**our the lentils in a large pot of cold water and boil over high heat for 5 minutes. Drain. Peel the onion and stud with the clove. Add more water to the large pot and boil the remaining bouquet garni, the onion, garlic, carrot, ground pepper, and fresh hot pepper, if using. Add the lentils, being sure there is enough water to cover. Simmer until firm, about 15 to 20 minutes. Five minutes before the end of the cooking, add salt to taste. Drain the lentils and remove the bouquet garni and the hot pepper. Return the lentils to the pot, add the meat, and simmer for 5 to 10 minutes. Gently drain and serve in a warm, deep serving dish.

NOTE BY **ALAIN DUCASSE** I like to brighten up the taste of lentils with finely chopped shallot, a dash of vinegar, and some freshly ground pepper. Leftovers of this dish can be served as a salad, with a strong mustard vinaigrette. The meat would then be thinly shredded over the vegetables.

Pork Loin with Milk and Potatoes

Carré de porc au lait, pommes de terre fondantes

⌂ ○

Alain Ducasse

Serves 4 ✦ Preparation time : 20 minutes ✦ Cooking time : 1 hour 45 minutes
3½ lbs. (1,5 kg) boneless pork loin ✦ salt and freshly ground pepper ✦ 10 new potatoes,
scrubbed ✦ 2 sprigs thyme, leaves only ✦ 2 white onions, each cut into 8 slices ✦ 5 garlic cloves,
crushed ✦ 6 cups (1,5 l) milk

Preheat the oven to 375°F (190°C). Season the pork roast with salt and pepper and place in a roasting pan. Arrange the potatoes, onion and garlic around the meat, sprinkle with thyme. Add enough milk to completely cover the meat. Roast for at least 1 hour 45 minutes, basting often. At the end of the cooking, the milk should be completely evaporated. Serve the pork roast on a platter, with the potatoes arranged around it. Add a turn or two of the pepper mill and salt, if necessary.

Cooking with milk works very well with pork, which dries quickly when fried or roasted in the oven. I love potatoes, and cooking them with the roast in milk makes them very tender indeed. This is the kind of dish I like, a family dish—simple, inexpensive, and delicious.

NOTE BY **FRANÇOISE BERNARD**

Veal

Veal is one of Alain Ducasse's favorite foods. This meat is truly a French specialty. It's possible to find excellent beef abroad—Kobe beef, for example—but you will not find quality veal anywhere else but in France. Milk-fed veal from a suckling calf is a uniquely French notion. Everywhere else, veal is red. Alain Ducasse likes the rib, simply fried in a pan. He loves the quasi, or rump roast, which he cooks in a pot with just a few cloves of garlic. The cut is tender and tasty, and Alain Ducasse is proud to have made it fashionable again by cooking it as a roast. His recipe for veal loin with coarsely chopped vegetables has been recreated in many places by many chefs.

Veal is the basis of traditional recipes—those simmered dishes that Françoise Bernard likes so much. "On a holiday, we would visit our aunts and cousins," she says. "We looked forward to eating the *blanquette de veau* [white veal stew] that we knew we would be having. Every one of my aunts had her own recipe. And we got a kick out of comparing them."

Veal jus is a staple in Alain Ducasse's cuisine—for simmering vegetable stews, braising meat, and as a base for sauces. He uses it by the ladleful, which is why he cannot give any precise quantities for moistening braised meat or cooking a vegetable. "Veal jus will mellow out the flavors," he repeats tirelessly to his cooking staff.

Although she does not make a sophisticated distinction between veal stock and veal jus—for her, jus is the liquid that comes out of a piece of roasted meat—Françoise Bernard makes her own meat bouillons. She prepares them in advance and stores them in her freezer. This way, she can use them as she needs them. Our two distinguished chefs have forever banished the commercial bouillon cube from their kitchens. Their tasty recipes will make you eager to follow their example.

Veal Scallopini au Gratin

Escalope gratinée au fromage

⌂ ∞

Françoise Bernard

Serves 4 ✦ **Preparation time : 15 minutes** ✦ **Cooking time : 15 minutes**
2 tbsp. flour ✦ **4 thin veal loin slices** ✦ **2 tbsp. (30 g) butter** ✦ **salt and pepper** ✦ **juice of 1 lemon**
✦ **3 oz. (80 g) Gruyère cheese** ✦ **2 slices of ham, each sliced in half**

Preheat the broiler or oven to 500°F (270°C). Lightly flour the veal slices and fry in butter for 4 minutes each side. Drizzle with the lemon juice and season with salt and pepper to taste. Reserve the cooking juice. Cut the Gruyère cheese into 4 thick slices. Place the veal in a baking dish and sprinkle with the cooking juice. Cover each with 1 half-slice of ham and 1 slice of cheese. Broil until the cheese melts and develops a brown crust, or bake on the upper shelf of a hot oven. Watch carefully to be sure that the scallopinis do not burn. Serve with tagliatelle or seasonal green vegetables, such as spinach, peas, green beans, or braised Belgian endives.

NOTE BY **ALAIN DUCASSE** For special occasions, spread a little truffle purée between the veal and the ham, and serve with a veal-truffle sauce. Thinly coat the scallopini with bread crumbs for a crisp, light texture. You can replace the thin cut with a thick medallion from the tenderloin, split it open and insert the garnish.

Veal Stew

Veau en casserole

⇧ ⇧ ⇧ ∞

Alain Ducasse

Serves 4 ✦ **Preparation time : 55 minutes** ✦ **Cooking time : 40 minutes**
2 thick veal rib steaks, about 1 lb. (450 g) each ✦ 4 medium carrots ✦ 4 small purple artichokes
✦ 4 medium turnips, with greens ✦ 8 scallions ✦ 2 baby zucchini, preferably round, quartered
and seeded ✦ 7 cups (1,7 l) veal stock (page 322) ✦ 7 oz. (200 g) button mushrooms, cleaned
and trimmed ✦ 7 oz. (200 g) chanterelle mushrooms, cleaned and trimmed ✦ 5 tbsp. (70 g)
butter ✦ ¾ cup (15 cl) crème fraîche ✦ juice of 1 lemon ✦ 4 tbsp. grapeseed oil ✦ sea salt and
pepper

Ask your butcher to debone the veal ribs, keeping the rim of outside fat and making
several slits in the fat. Flatten the meat by pounding it with the blade of a cleaver or
large knife. Peel the carrots and cut diagonally. Remove the artichoke leaves and
choke, saving only the bottoms. Peel the turnips and chop the greens. Peel the scallions. Quarter and seed the zucchinis. Cook the carrots, artichokes, turnips, turnip
greens, scallions, and zucchini in about 1½ cups (1,3 l) of veal stock for 20 to 30
minutes. Remove and drain each type of vegetable as soon as it is cooked. Cook the
mushrooms in 1 cup (20 cl) of stock and 2 tbsp. butter until the sauce reduces and
thickens to envelop the mushrooms, about 10 to 15 minutes. Reduce the remaining
stock over high heat until it coats the back of a spoon. Whisk in the cream and 3 tbsp.
butter. Whisk vigorously and add the lemon juice. Strain and blend. Reheat the vegetables in the sauce over low heat. Sauté the veal ribs in the grapeseed oil for 8 minutes
on each side, then let rest on a rack for 10 minutes. Slice the veal for your guests,
blanket with sauce and serve with the vegetables.

To simplify the list of ingredients, I would cook the vegetables in water rather than
stock. I would also cook the bouillon in a pressure cooker to save time.
NOTE BY
**FRANÇOISE
BERNARD**

Veal Shank with Carrots

Tendron de veau aux carottes

⌂ ○

Françoise Bernard

Serves 4 ♦ Preparation time : 35 minutes ♦ Cooking time : 1 hour 45 minutes
3 onions ♦ 3½ lbs. (1,5 kg) carrots, thinly sliced ♦ 3 tbsp. (40 g) butter ♦ ⅓ cup (40 g) flour
♦ 3½ lbs. (1,5 kg) veal shank, cut into 8 pieces ♦ 1 bouquet garni ♦ 5 sprigs parsley, minced ♦
salt and pepper

Slice 2 of the onions. Lightly caramelize the onions and carrots in 1½ tbsp. butter over high heat. Do not cover. **T**hinly slice the remaining onion. Pour some flour on a plate and coat the pieces of veal, gently shaking off the excess. Sauté the meat in the remaining butter. Transfer to a small casserole and add the sliced onion, 2 cups (40 cl) water, the bouquet garni, and salt and pepper to taste. Cover and simmer for 1 hour 30 minutes. Add the caramelized onions and carrots and simmer for 15 minutes. **A**range the meat and vegetables in a deep serving dish, drizzle with the cooking juice, and sprinkle with parsley.

NOTE BY **ALAIN DUCASSE** To add extra taste, cut the carrots into large pieces. They will soak up the veal juice and melt in your mouth. If the carrots are too finely cut, they will cook rapidly, without enough time to absorb the liquid.

Braised Veal Rump Roast with Spinach

Quasi de veau en cocotte aux épinards

⇧ ⇧ ◌◌◌ •

Alain Ducasse

Serves 4 ◆ Preparation time : 35 minutes ◆ Cooking time : 1 hour
2 tbsp. olive oil ◆ 1¾ lbs. (800 g) rump roast of veal ◆ 5 oz. (150 g) organ meats, such as liver, kidneys, and sweetbreads ◆ 7 tbsp. (90 g) butter ◆ 2¼ lbs. (1 kg) fresh spinach ◆ 2 garlic cloves ◆ 5 sprigs parsley, chopped ◆ ½ cup (10 cl) veal stock (page 322) ◆ salt ◆ white and black pepper

Preheat the oven to 375°F (200°C). **H**eat 1 tbsp. oil in a small casserole. Lightly sauté the veal on both sides and season with salt. Add the organ meats and 1½ tbsp. of the butter. Bake the casserole for 40 minutes, basting often. **R**emove the spinach stems and wash the leaves several times. Drain and pat dry with paper towels, being careful not to break the leaves. **M**elt about 2 tbsp. butter in a large skillet over low heat. As soon as the butter turns hazelnut brown, add the spinach leaves. Cook for 10 minutes. In the meantime, mix the remaining butter with the garlic and parsley. Season with salt and white pepper to taste. Add the garlic butter to the spinach toward the end of the cooking. **P**lace the meat on a rack set over a large dish. Cover the roast with aluminum foil and let rest for 15 minutes. Put the casserole back on the heat to brown the cooking juice and add the stock in 2 parts, stirring after each addition. Strain the sauce. Serve the roast with the spinach. Serve the veal sauce on the side in a sauceboat.

The quasi, or rump of veal, is the best cut for making a moist roast that can be easily cut into beautiful slices. To be sure that the roast is tender and flavorful, it is very important that the meat be allowed to rest at least 15 minutes before it is carved at the table.

NOTE BY
**FRANÇOISE
BERNARD**

Artichokes

Many people think that the artichoke, a relative of the thistle, is out of style—and a pain to prepare. Its choke has to be removed, and the vegetable has an unpleasant tendency to turn black. The artichoke is indeed a curious creature. Its choke is actually a thousand future flowers.

Alain Ducasse regards artichokes almost as he regards the truffle. Here, he might add a few strips of raw artichoke. There, he is thinking of an artichoke *brunoise* to sprinkle delicately on a crawfish bisque. To him, every good food is noble—the truffle, of course, but also the potato and the artichoke. The artichoke's subtle flavor has to be measured out artfully. The taste is at once astringent and metallic, and it leaves an unexpected, sweet sensation in your mouth if you drink water just afterward.

Françoise Bernard has cooked this vegetable often. She loves it—no, she adores it! Especially whole, with a tasty vinaigrette deep within its fleshy leaves. She cooks arti-

Marinière Mussels, a Specialty of Les Halles Paris Market, *page 30*

Creamed Mussels with Saffron, *page 31*

Sea Bream with Mushroom Stuffing, *page 80*

Salt-Crusted Sea Bream, *page 81*

Trout with Almonds, *page 84*

Trout with Sorrel, *page 85*

Country-Style Rabbit Terrine, *page 128*

Rabbit *Bocconcini* with Olives and Polenta, *page 129*

Artichokes à *la Barigoule, page 162*

Artichoke Ravioli with Goat Cheese, *page 163*

Country-Style Peas, *page 206*

Pea Soup with Garlic Bread Fingers, *page 207*

Zucchini Fritters, *page 234*

Zucchini Stuffed with Zucchini, *page 235*

Puff-Pastry Apricot Tart, *page 264*

Ice Cream with Half-Candied Apricots, *page 265*

Breton Baked Custard with Raisins, *page 284*

Grape Jelly, *page 285*

Orange Soufflé, *page 288*

Warm Tart with Orange Wine, *page 289*

chokes in the microwave, which is better suited to modern living and gives better results than the stovetop. With the microwave oven, there is no cooking stock to make and no cumbersome casserole. When microwaved in plastic wrap for 7 to 10 minutes, the artichoke is cooked just right: not too dry, not too moist. "I am not trying to make things difficult," she says. "I serve the artichoke with a vinaigrette or simply fried." Sometimes, she eats raw purple artichokes with just a few grains of salt. One of her chefs, who knows of her weakness, served her artichokes stuffed with mushrooms. This recipe, *à la barigoule*, is now famous, thanks to today's infatuation with Provençal cuisine, of which Alain Ducasse is one of the most famous proponents.

In his restaurant in Monaco, *Le Louis XV*, Alain Ducasse restores to the artichoke its Southern colors—in cannelloni with herbs or in a stew with bacon and potatoes. Our illustrious chef is very particular about this vegetable. He differentiates between a small violet artichoke and the so-called *barigoule* artichoke, which is larger. For him, there is nothing better than the thorny artichoke, which is found throughout Italy in autumn. He serves it juiced on a pan-fried sea-bass fillet that lies on a bed of raw artichoke leaves. Yet, whether whole or thinly sliced, the artichoke always retains its mystery.

Artichokes *à la Barigoule*

Artichauts à la barigoule

⌂ ⌂ ◯◯

Françoise Bernard

Serves 4 ◆ Preparation time : 35 minutes ◆ Cooking time : 1 hour 15 minutes
6 small artichokes ◆ 4 tbsp. (50 g) butter ◆ salt and pepper ◆ 3½ ounces (100 g) fresh or
smoked slab bacon, diced ◆ 1 large onion, chopped ◆ 2 tomatoes, cut into very small pieces,
or 6 tbsp. tomato paste ◆ 1 cup (20 cl) dry white wine

Wash the artichokes, remove the top third with a sharp knife, then slice each artichoke in half lengthwise. Remove the small violet leaves with scissors and cut out the choke. Sauté the half artichokes in 2 tbsp. of the butter for 5 to 8 minutes. Lightly season with salt and pepper. **S**auté the bacon and onion in the remaining butter. Add the tomatoes and reduce the heat to simmer. Season with a pinch of salt and a lot of pepper. When the liquid has evaporated, stuff each artichoke half with the mixture, filling the space left by the choke. Place the stuffed artichokes in a saucepan, sprinkle with the white wine, and cover. Simmer for about 1 hour.

NOTE BY **ALAIN DUCASSE** You can also add a little anchovy to this recipe. It will give the dish a Mediterranean flavor, and a spoonful of pesto will further brighten the taste. Anchovy and pesto work very well with artichoke. If you choose to add the anchovy, remember to season with less salt.

Artichoke Ravioli with Goat Cheese

Raviolis d'artichaut au chèvre

⌂ ⌂ ○

Alain Ducasse

Serves 4 ◆ **Preparation time : 1 hour 30 minutes** ◆ **Cooking time : 1 hour**
3 eggs ◆ **1 egg yolk** ◆ **1⅓ cups (200 g) flour** ◆ **2 tbsp. oil** ◆ **fine salt** ◆ **8 artichokes** ◆ **1 carrot,**
diced ◆ **2 garlic cloves, sliced** ◆ **3½ ounces (100 g) slab bacon, diced** ◆ **4 tbsp. olive oil** ◆ **2**
cups (40 cl) chicken stock (page 322) ◆ **1 sprig thyme** ◆ **2 bay leaves** ◆ **1 leek, white part only,**
thinly sliced ◆ **3 tbsp. (40 g) butter** ◆ **2 oz. (60 g) fresh goat cheese, crumbled** ◆ **¾ cup**
(100 g) grated Parmesan cheese ◆ **1 egg yolk** ◆ **pepper** ◆ **4 scallions, sliced** ◆ **2 carrots, sliced**
◆ **6 basil leaves** ◆ **juice of 1 lemon**

To make the ravioli dough, beat the eggs, egg yolk, flour, oil, and salt—by hand or with the bread hook of an electric mixer. Mix in a little cold water to make a smooth dough. To prepare the filling, cut off the tips of the artichoke leaves, cut the artichokes in half, and remove the chokes. Cube the hearts. Sauté the artichoke hearts with the carrot, garlic, and bacon in 1 tbsp. of the oil. Add 1½ cups (30 cl) of stock and the thyme, bay leaves, and salt to taste. Simmer, covered, for 25 minutes. Remove the artichokes, reserving the cooking juice, let cool. Cook the leek, covered, in 1 tbsp. oil and 1½ tbsp. of the butter over low heat until translucent. Mix the artichokes, leek, goat cheese, Parmesan cheese, egg yolk, and a little pepper. Divide the dough into 2 equal-size balls and roll them out. With a pastry or ravioli cutter, cut one sheet into 3 in. (8 cm). Leave the squares in place on the table after cutting. Spoon a bit of the artichoke filling in the center of each square. Brush a little water along the edges of the squares. Cover the squares with the second sheet of dough. With your fingers, press the sheet down around each mound of filling. Cut rows with the ravioli or pastry cutter to separate the sealed raviolis. Sauté the sliced scallions and carrots in 1 tbsp. of oil. Add the reserved juice and cook for 15 minutes. Drop the ravioli into boiling salted water and cook for 5 minutes. Drain. Pour the sauce over them, mixing well. Snip the basil leaves with scissors. Sprinkle the ravioli with the basil, lemon juice, and the remaining butter and oil.

Although this dish is very time-consuming to prepare, the end result will give you a great satisfaction. These ravioli may be prepared a little in advance (you don't have to refrigerate them) then reheated, covered, in the oven.

NOTE BY **FRANÇOISE BERNARD**

Artichokes in Vinaigrette

Artichauts vinaigrettte

⇧ ⇧ ○

Françoise Bernard

Serves 4 ◆ Preparation time : 15 minutes ◆ Cooking time : 50 minutes
4 artichokes ◆ 6 tbsp. vinegar ◆ 1 tsp. mustard ◆ 9 tbsp. oil ◆ salt and pepper ◆ 1 hard-boiled
egg yolk, optional

Remove the stems and outer leaves of the artichokes. Let the artichokes soak in cold
water and 2 tbsp. of vinegar for 5 minutes, top side down, to remove any dirt still in
the leaves. Rinse in cold water, gently opening the leaves to clean them. **D**rop the
artichokes into boiling salted water, cover, and cook for 40 to 45 minutes. Strain in a
colander, with the tips of the leaves pointing downward so the water drains out. **T**o
make a vinaigrette sauce, combine the mustard, oil, and 4 tbsp. of vinegar. Season
with salt and pepper to taste. If you prefer to make a smooth sauce, mash the hard-
boiled egg yolk and mix into the vinaigrette. Serve the artichokes warm with the sauce
on the side.

NOTE BY **ALAIN DUCASSE** You can cook artichokes for less time if you wish, especially fresh, young ones. With
less cooking, they will keep their crunchiness and distinctive taste. People always tend
to cook artichokes a little too long—they look so bulky, and fleshy leaves hide their
tender hearts.

Artichoke and Porcini Bouillon with Foie Gras Rissoles

Bouillon d'artichaut et de cèpe, rissoles de foie gras

⬠ ⬠ ⬠   ◯◯◯

Alain Ducasse

Serves 4 ◆ **Preparation time : 1 hour 15 minutes** ◆ **Cooking time : 1 hour** ◆ **Resting time : 30 minutes** ◆ **4 purple artichokes** ◆ **1 onion, thinly sliced** ◆ **3 tbsp. olive oil** ◆ **5 medium porcini mushrooms, cleaned and trimmed** ◆ **4 cups (80 cl) chicken stock (page 322)** ◆ **½ cup (10 cl) heavy cream, very cold** ◆ **2½ cups (250 g) flour, sifted** ◆ **¾ cup (15 cl) white wine** ◆ **½ ounces (15 g) truffle-skin peels** ◆ **4 ounces (120 g) foie gras** ◆ **1 quart (1 l) vegetable oil, for frying** ◆ **salt and pepper**

Trim the tops of the artichoke leaves, halve the artichokes, and remove the chokes. Cube 3 of the hearts. Cook the onion very slowly in 2 tbsp. oil over low heat, then add the artichoke cubes. Reserve 2 large porcini mushroom caps and cut the rest into pieces. Sauté the mushrooms with the artichokes, covered, until lightly colored but not brown—about 15 minutes. Boil the stock and pour over the vegetables. Simmer for 30 minutes. Mix in ¼ cup (5 cl) of the cream, bring to a boil, and remove from the heat. Mix and strain. **K**nead together the flour and wine, and let rest in a cool place for 30 minutes. Chop the remaining artichoke heart and sauté over low heat in 1 tbsp. of oil for 10 minutes. Add the minced truffle skin. Cut the foie gras into ½ in. (1,5 cm) cubes and add to the artichoke hearts. **T**hinly roll out the dough on a floured surface. Spoon small balls of the foie gras mixture onto the dough evenly spaced. Cut the dough into squares around each ball of filling. Fold the dough into triangles to make rissoles. Pinch down well. **W**hip the remaining cream. Slice the reserved mushroom caps. Season with salt and pepper and 1 tbsp. of oil and sauté in a skillet. **H**eat the vegetable oil, 350°F (177°C). Drop the rissoles into the oil to deep-fry them. Drain, then serve on a warm serving dish. Serve the broth in a soup tureen, adding 1 tbsp. of whipped cream. Portion the mushrooms and remaining whipped cream onto the plates. Add pepper and a drizzle of olive oil.

You can simplify this pretty starter by replacing the rissoles (which might open while cooking) with canapés, on which you can spread the foie gras mixture. This variation will be less risky, and much quicker, to make.   NOTE BY **FRANÇOISE BERNARD**

Asparagus

A harbinger of spring, asparagus arrives in mid-March and disappears in late June. The wild varieties are the earliest. Their tender, velvety tips look like buds of wheat.

Françoise Bernard's dish, Milanese asparagus, is proof that some tastes will never die. This recipe for asparagus sautéed with Parmesan cheese was very popular in the 1970s. Our chefs have reintroduced this starter in an even crunchier form. Today, asparagus is often not prepared as a starter but as a side dish, by itself or cooked over low heat with a few other vegetables. Alain Ducasse combines the violet Niçoise asparagus with peas, fava beans, and bacon.

Françoise Bernard has a predilection for simple, superb foods like asparagus. She enjoys them prepared in the classic style with a mousseline sauce or served lukewarm, covered in a vinaigrette or a thin mayonnaise with fresh chopped herbs. "The simpler, the better," she says, all the time. A sophisticated woman, she always eats her asparagus with a fork and knife, even though using one's fingers is acceptable.

The asparagus is an aristocratic vegetable. An array of utensils and dishes have been especially designed for it: an asparagus spoon, tongs, a dish with a detachable grate or honeycombs, and more. But to be eaten properly, the asparagus must first be correctly peeled. The tough part of the stalk must be broken off and the rest peeled with a potato peeler. You don't really need to peel fresh, young asparagus. The fresher the asparagus, the more tender it is. Refuse those with stems that are cracked or streaked with red—sure signs that they are beginning to dry out.

Alain Ducasse is especially fond of the so-called demoiselle asparagus, thin green asparagus that are very elegant as a garnish. He sautés them delicately in meat stock and sprinkles them with Parmesan cheese. The larger, more common asparagus, he first boils and then roasts in olive oil. Faithful to his habit of preparing different parts of the same food with different methods, Alain Ducasse serves asparagus stems in a lemon zabaglione and sprinkles the tips with Parmesan cheese. Perhaps the recipe that is dearest to his heart is Green Asparagus Roasted with Morel Mushrooms, dedicated to Alain Chapel.

Milanese Asparagus

Asperges à la milanaise

⌂ ∞

Françoise Bernard

Serves 4 ✦ **Preparation time : 20 minutes** ✦ **Cooking time : 20 minutes**
2¼ lbs. (1 kg) asparagus ✦ **½ cup (50 g) grated Parmesan cheese** ✦ **2 tbsp. (30 g) butter** ✦ **salt and pepper**

Preheat the oven to 375°F (200°C). Boil a large pot of salted water. Peel the asparagus with a potato peeler, from tips to ends. Break the stalks to take off the tough ends. Wash the spears, drop into boiling water, and cook for 12 to 15 minutes. Drain thoroughly. Place the asparagus side by side in a baking dish. Sprinkle Parmesan cheese on the tips and top halves of the spears. Melt the butter over low heat, making sure not to brown. Drizzle the asparagus with the butter. Bake for a few minutes in the top half of the oven. Watch to make sure that the cheese and butter do not get too brown. Remove from the oven when golden.

NOTE BY **ALAIN DUCASSE** Asparagus spears are usually tied in a bunch and cooked with their delicate tips up, so that they don't get crushed. After cooking, drain the asparagus, then quickly soak the tips in ice cold water. The cold water will stop the cooking and fix the bright green color.

Roasted Green Asparagus with Morel Mushrooms

Asperges vertes rôties aux morilles

⇞ ⇞ ◌◌

Alain Ducasse

Serves 4 ◆ Preparation time : 35 minutes ◆ Cooking time : 45 minutes
40 green asparagus spears ◆ 10 ounces (300 g) morel mushrooms, fresh ◆ 3 shallots, thinly
sliced ◆ 6 tbsp. (80 g) butter ◆ 2 garlic cloves, crushed ◆ salt and pepper ◆ 1 quart (1 l) chicken
stock (page 322) ◆ ¼ cup (30 g) grated Parmesan cheese

Peel the asparagus. Tie the spears in bunches of five and boil in salted water until al dente—about 6 minutes. Carefully remove the stems from the mushrooms and cut the larger caps in half lengthwise. Wash in a lot of water, 2 or 3 times if necessary. Gently sauté the shallots in 1½ tbsp. of the butter over low heat until translucent. Add the mushrooms and the garlic. Season lightly with salt and pepper. Add the stock and simmer over low heat for 10 to 15 minutes. Pour three quarters of the sauce into a small saucepan and reduce until smooth, about 30 minutes. Untie the asparagus bunches. Melt the remaining butter over low heat. Gently roll the asparagus in the butter and sprinkle with Parmesan cheese. Arrange the asparagus on plates, spoon on the mushrooms, and coat with the reduced sauce.

I always try to be careful not to clutter up my kitchen with dirty pots and pans—and limit the amount of cleaning up. I prefer to arrange the boiled asparagus on four plates, dot each with some softened butter (for which a small pan will suffice), sprinkle on the cheese, and serve the plates directly to my guests.

NOTE BY **FRANÇOISE BERNARD**

Asparagus in Mousseline Sauce

Asperge sauce mousseline

⛁ ⛁ ⛁ ◯◯◯

Françoise Bernard

Serves 4 ◆ **Preparation time : 40 minutes** ◆ **Cooking time : 30 minutes**
2¼ lbs. (1 kg) white asparagus ◆ 3 egg yolks ◆ salt and white pepper ◆ 3½ tbsp. butter, softened
◆ 2 tbsp. crème fraîche or sour cream

Boil salted water in a large pot. Break the asparagus stalks about 1 in. (2,5 cm) from the bottom and peel the whole white length with a potato peeler. Quickly wash the spears, tie into bunches of five or six, and drop into the boiling water. Boil until tender, about 20 to 30 minutes, then drain. Untie the asparagus, arrange on an oblong dish, and set aside in a warm place. **C**ombine the egg yolks with 3 tbsp. water in a heavy saucepan. Season with salt and pepper. Slowly heat the egg yolks over simmering water, whisking vigorously until the mixture thickens. Be careful that the saucepan does not become so hot as to burn your hand. Remove from the heat. **C**ut the butter into small pieces and whisk into the egg yolks, keeping the mixture over hot water. Just before serving, add the crème fraîche. Serve the warm asparagus with the mousseline sauce in a warm sauceboat on the side.

NOTE BY **ALAIN DUCASSE** You can make an emulsified sauce, such as a hollandaise or mousseline sauce, by stirring the whisk as if you were writing the numeral 8. Your hand motion must be quick enough to prevent the egg yolks from overcooking.

Parmesan Cheese Asparagus

Asperges au parmesan

☆ ○○○

Alain Ducasse

Serves 4 ◆ **Preparation time : 1 hour** ◆ **Cooking time : 5 hours**
1⅓ lbs. (600 g) beef chuck, cut into 2 in. (5 cm) cubes ◆ **3 tbsp. olive oil** ◆ **2 shallots, thinly**
sliced ◆ **1 garlic clove, crushed** ◆ **5 sprigs parsley, chopped** ◆ **1 small carrot, diced** ◆ **5 pieces**
of oxtail ◆ **1 cup (20 cl) red wine** ◆ **48 pitted olives** ◆ **20 green *demoiselles* asparagus (very**
thin spears) ◆ **1½ tbsp. (20 g) butter** ◆ **salt and freshly ground pepper** ◆ **⅓ cup (40 g) grated**
Parmesan cheese

Sauté the beef with 1 tbsp. of the oil. Add the shallots, garlic, parsley, and carrot.
Sauté for 10 minutes, drain the fat, and cover halfway with water. Reduce until the
liquid becomes syrupy and then add enough water to cover. Simmer for 1 hour 30
minutes. Let cool for about 20 minutes, strain, and reserve the beef juice. Preheat the
oven to 200°F (110°C). Heat 1 tbsp. of oil in an ovenproof casserole. Sauté the oxtail
pieces in the hot oil. When brown, carefully drain all the fat, add the wine, and reduce
to half its volume. Add enough cooled beef juice to cover, bring to a boil, and then
bake for 3 hours. Strain the juice, which should now be smooth and flavorful. Marinate
the olives in the warm juice. Diagonally cut the ends of the asparagus. Wash and pat
dry with paper towels. Sauté in the butter and the remaining 1 tbsp. of oil, rolling the
spears in the pan to cook uniformly. Season with salt and pepper. Check for doneness
with the point of a knife. Sprinkle with Parmesan cheese. Arrange on individual plates,
placing three spears on the bottom and two crosswise on top. Top with the warm
beef juice. Serve immediately.

This beef juice takes a particularly long time to make because you make it in two steps
(by first cooking the beef and then the oxtail)—but it will be very tasty and aromatic.
Make sure that the asparagus are only slightly cooked, depending, of course, on their
size. After washing, drain the spears on a clean cloth.

NOTE BY **ALAIN DUCASSE**

Belgian Endive

What a fantastic vegetable! Endive keeps marvelously and is easily sliced with a few cuts of the knife. And what a godsend as a salad! It is quick to clean and prepare. In Françoise Bernard's eyes, the endive only has virtues. She likes it mixed with a few slices of apple or some raisins. These sweet-and-sour combinations remind her of some of the dishes from the North, where she is from. When she is going to serve endive as a side dish, she cooks it meunière in a pan, sprinkled with a hazelnut butter that spreads its golden foam all over the caramelized vegetable. For children, she cooks it in a Mornay sauce with ham. They just love it.

Out of habit, Françoise Bernard still removes the cone-shaped core of the endive, although it is really no longer necessary—endive is much less bitter than it used to be. Not long ago, however, it was unthinkable to eat the core. She remembers that people added sugar, which even she recommended for a long time. In her early books, she also suggested removing the shriveled outside leaves. Today, the endive that is available is always beautiful and fresh—and so clean that one hardly dares wash it.

Alain Ducasse also removes the core, because it a little less tender than the rest. In his recipes, he contrasts the crunchiness of raw endive with the supple texture of cooked endive. In Paris, he serves endive in a bitter marmalade, with salmon and a lemon béarnaise sauce heightened with dabs of butter (so much better than ordinary melted butter)—a typically Northern dish, he says. The two, very different flavors of salmon and endive combine with the pungent béarnaise. The dish itself evokes for him the mellow aspect of the South and the lemon taste of the Riviera. This chef enjoys working with foods that allow him to create balanced dishes. The slightly bitter persistence of the endive—the bitterness of the North—is so far removed from Alain Ducasse's instincts that it helps him imagine contrasting flavors.

Broiled Belgian Endives with Beaufort Cheese

Endives Gratinées au Beaufort

♤ ♤ ○

Françoise Bernard

Serves 4 ✦ **Preparation time : 40 minutes** ✦ **Cooking time : 45 minutes**
2¼ lbs. (1 kg) Belgian endives ✦ 7 tbsp. (80 g) butter ✦ 1 onion, sliced ✦ juice of ½ lemon ✦
salt and pepper ✦ 1 heaping tbsp. flour ✦ 2½ cups (50 cl) milk, cold ✦ 3 pinches of grated
nutmeg ✦ about ⅓ cup (50 g) grated Beaufort, Comté, Emmental, or Swiss cheese ✦ thin slices
of boiled ham, optional

Remove any bruised leaves of the endives. With a sharp knife, hollow out each base
and discard the core. Rinse and immediately pat dry with paper towels. **M**elt 2 tbsp.
of the butter in a heavy saucepan over low heat. Add the endives and onion. Sprinkle
with the lemon juice to keep the endives from turning brown. Season with salt and
pepper. Cover and simmer over low heat for 35 minutes. Turn halfway through the
cooking. **M**elt 3 tbsp. of butter over low heat and whisk in the flour. Add the cold
milk all at once, while continuing to whisk rapidly. Sprinkle with nutmeg and season
with salt and pepper. Whisk the sauce until it boils and then cook for 5 minutes.
Remove from the heat and stir in the grated cheese. **P**reheat the broiler. **S**poon a few
tbsp. of the cheese sauce into a baking dish and spread evenly. Drain the endives and
place on top. Cover with the remaining sauce and dot with the remaining butter.
Brown under the broiler. Transform this vegetable dish into a main dish by rolling 1
slice of ham around each endive before broiling.

NOTE BY **ALAIN DUCASSE** To cook the endives more easily, split them in two lengthwise. The lemon juice, in-
tended to preserve the whiteness of the vegetables, is not really necessary. The sauce
will give them a beautiful golden color.

Cooked and Raw Belgian Endives with Truffles

Endives cuites et crues aux truffes

⌂ ⌂ ∞

Alain Ducasse

Serves 4 ♦ **Preparation time : 30 minutes** ♦ **Cooking time : 20 minutes**
12 Belgian endives, about 2 ounces (50 g) each ♦ **8 tbsp. (100 g) butter** ♦ **1 cup (20 cl) chicken stock (page 322)** ♦ **salt and freshly ground pepper** ♦ **2 tbsp. olive oil** ♦ **¼ cup (5 cl) balsamic vinegar** ♦ **juice of 1 lemon** ♦ **1 tbsp. truffle juice** ♦ **about 2 ounces (50 g) black truffles, chopped**

Remove 5 outer leaves from the endives and reserve in a cool place. Halve the endives in lengthwise and cut out the core. Lightly sauté the halved endives in the butter in a saucepan, making sure the butter does not burn. Add the stock and simmer for 15 minutes. At the end of the cooking, there shouldn't be any liquid left in the pan. Season with salt and pepper. **C**ut the reserved raw endive leaves in half widthwise. Season with the oil, vinegar, lemon juice, truffle juice, and salt and pepper to taste. Add the chopped black truffles. Serve with fish, arranging the cooked endive on the serving platter, beneath the fish, and the raw endive salad on top.

I find the presentation of cooked and raw endives on the same plate amusing. And I would never have dreamed of this very successful combination of a top-quality product like the truffle with as common a vegetable as the endive.

NOTE BY
FRANÇOISE
BERNARD

Belgian Endives, Ardennes-Style

Endives confites à l'ardennaise

⌂ ⌂ ∞

Françoise Bernard

Serves 4 ✦ **Preparation time : 30 minutes** ✦ **Cooking time : 1 hour**
2¼ lbs. (1 kg) Belgian endives ✦ 4 tbsp. (50 g) butter ✦ salt and pepper ✦ 5 oz. (125 g) lean
slab bacon, diced ✦ 3½ ounces (100 g) cured ham, such as prosciutto, chopped

Remove the bruised outer leaves of the endive. With a sharp knife, remove each core and discard. Rinse the endives and immediately pat dry on a paper towel. Heat the butter in a saucepan. Add the endives and 2 tbsp. of water and season lightly with salt and pepper. Cover and cook over very low heat for 30 minutes. Turn occasionally so that the endives are golden brown on all sides. Add the bacon and ham. Simmer for at least 20 minutes before serving.

NOTE BY **ALAIN DUCASSE** I like recipes that combine bacon and ham with vegetables. Here, I would replace the cured ham with a nice piece of salted bacon, diced into ¾ in. (1,5 cm) pieces.

Belgian Endives with Butter and Lemon

Endives meunière

⌂ ○

Alain Ducasse

Serves 4 ✦ **Preparation time : 20 minutes** ✦ **Cooking time : 45 minutes**
2¼ lbs. (1 kg) Belgian endives ✦ **juice of ½ lemon** ✦ **salt and freshly ground pepper** ✦ **10 tbsp.**
(140 g) butter

Remove the outer leaves of the endive and rinse rapidly in running water (soaking them will make them turn bitter). Hollow out each base and discard the core. Place the endives in a large pot and add the lemon juice, a pinch of salt, and 2 tbsp. of the butter. Add water to cover and bring to a boil over high heat. Cover the pot with a sheet of buttered wax paper, reduce the heat, and simmer for 35 minutes. Remove from the heat. Let the endives cool in their cooking juice, then squeeze gently to drain. Melt the remaining butter in a skillet. When the butter starts to foam, roll the endives in the pan to give them a beautiful golden color. Top with a twist of the pepper mill.

You might prefer to cook the endives in advance and sauté them in butter just before serving. Endives can accompany meat or fish or, wrapped in a thin slice of ham, become the entrée for a light meal.

NOTE BY
FRANÇOISE
BERNARD

Carrots

The carrot supposedly makes people friendly and gives them a clear complexion. Carrot bouillon is believed to be good for the sick. Not only is the carrot endowed with all these folkloric virtues, it can also, fortunately, be cooked in many different ways. Of course, as a child, Françoise Bernard ate carrot bouillon when she was feverish, and her mother's tender carrot purées, but her favorite recipe by far is carrots with onions and garlic, stewed in olive oil.

With the arrival of new varieties on the market, the carrot has been rejuvenated in recent years. As early as April, in markets everywhere, you can buy pretty bunches of carrot with their tops and the small, tender, aromatic bell carrots, which make the best Vichy Carrots. Sometimes Alain Ducasse livens up his pies with a few carrot greens. The carrots from Les Landes are also fashionable—they are large and especially long and smooth because they grow in sandy soil, unimpeded by obstacles.

So, the carrot plays the local card, the natural card, the card of freshness. Yet, this vegetable adds color to a pot-au-feu and mellow flavor to soups. Alain Ducasse always cooks a few carrots in his veal jus—an indispensable base in his cuisine—to sweeten it. He does not think that the carrot is enough by itself, however. He enhances the flavor with a dash of sherry vinegar or citrus juice or a pinch of cumin seeds.

The carrot loves mixing with other vegetables, and it is often sliced into very small pieces in a mosaic of turnips, leeks, and celery. Dicing it *en brunoise* or *en salpicon*, as the chefs call it, greatly annoys Françoise Bernard, for she hates wasting so much precious time. Whenever she sees her own chefs cutting a pile of carrots into tiny, almost identically sized dice, she cannot help saying as she passes by, "You don't have to take such great pains doing that!" They never pay any attention, however, for the arts of cutting and carving are a chef's privilege.

Vichy Carrots

Carottes Vichy

⌂ ○

Françoise Bernard

Serves 4 ◆ Preparation time : 15 minutes ◆ Cooking time : 45 minutes
2¼ lbs. (1 kg) carrots, thinly sliced ◆ 4 tbsp. (50 g.) butter ◆ 1 tsp. sugar ◆ salt ◆ 1 bottle vichy
(carbonated) mineral water ◆ 6 sprigs parsley, leaves only, minced

If the carrots are not tender, boil for 10 minutes. In a heavy saucepan, combine the carrots, butter, sugar, salt to taste, and enough vichy water to cover. Cover the pot and cook over very low heat until the liquid has almost completely evaporated—about 30 to 45 minutes. Transfer the carrots to a deep serving dish, sprinkle with parsley, and serve immediately. Vichy carrots are usually served with a poached fish or roast beef.

NOTE BY **ALAIN DUCASSE** Carrot and cumin go together particularly well, so you might want to add a few cumin seeds to the cooking water. Flat-leaf parsley will add a finishing touch of freshness and color to the dish.

Carrot and Pearl Onion Stew

Carottes et petits oignons en cocotte

⬠ ◯

Alain Ducasse

Serves 4 ✦ **Preparation time : 20 minutes** ✦ **Cooking time : 25 minutes**
4 tbsp. (50 g) butter ✦ **12 large carrots (2 bunches), sliced at an angle** ✦ **24 pearl onions, peeled**
✦ **8 cloves garlic, unpeeled** ✦ **¾ cup (15 cl) chicken stock (page 322)** ✦ **salt and pepper** ✦ **several**
sprigs flat-leaf parley, chopped ✦ **½ cup (10 cl) veal jus (page 323)**

Melt 3 tbsp. of the butter over low heat. Sauté the carrots, onions, and garlic until they are a beautiful golden color—about 10 to 15 minutes. Add the stock and simmer for 5 minutes. Prick the carrots with the tip of a knife to check that they are tender. At the end of the cooking, add the remaining butter. Season with salt and pepper to taste and sprinkle with parsley. **H**eat the veal jus and roll the carrots and onions in it to coat them. Serve the hot vegetables with a *blanquette de veau* or a roast.

These carrots are cut like diamonds and cooked in two steps—first in the stock, and then in the veal jus. I would simplify things: I would not slice the carrots at an angle, and I would finish the dish with fresh butter instead of veal jus. May the chef forgive me.

NOTE BY **FRANÇOISE BERNARD**

Braised Carrots with Pearl Onions

Carottes braisées aux petits oignons

⬆ ⬆ ◯

Françoise Bernard

Serves 4 ✦ Preparation time : 20 minutes ✦ Cooking time : 1 hour 10 minutes
4 tbsp. (50 g.) butter ✦ 2¼ lbs. (1 kg) carrots, thinly sliced ✦ 8 oz. (250 g) white pearl onions
✦ 2 garlic cloves, minced ✦ 1 bouquet garni ✦ salt and pepper ✦ 1 to 2 tbsp. crème fraîche or
sour cream, optional ✦ 6 sprigs chervil, leaves only, minced

Melt the butter over low heat in a heavy saucepan. Sauté the carrots and onions for a few minutes, mixing with a wooden spoon. Add the garlic, bouquet garni, salt and pepper to taste. Cover the pan with a soup plate filled with cold water. Simmer the carrots over low heat for about 1 hour. Add more water to the plate as it evaporates. If necessary, add 1 tbsp. of water to the pan to keep the carrots from sticking. If desired, add a bit of crème fraîche at the end of the cooking. Sprinkle with chervil and transfer to a deep serving dish. Serve with a roast or stew.

NOTE BY **ALAIN DUCASSE** This is the type of dish that I would love to eat as a casserole. The deliciously caramelized carrots would stick to the bottom slightly. I would serve the casserole with a veal roast. What a simple and friendly meal!

Braised Sweetbreads with Carrots

Ris de veau braisé aux carottes

⇧ ⇧ ∽∽

Alain Ducasse

Serves 4 ◆ Preparation time : 1 hour ◆ Resting time : 3 hours ◆ Cooking time : 50 minutes ◆ 1⅓ lbs. (600 g) sweetbreads ◆ salt and pepper ◆ 3 tbsp. olive oil ◆ 7 tbsp. (80 g) butter ◆ 1 lb. (500 g) carrots, cut at an angle ◆ 1 cup (20 cl) veal jus (see page 323) ◆ 5 garlic cloves, chopped ◆ 1 tsp. sherry vinegar

Remove the skin and nerves from the sweetbreads. Leave them under trickling cold water for 2 to 3 hours to clean. Blanch for 3 to 4 minutes in salted water, remove, and cool in cold water. Place them between two dish towels, under a weight, for 1 hour. Preheat the oven to 350°F (180°C). Season the sweetbreads with salt and pepper. Sauté in the oil and 4 tbsp. of the butter. Add the carrots and remaining butter and sauté for 5 minutes over low heat. Add the veal jus, bring to a boil, and add the garlic. Transfer the mixture to a baking dish and bake for 25 to 30 minutes, basting often. Remove from the oven, cover with aluminum foil, and set on a wire rack. Check the tenderness of the carrots with the tip of a knife. Correct the seasoning. Add water if the sauce is too thick or reduce slightly if it is too thin. Arrange the carrots in the center of individual plates, cover with 2 sweetbreads, and pour sauce on top. Sprinkle with a few drops of sherry vinegar to add a tangy flavor to the sauce.

As I always go for the simple approach, I would boil the sweetbreads in water for 15 minutes, remove them from the heat, and cool them under a weight (it does not have to be very heavy). Then I would slice them, roll them in flour, and sauté with some butter, adding parsley and lemon juice to finish. **NOTE BY FRANÇOISE BERNARD**

Cauliflower

Alain Ducasse does not share his colleague Joël Robuchon's passion for the cauliflower—although Robuchon's Cream of Cauliflower and Caviar makes Parisian gourmets faint in anticipation. Ducasse confesses that he is not crazy about this vegetable, and he has never put it on his restaurant menus. (He might have, had he been from Brittany.)

Here, Alain Ducasse offers two recipes for cauliflower, each of which adds a new dimension to this basically rustic vegetable. Ducasse has always been very fond of soups— and he always adds some little refined garnish to them. In his first recipe, he works with the concept of creaminess to create the Du Barry Cream of Cauliflower Soup, which is extremely smooth. In his second recipe, Cauliflower *à la Grecque*, he continues his ongoing search for balance. His imaginative talent shines brightly in this recipe. The traditional version of the dish consists of a few simple vegetables sautéed in olive oil and sprinkled with a spicy vinegar marinade. Ducasse binds the vegetables with meat stock and crème fraîche, to balance the vinegary cauliflower with smoother, milder flavors.

Françoise Bernard prepares cauliflower with great simplicity. She loves it au gratin or in a terrine. She often cooks it in Mornay sauce for her family, a hearty side dish that everybody likes. The Mornay sauce also smoothes the texture of the cauliflower, which is slightly dry. She sometimes prepares cauliflower as a purée, with potatoes and Gruyère cheese, or as fritters. Bernard insists on boiling her cauliflower twice, even though she knows that this is not necessary anymore. What is still essential, however, is choosing the best quality. The head must be very fresh and very white with tender, green leaves. Always choose one that still has its leaves—even if takes up a lot of room in your shopping basket—because it keeps much better that way.

Whether in the hands of the grand Parisian chef or of the queen of everyday cuisine, the cauliflower retains its country charm.

Cauliflower Loaf with Cheese

Pain de chou-fleur au fromage

⌂ ⌂ ○

Françoise Bernard

Serves 4 ✦ **Preparation time : 35 minutes** ✦ **Cooking time : 50 minutes**
2¼ lbs. (1 kg) cauliflower, trimmed and separated into florets ✦ **4 tbsp. (50 g) butter** ✦ **2 tbsp.**
flour ✦ **2½ cups (50 cl) milk, cold** ✦ **2 pinches of freshly grated nutmeg** ✦ **salt and pepper** ✦ **3**
eggs ✦ **½ cup (50 g) grated Swiss or Gruyère cheese**

Preheat the oven to 350°F (180°C). **B**oil salted water. Drop the florets into the pot and
cook for 12 to 15 minutes. **T**o make a béchamel sauce, melt 3 tbsp. of the butter in
a skillet over low heat. Stir in the flour. Slowly add the milk, stirring or whisking constantly until the sauce thickens. Add the nutmeg, salt and pepper to taste. **S**eparate
the eggs. Drain the cauliflower and purée in a blender or food processor. Combine
the purée with the béchamel sauce, egg yolks, and grated cheese. Let cool. Beat the
egg whites until stiff and fold into the purée. Butter a soufflé mold, pour in the
mixture, and bake for 40 minutes. Serve as soon as it comes out of the oven, without
unmolding.

NOTE BY
ALAIN
DUCASSE
To add a fresh, crunchy accent to this dish, serve it with a salad of tiny, raw cauliflower
florets, seasoned with olive oil, lemon juice, and salt. For color, sprinkle with diced,
bright-red tomatoes.

Cauliflower *à la Grecque*

Chou-fleur à la grecque

⌂ ○

Alain Ducasse

Serves 4 ✦ **Preparation time : 35 minutes** ✦ **Cooking time : 45 minutes**
10 whole coriander seeds ✦ **10 black peppercorns** ✦ **1 garlic clove, crushed** ✦ **1¾ lbs. (800 g)**
cauliflower, trimmed and separated into florets ✦ **2 tbsp. olive oil** ✦ **juice of 2 lemons** ✦ **½ cup**
(10 cl) white wine ✦ **1 bouquet garni** ✦ **¾ cup (15 cl) chicken stock (page 322)** ✦ **½ cup**
(10 cl) heavy cream ✦ **salt and freshly ground pepper**

Wrap the coriander seeds, peppercorns, and garlic in a piece of cheesecloth and tie
with string. Reserve one quarter of the cauliflower florets and sauté the rest in 1 tbsp.
of oil for 5 minutes. Do not brown. Add half of the lemon juice, the wine, the cheesecloth bag, and the bouquet garni. Reduce to half its volume and add ½ cup (10 cl) of
the stock. Cook, covered, for 25 to 30 minutes, making sure that the liquid does not
reduce too much (add a little water if needed). **R**emove the florets with a slotted spoon.
Remove the bouquet garni and cheesecloth bag and reduce slightly. Add the remaining
lemon juice and 1 tbsp. of the oil. Reduce until the sauce is smooth. Pour over the
cauliflower. **C**ook the reserved florets in the heavy cream and ¼ cup (5 cl) stock for
10 minutes. Season with salt and pepper. Blend to a fine purée in a food processor.
Cover the cauliflower with this hot purée, and cool in the refrigerator. Serve cold in
stem glasses.

Before cooking cauliflower, I blanch it in boiling water—it only takes a minute and will
help your guests to digest the vegetable more easily. I love this very modern presentation of the cauliflower in glasses.

NOTE BY
FRANÇOISE
BERNARD

Cauliflower au Gratin

Chou-fleur au gratin

⌂ ○

Françoise Bernard

Serves 4 ◆ Preparation time : 25 minutes ◆ Cooking time : 30 minutes 2¼ lbs. (1 kg) cauliflower, separated into florets ◆ 3 tbsp. (50 g) butter ◆ ¼ cup (30 g) flour ◆ 2½ cups (50 cl) milk, cold ◆ salt and pepper ◆ About ½ cup (50 g) grated cheese

Boil salted water. Drop the florets into the pot and cook for 15 to 20 minutes. To make a béchamel cheese sauce, melt 2 tbsp. of the butter in a saucepan over low heat. Stir in the flour for a few seconds, until the mixture foams. Add the milk all at once, stirring or whisking until the sauce thickens. Season with salt and pepper to taste. Cook for 10 minutes over very low heat. Remove from heat and stir in half of the grated cheese. Preheat the broiler. Cut the remaining butter into small pieces. Gently drain the florets, arrange in a baking dish, and cover with the béchamel cheese sauce. Sprinkle with the remaining grated cheese. Brown the dish under the broiler for a few minutes. This recipe is ideal for using up leftover cauliflower. The dish can also be served with a few boiled potatoes, hard-boiled eggs, and slices of haddock.

NOTE BY ALAIN DUCASSE This family dish will be absolutely delicious with some meat juice or beef casserole sauce served on the side. Vegetables often taste better with meat juice or a few pieces of bacon—the meat stimulates their flavor.

Du Barry Cream of Cauliflower Soup

Crème Du Barry

⌂ ○

Alain Ducasse

Serves 8 ✦ **Preparation time : 35 minutes** ✦ **Cooking time : 1 hour**
2½ lbs. (1,2 kg) cauliflower, separated into florets ✦ **4 cups (80 cl) veal stock (page 322)** ✦ **1**
leek, white part only, finely sliced ✦ **7 tbsp. cup (80 g) butter** ✦ **salt and white pepper** ✦ **½ cup**
(10 cl) crème fraîche ✦ **chopped chervil, for garnish, optional**

Reserve about 1 cup (200 g) of the smallest florets. Bring the stock to a boil. Lightly
sauté the leek in the butter, making sure not to brown. Slowly add the stock. Add the
remaining florets and season with salt. Cook, covered, for 30 minutes. Add the crème
fraîche and a little white pepper. Boil gently for 20 minutes. Blend to a smooth cream
in the food processor. Strain. Drop the reserved florets into boiling salted water and
boil vigorously for about 5 minutes. Remove from heat, rinse under cold water, and
drain. Portion the florets into 8 individual soup plates and cover with the boiling cream.
If desired, sprinkle with chopped chervil.

Everything in this soup is white: the meat stock, the cauliflower, the leek, and the   NOTE BY
pepper. Although I am less particular about presentation than Alain Ducasse, I approve   **FRANÇOISE**
of his attentive choice of the best ingredients for his soups. They produce a beautiful   **BERNARD**
and appetizing color.

Chanterelle Mushrooms

Françoise Bernard remembers the days when you could easily treat yourself to a panful of fried chanterelles without ruining yourself. These mushrooms have, unfortunately, become very expensive. She likes them fried in butter, with just a sprinkling of chopped parsley or some meat juice.

For Alain Ducasse, only three forest mushrooms are worth eating: morels, porcini, and chanterelles. Horn-of-plenty mushrooms are acceptable only when mixed with other mushrooms. *Pieds-de-mouton* mushrooms require a lot of garlic and parsley—unacceptable for the great chef. The delicate, apricot-scented, orange-yellow chanterelle has nothing in common with these sorry forest characters. Erroneously called common, the chanterelle is sufficient unto itself. Fried. Casually sprinkled with veal jus. Simmered, perhaps, in a dollop of crème fraîche. At most, mixed with a few scrambled eggs. The chanterelle requires discretion. The young ones only need to be dusted with a soft brush. The others must be rinsed rapidly so that they do not become saturated with water. Cover the pan when you start cooking so as to preserve their aroma, which is so volatile that it begins to evaporate as soon as the mushrooms are picked. Sometimes, the chanterelle develops stem aromas, in which case its juice will be rather bitter. Cap aromas give them a mellow taste, as good as candy.

How do you track down these denizens of the woods? Outfit yourself with a pair of boots, a stick, a pocket knife, and, of course, a solid basket. Progress slowly into the woods, carefully watching where you put your feet. The chanterelle grows close to beech, oak, pine, and eucalyptus trees. When you spot a mushroom, do not pick it immediately. Use your stick to push aside the surrounding grasses and moss that may be covering other specimens. Rather than pick the small, young mushrooms, return two days later. The closer together a chanterelle's gills are under its corolla, the younger it is. Pick the more mature ones delicately, cutting above their base, so as not to destroy the mycelium that allows them to reproduce. Then, gently close the moss again.

Chanterelle Mushrooms with Cream

Girolles à la crème

☐ ☐ ◯◯◯

Françoise Bernard

Serves 4 ✦ **Preparation time : 30 minutes** ✦ **Cooking time : 30 minutes**
3 lbs. (1,5 kg) chanterelle mushrooms, trimmed ✦ **1 tsp. vinegar** ✦ **7 tbsp. (80 g) butter** ✦ **salt and pepper** ✦ **½ cup (100 g) crème fraîche or sour cream** ✦ **5 sprigs parsley or chervil, leaves only, chopped**

Wash the mushrooms several times in water and vinegar, but do not soak. Gently drain in a colander. **M**elt 2 tbsp. of the butter over low heat. Sauté the mushrooms over medium heat for 5 minutes. Drain in a colander. Return the mushrooms to the skillet with the remaining butter. Season with salt and pepper. Simmer, covered, for 15 minutes. Add the crème fraîche and boil for 3 minutes, stirring with a wooden spoon. Sprinkle with parsley and serve immediately. These mushrooms are perfect with a veal roast or veal scaloppini.

NOTE BY
ALAIN
DUCASSE
To retain the delicate taste of the chanterelles, clean them by scraping them with a knife and then wiping with a moist cloth. Washing causes them to lose some of their aroma—but, unfortunately, it is necessary if the mushrooms are very dirty.

Chanterelle Mushrooms with Chervil in Crawfish Stew

Girolles au cerfeuil, ragoût d'écrevisses

☆ ☆ ☆   ◯◯◯

Alain Ducasse

Serves 4 ◆ Preparation time : 45 minutes ◆ Cooking time : 50 minutes
24 red-clawed crawfish ◆ ½ cup (10 cl) olive oil ◆ 4 garlic cloves, crushed ◆ 1 scallion, thinly
sliced ◆ 1 tsp. tomato paste ◆ 3 tbsp. cognac ◆ ½ cup (10 cl) white wine ◆ 2½ cups (50 cl)
chicken stock ◆ juice of 1 lemon ◆ 1⅓ lbs. (600 g) medium chanterelles, trimmed and cleaned
◆ 7 tbsp. cup (80 g) butter ◆ 5 sprigs chervil, leaves only ◆ sea salt and freshly ground pepper
◆ truffle peelings, optional

Drop the crawfish into boiling water for 2 minutes. Drain. Reserve 4 and peel the others. Crush the heads in a mortar and sauté in a saucepan with 1 tbsp. of the oil. Add the garlic, scallion, and tomato paste and continue to sauté. Add the cognac and wine and reduce almost entirely. Add enough stock to cover and reduce to two-thirds its volume over low heat, skimming carefully and often. Remove from heat, strain, and cool. Stir in a dash of lemon juice and 1 tbsp. oil. **S**auté the mushrooms in the remaining oil. Add 1 ladleful of stock and cook for about 10 minutes. Whisk in 1 tbsp. of butter to bind the sauce. If you have some truffle peelings, chop them and mix into the mushrooms. **S**auté the 4 reserved crawfish and the crawfish tails in 2 tbsp. of hot butter. Spoon the mushrooms into a serving dish and arrange the tails on top. Sprinkle with the chervil leaves and a little of the cooking juice. Decorate the dish with the 4 whole crawfish.

This elegant starter seems the perfect dish for a holiday, first communion, or wedding celebration. You can create a less festive dish—although it will still be very elegant—by replacing the crawfish with large tropical prawns.

NOTE BY
FRANÇOISE
BERNARD

Pan-Fried Chanterelle Mushrooms

Poêlée de girolles sautés

⇧ ⇧ ◯◯◯

Françoise Bernard

Serves 4 ✦ **Preparation time : 20 minutes** ✦ **Cooking time : 30 minutes**
3 lbs. (1,5 kg) chanterelles, trimmed ✦ **1 tsp. vinegar** ✦ **4 tbsp. oil** ✦ **1 shallot or 1 garlic clove,**
finely chopped ✦ **salt and pepper** ✦ **6 sprigs parsley, leaves only, chopped**

Wash the mushrooms several times in water and vinegar, but do not soak. Gently drain in a colander. Heat 3 tbsp. of oil, add the mushrooms, and sauté for 5 minutes. Drain in the colander. Do not wash the pan. **H**eat the remaining oil in the same pan. Add the chanterelles and the shallot. Season with salt and pepper. Sauté for a few minutes over high heat. Cover, lower the heat, and simmer for 20 minutes. Sprinkle with parsley just before serving.

NOTE BY **ALAIN DUCASSE** A little *persillade* (parsley and garlic garnish) will add a fresh taste to your fried chanterelles. Chop the parsley with 2 cloves of garlic and sprinkle the garnish on the mushrooms before serving. I would sauté the mushrooms in olive oil.

Chanterelle Tartlets

Petites tartes aux girolles

⌂ ◌◌◌

Alain Ducasse

Serves 6 ◆ Resting time : 30 minutes ◆ Preparation time : 20 minutes ◆ Cooking time : 25 minutes ◆ about 1½ cups (230 g) flour ◆ 9 tbsp. butter, (120 g) softened ◆ salt and pepper ◆ 1 egg yolk ◆ 3 eggs ◆ 1 cup (20 cl) crème fraîche or sour cream ◆ 1 cup (20 cl) milk ◆ ½ cup (50 g) grated Parmesan cheese ◆ 5 sprigs flat-leaf parsley, leaves only, finely chopped ◆ 5 sprigs chervil, leaves only, finely chopped ◆ grated nutmeg ◆ 5 oz. (150 g) foie gras, diced ◆ 10 oz. (300 g) chanterelle mushrooms ◆ 1 shallot, finely chopped ◆ 2 tbsp. olive oil

Preheat the oven to 350°F (180°C). **M**ix 1⅓ cups (200 g) flour, 8 tbsp. butter, 3 pinches of salt, the egg yolk, and 3 tbsp. water. Knead into a pastry dough. Do not work too much. Refrigerate for 30 minutes. **B**eat the 3 whole eggs. Add the crème fraîche, milk, and Parmesan cheese. Beat in the parsley, chervil, and nutmeg. Season with salt and pepper to taste. Set aside. **S**auté the diced foie gras in a pan without adding any fat. In a separate pan, sauté the chanterelles and shallot in the oil. **R**oll out the dough on a floured surface. Cut out pastry rounds to line 12 small, buttered tart pans. You can also make a single tart in 9 in. (24 cm) tart pan. To make a large tart, pre-bake the pastry. Line the pie plate with dough, cover with a sheet of wax paper, fill with dried beans, and bake for 20 minutes. Remove from the oven and discard the paper and beans. **S**poon the foie gras and chanterelles into the dough or pastry. Cover with the egg custard and bake for 9 to 20 minutes, depending on the size of the pans. Serve hot with a Belgian endive salad.

Individual tarts seems preferable to me than one large tart. They will demand a bit more work in the beginning, but will be much easier to serve because the foie gras melts while cooking. Small tarts are also much more elegant, which seems appropriate for such a refined filling.

NOTE BY **FRANÇOISE BERNARD**

Green Beans

In France, we have the *haricot pape*, a large flat green bean used in Provençal pesto soup; the *mange-tout*, or snap bean, a fleshy green bean, which is both tasty and beautiful; the tender yellow wax bean; and, of course, the string bean, which is very popular among the French, who prefer it to be as slender as possible—they're crazy about the so-called *haricot vert*.

When Françoise Bernard worked for Astra (the margarine company), she asked the chefs that she was interviewing to take a seemingly simple little test: Boil green beans. If the chef added salt to the boiling water with the beans to fix their color—and not before—he won a point. If he chose a large pot, he won another point, because beans require a large volume of water. The texture is also effected by the cooking time. The younger the bean, the quicker it cooks; 5 minutes are enough for beans that are very thin and freshly picked. In Françoise Bernard's family, it was considered a sin to overcook beans. She eats them cold as a salad, sautéed, drizzled with meat juice or crème fraîche, or sprinkled with chopped garlic and herbs.

Although Alain Ducasse cannot resist a good plate of green beans—seasoned with thick crème fraîche, lemon juice, and shallots—he also ardently defends freshly shelled beans, in particular, the coco beans from the Nervia valley in Liguria. These Italian beans have almost no skin and literally melt in your mouth. Of course, they are almost impossible to find, unless you are a chef like Ducasse. In France, you can always fall back on the *Paimpol coco*, the ingot bean, the giant *Soissons* bean, or the white bean from Tarbes, which is so creamy in soup. These varieties were introduced to Europe by Christopher Columbus. As have all dried vegetables, they have become popular again and are served in salads or soup. Under the culinary leadership of chefs, these rustic foods have reclaimed their place in the vegetable aristocracy.

Vegetable Jardinière

Jardinière de légumes

⌂ ∞

Françoise Bernard

Serves 4 ◆ Preparation time : 45 minutes ◆ Cooking time : 55 minutes
2 tbsp. (30 g) butter ◆ 1 bunch new carrots, sliced ◆ 3 baby turnips, diced ◆ 7 oz. (200 g) green
beans, tips and strings removed ◆ 8 oz. (250 g) peas, shelled ◆ 1 small lettuce head ◆ 3 sprigs
chervil or parsley, tied ◆ salt and pepper ◆ 8 oz. (250 g) new potatoes, peeled and diced ◆ 1
tbsp. crème fraîche or sour cream

Melt the butter over low heat. Add the carrots, turnips, green beans, peas, and lettuce.
Stir in 4 tbsp. water, the chervil, and salt and pepper to taste. Cover the pot with a
soup plate filled with cold water and simmer for 20 minutes. Add the potatoes to the
pot and cook for 30 minutes. Add more water to the plate as it evaporates. Before
serving, remove the chervil and mix in the crème fraîche.

NOTE BY **ALAIN DUCASSE** This is the kind of dish that was once ladled out of a stew pot blackened by a fire.
You could replace the crème fraîche with thick creamed peas, made by mixing the
cooked peas with veal stock and cream.

Green Beans and Lemon Cream

Haricots verts, crème citron

⟰ ◯

Alain Ducasse

Serves 8 ✦ **Preparation time : 35 minutes** ✦ **Cooking time : 20 minutes**
1½ lbs. (700 g) green beans, tipped ✦ **ice water** ✦ **½ cup (10 cl) crème fraîche or sour cream**
✦ **juice of 1 lemon** ✦ **3 shallots, sliced** ✦ **fine salt and freshly ground black pepper** ✦ **crushed ice**

Drop the green beans in boiling salted water and cook for about 20 minutes. Drain and refresh in ice water to preserve their color. Drain and set aside. **I**n a large bowl, combine the crème fraîche, lemon juice, shallots, and salt to taste. Rest the bowl in another bowl full of ice. Gently stir in the green beans, add a good twist of the pepper mill, and serve. You can serve this dish with a lettuce salad seasoned with virgin olive oil and lemon juice.

I like my green beans a bit firm. I also like that these take so little time to prepare. I would not cool them off in ice water, however—it's bad for the color. Personally, I think that they taste even better if still a bit warm when mixed with this excellent lemon cream. NOTE BY **FRANÇOISE BERNARD**

Sautéed Green Beans

Haricots verts sautés

⌂ ○

Françoise Bernard

**Serves 4 ◆ Preparation time : 35 minutes ◆ Cooking time : 20 minutes
2¼ lbs. (1 kg) green beans, tips and strings removed ◆ salt and pepper ◆ 4 tbsp. (50 g) butter
◆ 1 garlic clove, minced ◆ 5 sprigs parsley, minced**

Boil a lot of unsalted water in a large pot. Drop the beans into the boiling water. Season with salt and bring to a rolling boil, uncovered. Boil for 5 to 10 minutes, depending on the variety. Remove the beans while they are still a bit firm and drain. **M**elt the butter in a large saucepan over low heat. Quickly sauté the green beans and pepper—they should not get too brown. Add the garlic, sprinkle with parsley, and serve immediately.

NOTE BY **ALAIN DUCASSE** I recommend cooling green beans in cold water immediately after cooking, in order to preserve their green color, and then drain them right away. I know that my method contradicts Françoise Bernard's—so it is up to you to decide.

Green Bean and Lobster Salad

Salade de haricots verts au homard

♙ ♙ ∞

Alain Ducasse

Serves 4 ♦ Preparation time : 1 hour ♦ Cooking time : 20 minutes
2 lettuce hearts ♦ vinegar, for washing ♦ 7 oz. (200 g) green beans ♦ salt ♦ 2¼ lbs. (1 kg)
almonds, in shells ♦ 7 oz. (200 g) medium-size waxy potatoes, scrubbed ♦ 4 female lobsters,
with the coral, about 1 lb. (450 g) each ♦ 1 tbsp. balsamic vinegar ♦ 3 tbsp. wine vinegar ♦ ½
cup (10 cl) olive oil ♦ 2 tbsp. olive oil vinaigrette dressing

Wash the lettuce hearts in water and vinegar. Cut into ½ in. (1 cm) thick slices. Cook the green beans in boiling salted water. Crack the almonds open and remove the nuts. Cook the potatoes for about 15 minutes in boiling salted water. **D**rop the lobsters in boiling salted water. Cook for 7 minutes and then shell them. Remove the coral and mash in a bowl with a fork. Whisk in the vinegars and drizzle in the oil, whisking vigorously until the mixture is smooth. Shell and thinly slice the lobster tails. Marinate them, rounded sides up, in the coral vinaigrette. **A**rrange the lettuce leaves in a rose pattern on the plates and sprinkle with the vinaigrette. Peel and thinly slice the potatoes. Fan the lobster on the lettuce, alternately placing the green beans, potato, and almonds. Brush the lobster meat with vinaigrette and serve.

You might be tempted to make this recipe with frozen lobster tails because they are easier to work with and cheaper. But, remember, they are nowhere near as tasty— and you won't have any coral for your vinaigrette.

NOTE BY **FRANÇOISE BERNARD**

Peas

Françoise Bernard feels good about the pea. Actually, she is crazy about those tender little green balls, fresh or frozen. The pea is one vegetable that keeps its flavor when frozen, although the varieties selected by the food industry are still a little too large for her taste. Frozen peas are more or less crunchy, depending on the brand. The fresh pea season is short indeed—from May to June—and it must not slip by. Shelling peas, far from being a chore, is rather fun. "Peas taste even better today than before, it seems to me," she says. "Before, you had to add sugar when cooking to sweeten them. You don't have to do that anymore."

Alain Ducasse does not differentiate between types of peas. Small or large, he loves them all, as long as they are freshly picked and their pods are smooth and shiny. Actually, he does have a favorite: the so-called telephone pea. The telephone pea is a very sweet, large variety that he gets from farmers around Ventimiglia, the flower town of Liguria. He serves them in *Le Louis XV*, his restaurant in Monaco. For Alain Ducasse, boiling peas in water is heresy. He prefers to simmer them with small new potatoes, hearts of lettuce, and bacon. This method of cooking is actually a traditional recipe, *Petits Pois à la Française*, to which he has added bacon for more flavor. You can also mix peas with Swiss chard, spinach, and pearl onions—but don't forget, cook them only for 3 to 4 minutes, 5 at most. Alain Ducasse makes use of the entire pea. The pods color his green risotto and brighten his pea cream. This vegetable may be small, but it is certainly versatile, isn't it?

French-Style Peas

Petits pois à la française

⌂ ⌂ ○

Françoise Bernard

Serves 4 ◆ Preparation time : 30 minutes ◆ Cooking time : 45 minutes
4½ lbs. (2 kg) fresh peas, shelled ◆ 4 tbsp. (50 g) butter ◆ 6 white pearl onions, peeled ◆ 1
lettuce heart ◆ 5 sprigs parsley ◆ 3 sprigs chervil ◆ salt and pepper ◆ boiling water, optional

Put the peas in a saucepan with 2 tbsp. of butter, the onions, lettuce heart, parsley, chervil, 1 tbsp. of water, salt and pepper. Cover the pan with a soup plate full of cold water and cook over very low heat for about 45 minutes. Add 2 to 3 tbsp. of boiling water to the pan if the peas start sticking to the bottom. Add more cold water to the soup plate as the peas cook, to condense the vegetable juices in the pan below. Just before serving, remove the parsley and chervil, and gently stir in the remaining butter. This dish should be made with young peas, which are very tender.

NOTE BY **ALAIN DUCASSE** Consider reducing the cooking time if you want the young peas to remain whole. Add a fresh note by sprinkling the cooked peas with some snipped herbs, such as parsley, chervil, tarragon, and arugula.

Garden Pea and Potato Stew

Cocotte de petits pois aux pommes de terre

⌂ ○

Alain Ducasse

Serves 4 ✦ **Preparation time : 55 minutes** ✦ **Cooking time : 35 minutes**
12 small new potatoes, scrubbed ✦ 3 tbsp. olive oil ✦ 8 scallions, peeled ✦ 2¼ lbs. (1 kg) peas,
shelled ✦ 20 fava beans in their pods, shelled, optional ✦ 12 salad leaves, such as radicchio,
romaine, or Bibb lettuce ✦ 1 cup (20 cl) chicken stock (page 322) ✦ salt and white pepper

Sauté the potatoes in a heavy casserole in 2 tbsp. of oil for about 15 minutes. Add
the scallions and sauté for about 30 seconds. Add the peas and cook for another 5
minutes. Add the salad leaves and the fava beans, if using, and sauté, stirring gently.
Add the stock and cook for about 10 minutes. Do not overcook, or the vegetables will
soften and lose shape. Season with salt and a twist of the pepper mill. Just before
serving, drizzle with the remaining olive oil. This stew is particularly good served with
a roast, but it can also be eaten alone—it's quite filling.

You can smell the aromas of spring even before you begin cooking! This recipe really
inspires you to cook vegetables—and to give them star treatment, which hardly ever
happens in most restaurants and homes.

NOTE BY
**FRANÇOISE
BERNARD**

Country-Style Peas

Petits pois à la paysanne

⌂ ○

Françoise Bernard

Serves 4 ♦ **Preparation time : 30 minutes** ♦ **Cooking time : 1 hour**
2 tbsp. (30 g) butter ♦ **3 tbsp. flour** ♦ **3½ lbs. (1,5 kg) fresh peas, shelled** ♦ **10 pearl onions,**
peeled ♦ **3 carrots, sliced** ♦ **1 small lettuce head** ♦ **1 sprig thyme** ♦ **2 sprigs tarragon or savory**
♦ **salt and pepper** ♦ **5 oz. (150 g) smoked bacon, optional**

Melt the butter in a large saucepan over low heat. Stir in the flour with a wooden
spoon. Add the peas, onions, carrots, lettuce, thyme, tarragon, and enough cold water
to cover. Season with salt and pepper. Bring to a boil and stir. Cover and simmer over
low heat for about 45 to 50 minutes. Remove the thyme and tarragon before serving.
This recipe is particularly suited to the end of the season, when the peas are large and
a bit tough. You can also add smoked bacon to this dish.

NOTE BY **ALAIN DUCASSE** Peas should be cooked quickly so that they remain a beautiful green. They also should
not crush under the pressure of a finger. This stew is similar to mine. I would serve it
with small, unpeeled new potatoes.

Pea Soup with Garlic Bread Fingers

Soupe de petits pois et mouillettes aillées

⌂ ○

Alain Ducasse

Serves 4 ✦ Preparation time : 50 minutes ✦ Cooking time : 30 minutes
4 leeks ✦ 2 onions, thinly sliced ✦ 4 garlic cpves ✦ 4 tbsp. olive oil ✦ salt and pepper ✦ 7 oz.
(200 g) peas, shelled ✦ 6 cups (1,5 l) chicken stock (page 322) ✦ crushed ice ✦ 7 oz. (200 g)
snow peas ✦ about 2 cups (100 g) radish leaves ✦ ice water ✦ 3 carrots ✦ ¼ bulb celeriac ✦ 4
thick slices whole wheat bread ✦ 2 tbsp. ham fat or butter ✦ several sautéed wild mushrooms,
optional ✦ ¾ cup (15 cl) crème fraîche or sour cream

Thinly slice 1 of the leeks. Sauté the sliced leek, onions, and 1 garlic clove in 2 tbsp. of the oil. Season with salt and pepper. Add the peas and stock. Boil for 20 minutes and then quickly place the pan on the crushed ice to cool. Cook the snow peas and radish leaves in boiling salted water for 10 minutes. Cool them by placing in a bowl of ice water. Drain. Add these vegetables to the pea soup. Dice the carrots, celeriac, and remaining leeks. Sauté with 2 garlic cloves in 1 tbsp. of oil, without browning. Season with salt and pepper. Brown the bread slices and the remaining garlic in the ham fat. Cut each slice into 4 or 5 *mouillettes*, or bread fingers. Spoon the diced vegetables into individual soup plates (you can also add a few sautéed wild mushrooms, if you wish). Bring the soup to a boil, add the crème fraîche, and check the seasoning. Ladle the soup over the diced vegetables. Serve the bread fingers on the side.

I would not serve this dish in soup plates but rather in calottes, which are rimless soup bowls, to call attention to the fresh-almond green color of the soup and to make it easy to serve.

NOTE BY
FRANÇOISE
BERNARD

Porcini Mushrooms

The king of autumn, the porcini—or *cèpe*, in French—is one of the few mushrooms that Alain Ducasse considers to be excellent, in the company of the morel and the chanterelle. For him, there is nothing better than roasted porcini, although this does not stop him from cooking it a thousand other ways—grilled, for example, as in his Artichoke Bouillon with Grilled Porcini. His most original way to prepare porcini is in a casserole with chestnut leaves. Whether a country-minded soul or a trendy cook looking for unheard-of pleasures, no one is indifferent to this dish. Just imagine slices of porcini caps braised between two beds of chestnut leaves! The cap is the part of the porcini that Alain Ducasse prefers. He chops the stems, which are often stringy, and adds them to the pan at the end of the cooking, or he mixes them into a stuffing.

In Françoise Bernard's family, which comes from the North, porcini are rarely eaten. This mushroom prefers the shade of southwestern trees. In that region, it is often served as a fricassee with a few Sarlat apples. Françoise Bernard has learned to like porcini, but she is still rather reluctant to use them, due to their high price. She advises her readers to use preserved porcini in her recipes. Also, she is not always confident about a market's sources for fresh porcini—all too poorly indicated, according to her—or about the mushroom's appearance and quality.

Fresh porcini are often dirty. Caps perforated with small holes are a sure sign that the mushrooms were home to a few worms. You can get rid of these uninvited guests by spreading the mushrooms in a shallow dish and covering it with a very tight layer of plastic wrap. The worms will come up for air after 1 hour and stick to the plastic wrap, which you then only have to throw away. The base of the stem should be discarded (the entire stem if it is stringy), and the rest cleaned with a soft brush. Very dirty porcini should be washed in running water and dried immediately.

The three most common varieties of porcini in France are the Bordeaux porcini, the tan porcini (also known as tête-de-nègre, or black cap), and the pine porcini. Like all mushrooms, the best porcini are young, compact, and firm. The cap of a very young porcini has a white underside. If the underside is lemon yellow—which is best—the mushroom is about one day old and will be a pure delight with a parsley and garlic sauce. Older porcini should be saved for a risotto or cooked with potatoes.

Porcini Mushrooms, Bordeaux-Style

Cèpes à la bordelaise

⇧ ⇧ ∞

Françoise Bernard

Serves 4 ◆ **Preparation time : 25 minutes** ◆ **Cooking time : 20 minutes**
1½ lbs. (600 g) very firm porcini mushrooms ◆ **1 tbsp. vinegar** ◆ **2 small shallots** ◆ **3 sprigs**
parsley, leaves only ◆ **3 tbsp. oil** ◆ **4 tbsp. (50 g) butter or duck fat** ◆ **1 tbsp. bread crumbs,**
made from stale bread ◆ **salt and pepper** ◆ **juice of ½ lemon**

Remove the ends of the mushroom stems. Drop the porcini into vinegar water, quickly
remove, and pat dry with paper towels. Slice the mushrooms. Mince the shallots and
parsley together. **H**eat the oil in a pan. Sauté the porcini over medium-high heat for
10 minutes. Add the butter, bread crumbs, and shallot-parsley mixture. Season with
salt and pepper. Cook over medium heat, 5 to 10 minutes, being careful not to burn.
At the end of the cooking, add a little lemon juice. Serve with an omelet, poultry, or
beef.

NOTE BY **ALAIN DUCASSE** To spice up the flavor, I would add 2 cloves of garlic to the minced shallot-parsley mixture. And why not add a bit of chopped ham, too? (Don't season the dish with as much
salt if you do.) The porcini mushroom has a strong personality—it is not afraid to be
combined with other full-flavored ingredients, like garlic, ham, olive oil, or truffles.

Porcini Mushroom Truffle Marmalade

Marmelade de cèpes truffée

⇧ ⇧ ◯◯◯

Alain Ducasse

Serves 1 ◆ Preparation time : 15 minutes ◆ Cooking time : 20 minutes
1 large porcini mushroom ◆ ½ cup (10 cl) chicken stock (page 322) ◆ ¼ cup (5 cl) pheasant
jus (page 323) ◆ 2 tbsp. olive oil ◆ ⅓ oz. (10 g) truffle peelings, chopped ◆ 1 tbsp. truffle juice
◆ 2 shallots, thinly sliced ◆ sea salt and freshly ground pepper ◆ 3 tsp. red wine vinegar

Clean the mushrooms, chop the stems, and dice the caps. Combine the chopped stems, diced caps, stock, pheasant jus, and olive oil in a skillet. Reduce to half its volume. Add the truffle peelings, truffle juice, and shallots. Season with salt and pepper, simmer 5 minutes, then sprinkle with vinegar. This mixture can be served on Potato Gnocchi (page 217), spaghetti, or poached chicken. Adjust the quantity, depending on what you decide to serve it with.

This is a fine condiment to serve with a pheasant hen on a special occasion—or with any other type of game, for that matter. I think that you would also obtain excellent results without adding the truffle peelings.

NOTE BY **FRANÇOISE BERNARD**

Turkey Stuffed with Porcini Mushrooms

Dinde farcie aux cèpes

☖ ◯◯◯

Françoise Bernard

Serves 10 to 12 ✦ Preparation time : 50 minutes ✦ Cooking time : 3 hours ✦ Resting time : 20 minutes ✦ 1 lb. (500 g) canned porcini mushrooms ✦ ½ cup (50 g) bread cubes ✦ ¾ cup (15 cl) milk, warm ✦ 1 egg ✦ 10 oz. (300 g) very finely ground pork and veal ✦ 1 turkey liver, diced ✦ ¾ cup (15 cl) port wine ✦ salt and pepper ✦ 1 small turkey, about 9 lbs. (4 kg) ✦ 4 tbsp. (50 g) butter, softened

Preheat the oven to 350°F (180°C). Rinse the mushrooms and pat dry with paper towels. Dice the caps and chop the stems. Place the bread in a bowl and pour on the warm milk. Beat the egg slightly and add to the mixture. Add the mushrooms, ground meat, diced liver, and ⅔ cup (13 cl) of the wine. Season with salt and pepper, mix well. Pack this stuffing inside the turkey cavity, without overfilling. Sew closed or stuff a crumpled sheet of aluminum foil into the opening as a stopper. Place the turkey on its side in a large roasting pan or deep-sided oven tray. Brush the bird with butter, season with salt and pepper. Bake for 1 hour on each side, then place the turkey on its back and bake for about 45 minutes. Baste frequently with the cooking juice. When the turkey is done, turn off the heat and let it rest in the oven for 20 minutes. Scrape the bottom of the roasting pan and pour the cooking juice and drippings into a small saucepan. Bring to a boil and skim off the fat. Add ¼ cup (5 cl) water, reduce over high heat for 5 minutes, and add the remaining wine. Place the turkey on a large, warm serving platter and serve the sauce in a sauceboat on the side.

NOTE BY **ALAIN DUCASSE** You must baste a turkey frequently while it roasts. Here's a tip from a chef: The turkey is very nearly done when the meat of the wings gives way under the pressure of your fingertip. If you cook it much longer, it might be too dry.

Porcini Mushrooms in Chestnut Leaves

Cèpes cuits en feuilles de châtaignier

⇧ ⇧ ⇧ ∞

Alain Ducasse

Serves 4 ✦ **Preparation time : 20 minutes** ✦ **Cooking time : 20 minutes**
2¼ lbs. (1 kg) porcini mushrooms ✦ **2¼ lbs. (1 kg) chestnut leaves** ✦ **3 shallots, chopped** ✦ **1½ cups (30 cl) olive oil** ✦ **salt and pepper**

Preheat the oven to 400°F (210°C). Clean the mushrooms with a moist towel and remove the ends of the stems. Separate the caps from the stems. Slice the stems and set aside in a bowl. Lay chestnut leaves on the bottom of 4 small baking dishes, preferably glass, with lids. Spread some of the shallots on the leaves and sprinkle with the oil. Cover the leaves with the mushroom caps. Season with salt and pepper to taste. Season the sliced stems with salt and pepper and arrange in small mounds on top of the caps. Cover with chestnut leaves and then with aluminum foil. Bake, with the lids on, for 20 minutes. Serve the mushrooms in the baking dishes as soon as you remove them from the oven.

This is a magnificent autumn dish. You will feel as though you are in the heart of the forest, not in your own kitchen. What an excellent recipe to raise the spirits of a city dweller who longs for nature! As soon as you lift the lid of the baking dish, the chestnut leaves send out their woodsy aroma, which blends marvelously with the fragrance of the porcini mushrooms.

NOTE BY **FRANÇOISE BERNARD**

Potatoes

It is hard to imagine a prestigious chef like Alain Ducasse—the only chef in France ever to have been awarded six stars—with a potato and peeler in hand. Yet, there he is: the aficionado of white truffle and foie gras, cooking potatoes. He transforms the mealier potatoes, the Mona Lisa, for example, into gnocchi, which he seasons with white truffles. He cooks the firmer ones in earthenware pots, like those our grandmothers used, bulging with warm aromas. He is particularly fond of this potato-cooking method: Forget them in the oven for about 20 hours. These baked potatoes are breathtakingly mild.

Françoise Bernard has a radically different approach to cooking potatoes. When she is in a hurry, she quickly slices some potatoes on a plate, drizzles olive oil over them, adds salt and pepper, covers them with plastic wrap, and puts the plate in the microwave for a few seconds. This impromptu dish is delicious served with a green salad. "I love the practical side and the fun side of the potato," she confides to Alain Ducasse, who, far from disagreeing with her, presents her with his recipe for mashed potatoes with olive oil. For this dish, he uses yellow Manosque potatoes, which are, unfortunately, very rare. "Fast" and "gourmet' are not irreconcilable terms for our chefs.

Alain Ducasse roasts Grenaille potatoes over coarse salt. He also cooks these new mountain potatoes, each one no larger than an egg, in duck fat for a very long time over low heat, and then grills them. He carves large sticks for his french fries from the Bintje or the Agria varieties. They are real fries, crunchy on the outside and soft on the inside, nothing like those skinny fries that only crunch. These two chefs prove, if it is still necessary to do so, that the potato has infinite facets. This little darling of Parmentier, who cultivated the vegetable in eighteenth-century France, the potato has not yet had its last word.

Scalloped Potatoes *Dauphinois*

Gratin Dauphinois

⏶ ⏶ ⏶

Françoise Bernard

Serves 4 ✦ Preparation time : 35 minutes ✦ Cooking time : 1 hour
2¼ lbs. (1 kg) medium-size potatoes ✦ 1 garlic clove, crushed ✦ 2 tbsp. (30 g) butter, softened
✦ 2 cups (40 cl) milk ✦ about ½ cup (50 g) grated Gruyère cheese ✦ 1 egg ✦ salt and pepper

Preheat the oven to 400°F (210°C). Peel and wash the potatoes and pat dry with paper towels. Cut into thin, even slices with a knife or vegetable cutter. Select a glass baking dish that is large enough to hold all the potato slices in a single layer. Rub the inside of the dish with garlic, then grease with butter. Bring the milk to a boil. Arrange the potato slices in the dish and cover with ⅓ cup (17 g) of the cheese. Pour 1½ cups (30 cl) of the boiling milk on top. Season with salt and pepper. Bake 50 to 60 minutes. Just before the cooking is done, beat the egg with the remaining milk, season with salt and pepper. Pour this mixture over the potatoes, sprinkle with the remaining cheese, and dot with butter. Lower the oven temperature to 350°F (180°C) and bake until the mixture has thickened. Remove and serve immediately with roasted or broiled beef or poultry.

NOTE BY **ALAIN DUCASSE** The success of this dish depends on how thin the potato slices are. The second rule: Bake the slices in single layer. Be sure you have a large enough baking dish to spread them out.

Potato Gnocchi

Gnocchis de pommes de terre

⇧ ⇧ ○

Alain Ducasse

Serves 4 ✦ **Preparation time : 45 minutes** ✦ **Cooking time : 50 minutes**
3 large potatoes, scrubbed ✦ **coarse salt, for roasting** ✦ **4 tbsp. olive oil** ✦ **1⅓ cups (240 g) flour**
✦ **1 egg** ✦ **coarse salt and pepper** ✦ **grated Parmesan cheese, optional**

Preheat the oven to 350°F (180°C). **R**oast the potatoes on a bed of coarse salt for 45 minutes. Check for doneness with the tip of a sharp knife. Peel and rice the potatoes onto a floured surface. Drizzle with 2 tbsp. of the oil, sift the remaining flour on top, and add the egg. Mix the dough into a ball with your fingertips. Season with salt and pepper and cut into quarters. Roll each quarter between your hands to make ropes about ½ in. (1 cm) thick. Cut the ropes into ¾ in. (1,5 cm) pieces. One by one, roll the pieces with a fork, pressing down with the tip of your thumb or index finger to form ribs with the fork tines. **D**rop the gnocchi into a pot of boiling salted water. Remove with a slotted spoon as they rise to the surface. Serve hot, simply seasoned with the remaining olive oil and some grated Parmesan cheese. You can also toss them with tomato sauce, meat stew, Porcini Mushroom Truffle Marmalade (page 211) or pesto.

Roasting unpeeled potatoes on a bed of coarse salt is an excellent idea. Their texture reminds me a little of the potatoes I ate as a child in the North. Those were baked in the coal stove under an bell-shaped earthenware cover placed directly on the embers. They were so good! My aunt served the potatoes warm with a bacon and frisée lettuce salad loaded with garlic.

NOTE BY **FRANÇOISE BERNARD**

Potato Pancakes

Crêpes de pommes de terre

☗ ☗ ○

Françoise Bernard

Serves 4 ✦ **Preparation time : 35 minutes** ✦ **Cooking time : 15 minutes**
1½ lbs. (600 g) potatoes, peeled, grated, rinsed, and dried ✦ 2 eggs ✦ 1 tbsp. flour ✦ 4 pinches
of grated nutmeg ✦ salt and pepper ✦ 4 tbsp. oil

Combine the grated potatoes with the eggs, flour, and nutmeg. Season with salt and
pepper to taste and mix well with a fork. Heat 2 tbsp. of the oil in a large pan. When
the oil is very hot, place 3 to 4 individual tablespoonfuls of the mixture in the pan,
spacing them so they don't touch each other. Flatten each mound into small pancakes.
Sauté quickly on 1 side, turn with a spatula, and sauté the other side. Add a little more
oil to the pan, as needed, and continue to make pancakes with the remaining mixture.
Serve hot. If necessary, keep the pancakes warm in the oven or between 2 plates on
a pot of boiling water.

NOTE BY **ALAIN DUCASSE** In classic cuisine, these pancakes are called pommes darphin. They can be served as a
side dish or used as the base for another recipe, like a slightly unorthodox tart.

Fork-Mashed Potatoes

Pommes de terre écrasées à la fourchette

⌂ ○

Alain Ducasse

Serves 4 ✦ **Preparation time : 30 minutes** ✦ **Cooking time : 45 minutes**
coarse salt ✦ **2¼ lbs. (1 kg) mealy potatoes, of equal size, scrubbed** ✦ **2 tbsp. (30 g) butter,**
very soft ✦ **3 tbsp. olive oil** ✦ **fine salt** ✦ **2 sprigs of flat-leaf parsley, leaves chopped**

Preheat the oven to 350°F (180°C). **S**prinkle the bottom of a baking sheet with coarse salt and place the potatoes, side by side, on top. Bake until a knife blade slides in easily—about 45 minutes. **C**ool and peel the potatoes. Place them in a deep serving dish, add the butter, and mash with a fork. Add the oil and sprinkle with fine salt. Mix gently, without mashing too much—the mixture should remain airy. Sprinkle with the parsley and serve immediately. This potato dish goes with just about anything.

This is a purée as I love purées—not too smooth. This mealy potato, mashed with a fork and fluffed with olive oil, seems to me to be the antithesis of Joël Robuchon's great success—his cream and butter purée. These two great chefs have brilliantly demonstrated to us how to obtain very different results with the same food and a similar recipe.

NOTE BY **FRANÇOISE BERNARD**

Spinach

The French say that a financial windfall puts butter on your spinach. Françoise Bernard echoes that sentiment when she says, "Spinach calls for butter or cream." When she is not simmering spinach in crème fraîche, she is cooking it with a little bacon and crushed garlic. To enhance this simple dish, she adds a few beaten eggs, some Gruyère and grated Parmesan cheese, and browns it in the oven.

Although he recognizes that spinach with cream is a marvelous classic dish, Alain Ducasse mostly considers this vegetable as an ingredient. He rarely gives it the spotlight, except for his crusted Roasted Spinach, which is served as a starter or as an accompaniment to veal loin. He prefers mixing spinach with something else—in a stuffing for an herb pie, for example, or with pasta, or into the pasta itself, as in his delicious Spinach Tagliatelle. He never blanches spinach before cooking. He prefers to add it to brown butter and simply let it cook there, stirring from time to time. He also likes to brighten the flavor with a bit of meat jus and cream. The idea then is to obtain a beautiful creamy aspect, cooking over low heat to keep the cream from separating. And what about raw spinach salads? Is Alain Ducasse's passion for "the raw with the cooked" not aroused in this case? Times have changed since Alexander Dumas claimed that spinach should never be eaten unless cooked. Now, at the turn of the millennium, salads of young spinach shoots with thin slices of haddock or sprinkled with chicken livers are more popular than ever.

Neither of our chefs can tolerate spinach that is not absolutely fresh. They consider canned spinach as "atrocious" and frozen spinach as "barely acceptable"—nothing like the beautiful, dark green, fresh leaves.

Spinach, Roman-Style

Epinards à la romaine

⇧ ⇧ ∞

Françoise Bernard

Serves 4 ◆ Preparation time : 35 minutes ◆ Cooking time : 30 minutes
3½ lbs. (1,5 kg) spinach ◆ 1 thin slice of lean bacon, diced ◆ 1½ tbsp. (20 g) butter ◆ 1 clove
garlic, crushed ◆ salt and pepper ◆ 2 eggs ◆ ¾ cup (15 cl) milk ◆ ¼ cup (25 g) grated Parmesan
cheese ◆ ¼ cup (25 g) grated Gruyère cheese ◆ 2 oz. (50 g) Gruyère cheese, sliced

Preheat the oven to 425°F (220°C). Boil water in a large pot. Discard the spinach stems and wash the leaves. Blanch the leaves for 5 minutes, drain thoroughly, and chop coarsely. Sauté the bacon in the butter. Add the spinach, garlic, salt, and pepper. Cover, simmer for 5 minutes, transfer to a baking dish. Beat together the eggs, milk, Parmesan cheese, and grated Gruyère cheese. Season with salt and pepper and pour over the spinach. Lay slices of Gruyère cheese in a lattice pattern on top and bake for 15 minutes.

NOTE BY **ALAIN DUCASSE** When you are cooking large quantities of spinach, it's best to cook it in several batches rather than all at once. I prefer to cook spinach in brown butter with crushed garlic, covered, over low heat. I do not blanch it.

Roasted Spinach

Rôties d'épinards

⌂ ○

Alain Ducasse

Serves 4 ✦ **Preparation time : 25 minutes** ✦ **Cooking time : 20 minutes**
2¼ lbs. (1 kg) fresh spinach ✦ **4 tbsp. (50 g) butter** ✦ **1 garlic clove, peeled** ✦ **1 cup (20 cl)**
crème fraîche or sour cream ✦ **¾ cup (15 cl) meat jus (page 323)** ✦ **salt and white pepper** ✦ **8**
pieces of French bread, for croutons

Preheat the broiler. **D**iscard the spinach stems. Wash the leaves several times in large
amounts of water. Drain well, being careful not to break the leaves. Melt the butter
in a skillet over low heat. When the butter starts to turn light brown, add the spinach.
Sauté, stirring with a fork that has the garlic stuck in the tines. Add the crème fraîche
in 2 or 3 parts, stirring after each addition. Reduce over low heat, so the cream does
not curdle-about 5 minutes. Add the meat jus and simmer for 10 minutes. Season
with salt and pepper. Toast the bread. Arrange the toast in a baking dish, cover with
the spinach mixture, and brown under the broiler for 5 to 10 minutes.

This recipe opens the door onto many new, gourmet adventures. Can't you easily
imagine this roasted spinach as a starter, accompanied by a poached or fried egg? It
would also be delicious as a garnish for a roast. How about adding a few pine nuts or
slices of half-dry Crottin de Chavignol cheese? If you prefer regular shapes, make the
croutons from slices of white sandwich bread. I just love recipes that free you to create
anything you fancy!

NOTE BY
FRANÇOISE
BERNARD

Spinach with Cream

Epinards à la crème

☞ ∞

Françoise Bernard

Serves 4 ♦ **Preparation time : 15 minutes** ♦ **Cooking time : 20 minutes**
4½ lbs. (2 kg) spinach ♦ **2 tbsp. (30 g) butter** ♦ **¼ cup (60 g) crème fraîche** ♦ **salt and pepper**

Boil water in a large pot. Discard the spinach stems and wash the leaves in a large amount of water. Blanch for 5 minutes. Drain well, squeezing with your hands to remove the excess water. Coarsely chop the leaves. Cook the spinach in the butter over high heat for 2 to 3 minutes, stirring with a wooden spoon. The spinach must be completely dry, or the water will dilute the crème fraîche. Reserve 1 tbsp. of the crème fraîche and pour the rest over the spinach. Season with salt and pepper. Mix well, cover, and simmer for 10 minutes. Just before serving, stir in the rest of the crème fraîche.

NOTE BY **ALAIN DUCASSE** Spinach with cream is the ideal side dish for roasted meat—a tender piece of suckling veal from Limousin, for example. You can also serve it with a country omelet, with a few croutons of fried bread and some crispy bacon bits.

Tagliatelle with Spinach and Truffles

Tagliatelle aux épinards et aux truffes

⭫ ∞

Alain Ducasse

Serves 4 ✦ Preparation time : 1 hour ✦ Resting time : 12 hours ✦ Cooking time : 10 minutes ✦ 3⅓ cups (500 g) flour ✦ 8 oz. (250 g) spinach, puréed ✦ 3 eggs ✦ 1 tbsp. olive oil ✦ ½ cup (10 cl) chicken stock (page 322) ✦ 1 cup (20 cl) truffle juice ✦ 8 tbsp. (100 g) butter ✦ 1 tsp. truffle peelings, chopped, optional ✦ salt ✦ about 1 cup (100 g) freshly grated Parmesan cheese

Sift the flour. Knead into the puréed spinach and eggs, without overworking. The dough should not be too elastic. Cover with plastic wrap and let rest in the refrigerator for 12 hours. **T**he next day, make flat, thin tagliatelle noodles with a pasta machine set at ⅛ in. (1 mm). As the dough comes out of the machine, cut a sheet every 6 in. (15 cm). Cover with a clean cloth and refrigerate. Just before cooking, cut the sheets into ¼ in. (5 cm) noodles with a knife. Boil for about 3 minutes in the oil and a large amount of salted water. Drain well. **B**oil the stock and truffle juice in a large saucepan. Stir in the butter, truffle peelings, if using, and the pasta. Carefully mix until the noodles are well covered. Adjust the seasoning with salt. Serve the pasta with Parmesan cheese on the side.

Because I don't like frozen puréed spinach, I suggest you prepare a homemade purée by steaming the spinach and mixing it in a blender. If you prefer to boil the spinach rather than steam it, dry the purée over low heat or with a piece of cloth—this way, the pasta will not be too moist. If you are in a hurry, you can always buy plain tagliatelle and serve it over spinach cooked in brown butter.

NOTE BY **FRANÇOISE BERNARD**

Tomatoes

All the books written by Alain Ducasse praise the tomato. This vegetable embodies all that he passionately loves—freshness, acidity, color, the Mediterranean. The tomato lends itself to every type of culinary adventure. You can "drink it and eat it too," as they say. According to botanists, the tomato is a fruit. It can be eaten raw or half-cooked; cut into rounds over a thin tart or toasted bread; baked in olive oil for hours in a very slow oven. You can use it in cold or hot soups, in "sauces to be eaten" (a specialty of Alain Ducasse), or in a Bloody Mary on a moody evening. You can play with textures by combining dried pasta with a cooked-tomato coulis, slices of baked tomato, and diced fresh tomato. What a tasty trio! And there's the "multi-ethnic" tomato salad served at *La Bastide de Moustiers*, made with tomatoes of all colors and all shapes! Did you know that there are even black tomatoes?

The tomato is, without a doubt, Alain Ducasse's favorite

vegetable, and this book is not long enough for him to sing all its praises. Françoise Bernard feels the same—as a child, she would marvel at seeing her aunts' green tomatoes redden on the windowsills where they were left to ripen. What a pleasure to watch a fruit gradually turn red!

Today, everyone loves baked tomatoes, either as an antipasto or in a thin tart. The best recipes accentuate the sweet flavor of the tomato but also respect its freshness—such as the Catalan bread spreads, toasts rubbed with garlic and fresh tomato, or the pasta seasoned with a tomato sauce that Françoise Bernard once ate at a Sardinian restaurant.

There is only one problem: The tomato has become prettier over the years, but as soon as the frost arrives, beautiful tomatoes are deceptive. "Don't talk to me about those so-called branches of tomatoes on the vine. 'They are too beautiful to eat.' They're nothing but skin and water!" Once she has calmed down, Françoise Bernard explains that she prefers the flavor of tomatoes that grow in soil to those that are force-fed. Field tomatoes certainly make the most beautiful salads and the best sauces in the world.

Tomato Stuffed with Meat

Tomate farcie à la viande

⬡ ⬡ ◯

Françoise Bernard

Serves 4 ◆ Preparation time : 40 minutes ◆ Cooking time : 40 minutes
4 large, firm tomatoes ◆ salt and pepper ◆ ½ cup (10 cl) milk, hot ◆ ½ cup (50 g) diced stale
white sandwich bread ◆ 5 sprigs parsley, leaves only, chopped ◆ 1 onion ◆ 1 clove garlic ◆ 7
oz. (200 g) ground meat, such as leftover pot roast or roast beef ◆ 1 egg ◆ (25 g) butter ◆ ½
cup (50 g) bread crumbs or cracker crumbs

Preheat the oven to 350°F (180°C). Remove and reserve the cap of each tomato. Scoop out the flesh with a teaspoon, making sure not to pierce the skin. Strain and set the juice aside. Season with salt then drain, upside down, on a dish or a rack set over a plate. Put the bread in a small bowl and pour the hot milk on top. Chop the parsley, onion, and garlic. Squeeze out the milk and place the bread in a larger bowl. Add the parsley, onion, garlic, ground meat, egg, salt, pepper. Add a little of the tomato juice if the stuffing is too dry. Mix well and stuff the tomatoes. Arrange the tomatoes in a small, buttered baking dish, setting them close together so they won't fall apart while baking. Sprinkle each one with bread crumbs and dot with butter. Bake for 30 minutes. Place a cap on each tomato and bake for 10 more minutes. Serve very hot.

NOTE BY **ALAIN DUCASSE** Rather than stuffing the vegetable with meat, I prefer to stuff it with vegetables. I like to heighten the flavor of the tomato with a tomato stuffing.

Tomatoes Stuffed with Tomato

Tomates farcies à la tomate

⌂ ○

Alain Ducasse

Serves 4 ◆ Preparation time : 35 minutes ◆ Cooking time : 1 hour 10 minutes
16 tomatoes ◆ salt and pepper ◆ 4 white onions, chopped ◆ 4 tbsp. olive oil ◆ 4 cloves garlic,
unpeeled ◆ 1 sprig rosemary ◆ 1 sprig thyme ◆ 2 oven-dried tomatoes (page 231), chopped ◆ 1
tbsp. grated Parmesan cheese ◆ 1 tbsp. flat-leaf parsley, leaves, chopped ◆ 1 tbsp. basil, leaves,
shredded ◆ 2 tbsp. juice from a roast chicken

Preheat the oven to 400°F (210°C). Cut off the top third of 8 tomatoes. Scoop out
the flesh and reserve the caps. Season the insides with salt and pepper, turn the
tomatoes upside down on a wire rack, and drain for 20 minutes. Peel and seed the
remaining tomatoes. Lightly sauté the onions in 1 tbsp. of the oil over low heat. Heat
1 tbsp. of oil in a heavy casserole. Add the seeded tomatoes, garlic, rosemary and
thyme sprigs, season with salt and pepper. Bake to the consistency of a tomato jam,
about 30 minutes. Remove from the oven. Remove and discard the garlic, rosemary,
and thyme. Add the onions, oven-dried tomatoes, Parmesan cheese, parsley, basil, a
drizzle of oil, and salt and pepper to taste. Lower the oven temperature to 350°F
(180°C). Stuff the tomatoes and replace their caps. Arrange in a baking dish and
sprinkle with the chicken juice and some oil. Bake for 25 minutes, basting frequently.
Remove from the oven. Season with pepper, add the remaining oil, and serve in the
baking dish. If you prefer to serve this dish cold, cook the tomatoes before you stuff
them.

I would double the proportions of this recipe so that I could reserve the tomatoes as
a starter for another meal. I would also serve these tomatoes with Zucchini Stuffed
with Zucchini (page 235) as an accompaniment to poultry or a veal roast.

NOTE BY **FRANÇOISE BERNARD**

Provençal Tomatoes

Tomates provençales

⌂ ○

Françoise Bernard

Serves 4 ◆ **Preparation time : 15 minutes** ◆ **Cooking time : 15 minutes**
6 very firm tomatoes ◆ **salt and pepper** ◆ **6 tbsp. (80 g) butter** ◆ **4 garlic cloves** ◆ **1 bunch**
parsley ◆ **3 tbsp. bread crumbs or cracker crumbs**

Halve the tomatoes, season with salt, turn upside down on a plate to drain. Heat 1 tbsp. of the butter and place the tomatoes in the skillet, cut side down. Sauté over high heat for 2 minutes, turn, and sauté the other side for 2 minutes. Season with salt and pepper. Peel the garlic and wash the parsley. Chop the garlic and parsley and mix with the bread crumbs. Spoon the mixture onto the halved tomatoes. Top each with a dab of butter, cover the skillet, and cook over medium heat for 10 minutes. These tomatoes are especially good with veal scaloppini and veal ribs.

NOTE BY **ALAIN DUCASSE** This seemingly simple dish can turn into the best, or worst, dish ever. For even cooking and softer texture, blanch and peel the tomatoes, spread the stuffing on top, and place under a broiler. This method will preserve the freshness of the tomato and the crustiness of the parsley bread crumbs.

Oven-Dried Tomato Tart

Tarte aux tomates confites

⌂ ⌂ ○

Alain Ducasse

Serves 6 ◆ Preparation time : 55 minutes ◆ Resting time : 2 hours ◆ Cooking time : 4 hours ◆ 2 cups (280 g) flour ◆ 11 tbsp. (150 g) butter, softened ◆ 2 tbsp. (30 g) lard ◆ 2 small egg yolks ◆ ¼ cup (5 cl) water ◆ 4½ lbs. (2 kg) tomatoes, peeled, seeded, and quartered ◆ 5 garlic cloves, crushed ◆ 5 sprigs thyme, leaves only ◆ 1 cup (20 cl) olive oil ◆ sea salt and pepper ◆ 3 handfuls (100 g) arugula ◆ 1 handful (50 g) frisée ◆ 1 handful (50 g) mesclun ◆ 4 sprigs basil, leaves only

Make a well in 1¾ cups (245 g) of the flour. Put the butter, lard, 1 egg yolk, and the water in the center. Mix the butter into the flour with the palm of your hand. Roll the dough into a ball, wrap in plastic wrap, and refrigerate for 2 hours. Preheat the oven to 170°F (75°C), leaving the door ajar. Place the tomatoes in an oiled baking dish and sprinkle with the garlic, thyme, 2 tbsp. of oil, and salt. Bake for 3 to 4 hours, turning the pieces after 1½ to 2 hours. Remove from the oven. Raise the oven temperature to 400°F (210°C). On a floured surface, roll out the dough as thin as possible. Cut out a 10 in. (26 cm) circle and place on a baking sheet lined with parchment paper. Prick the dough with a fork. Bake for 20 minutes. Remove from the oven. Beat the remaining egg yolk and brush it on the crust. Bake for 5 more minutes. Remove from oven and let cool. Clean the arugula, frisée, and mesclun. Arrange the greens in the center of the cooled crust. Spoon the oven dried tomatoes on top and decorate with basil. For a finishing touch, add some Parmesan cheese and a few zucchini swirls, made with a vegetable peeler—sauté the zucchini in butter.

The simplest decoration is often the most successful. A sprinkle of zucchini peels will have a beautiful effect on the baked tomatoes. Green and red go together so well.   NOTE BY **FRANÇOISE BERNARD**

Zucchini

Zucchini is the vegetable that smoothes the flavor of rata-
touilles left to simmer on back burners. Ratatouille is a vegetable cocktail, popular with old and young. "I am the queen
of ratatouille," Françoise Bernard claims with a laugh. It is
truly refreshing served cold in the summer. In winter, its
warm and colorful flavors brighten all types of meats and
vegetables. Françoise Bernard usually prefers to mix zucchini with other vegetables, as does Alain Ducasse. Sometimes, she fries it as a quick garnish or prepares it as fritters,
which adds some structure to its watery pulp. When the zucchini is small and young, she serves it raw, with a dash of
lemon and a drizzle of hazelnut oil.

Alain Ducasse's preferred varieties have astonishing
names: the giant trumpet zucchini, also known as butter zucchini, which has a surrealistic shape; and the elegant violin
zucchini, which ends in a blossom. Everything about these
varieties is good—which is far from true of the Parisian zuc-

chini. Many consider this zucchini to be green, but Alain Ducasse insists it is gray, and he claims its consistency is cottony and its pulp is waterlogged. Not a flattering description! For him, its only redeeming quality is its zebra-striped skin, which he slices into a perfect *brunoise*—first lengthwise into thin strips, then into tiny jewel-like dice.

The type of zucchini that Ducasse finds worthy is picked under the hot Southern sun. He cooks it in a risotto, in a cream, in a pie, in a thick pancake, or as fritters. He simply washes the young ones and eats them raw, or he braises them rapidly. His specialty is to stuff vegetables with themselves— tomatoes with tomatoes and zucchini with zucchini. For this dish, he chooses round zucchini. This variety is not limited to a Southern chef; it has become more common in markets. Alain Ducasse sets his risottos ablaze with the sun-yellow blossom, when he doesn't turn it into an airy fritter. The zucchini blossom is usually treated as a delicacy—but Alain Ducasse does not always do so. In some of his recipes, the zucchini blossom becomes an ingredient like any other, sliced in a chiffonade, as if it were lettuce.

Zucchini Fritters

Beignets de courgette

⭓ ⭓ ⭓ ◯

Françoise Bernard

Serves 4 ✦ Preparation time : 15 minutes ✦ Resting time : 1 hour ✦ Cooking time : 15 minutes ✦ 1¼ cups (180 g) flour ✦ 1 whole egg ✦ 2 egg whites ✦ 1 tbsp. oil ✦ salt and pepper ✦ ¾ cup (15 cl) beer or water ✦ 2 quarts (2 l) vegetable oil, for frying ✦ 4 zucchini, about 1¾ lbs. (750 g)

Mix 1 cup (144 g) flour, the whole egg, egg whites, oil, and ½ tsp. salt in a large bowl. Gradually stir in the beer. The mixture should be sticky, like pancake batter. Let rest for 1 hour. **H**eat the vegetable oil in a large pot or deep fryer until very hot but not smoking. While the oil is heating, peel the zucchini and cut into rounds about ¼ in. (5 cm) thick. Season with salt and pepper. Pour the remaining flour into a plate. Lightly dredge the rounds with flour, dip in the batter, and drop into the hot oil. Cook for 4 to 5 minutes. When they rise to the surface, golden brown, remove with a slotted spoon and drain on paper towels. Do not cook too many at the same time; they should fry without touching one another to be perfectly golden brown all over. Season with salt and pepper. Serve hot.

NOTE BY **ALAIN DUCASSE** If you are lucky enough to have zucchini with blossoms, you can make zucchini blossom fritters. Serve with some chopped raw zucchini, simply seasoned with olive oil, lemon juice, and salt.

Zucchini Stuffed with Zucchini

Courgette farcie à la courgette

⌂ ⌂ ○

Alain Ducasse

Serves 4 ♦ Preparation time : 40 minutes ♦ Cooking time : 30 minutes
4 small round zucchini ♦ salt and pepper ♦ 2 long green zucchini ♦ 4 tbsp. olive oil ♦ 4 white
onions, sliced ♦ crushed ice ♦ 1 tbsp. pine nuts ♦ 1 tbsp. ricotta cheese ♦ 1 tbsp. Parmesan
cheese, grated ♦ 3 sprigs flat-leaf parsley, leaves only, minced ♦ 1 garlic clove, minced ♦ ¾ cup
(15 cl) chicken stock (page 322) ♦ diced ham, for stuffing, optional

Preheat the oven to375°F (190°C). Wash the zucchini, cut off the top third of each,
and remove the pulp with a tsp.. Season with salt and pepper, inside and out. Turn
upside down on a rack to drain. Wash and chop the long zucchini, without peeling.
Heat half of the oil in a saucepan, add the onions, and stir. After 30 seconds, add the
chopped zucchini, season with salt and pepper. Sauté over high heat until the onions
are translucent. Remove from the heat. Cool rapidly on a bed of ice, to preserve the
bright green color. Toast the pine nuts in the oven or a dry skillet for 2 minutes. Chop
the nuts and mix into the sautéed vegetables. Stir in the ricotta, Parmesan cheese,
parsley, garlic, and diced ham, if desired. Stuff the zucchini with this mixture. Place
the zucchini in a baking dish and drizzle each with a little oil. Add some stock and
bake for 20 minutes, basting often. Arrange the stuffed zucchini on individual plates.
Top with the cooking juice and a drizzle of oil. You can serve these small stuffed
zucchini with a tomato coulis.

The round zucchini are much prettier than the long ones. They have the charm of the
unexpected, especially if they are small. They are also much easier to stuff.

NOTE BY
**FRANÇOISE
BERNARD**

Zucchini in a Niçoise Ratatouille

Courgettes en ratatouille niçoise

👨‍🍳 👨‍🍳 ∞

Françoise Bernard

Serves 4 ✦ **Preparation time : 40 minutes** ✦ **Cooking time : 1 hour**
½ **cup (10 cl) olive oil** ✦ **2 eggplants, peeled and cut into pieces** ✦ **8 zucchini, peeled and cut
into pieces** ✦ **1 lb. (500 g) tomatoes, peeled, squeezed, and cut into pieces** ✦ **2 sweet peppers,
cut into strips** ✦ **2 onions, sliced** ✦ **1 fennel bulb, cut into strips** ✦ **2 garlic cloves, minced** ✦ **1
bouquet garni** ✦ **salt and pepper**

Heat 3 tbsp. of the oil in a large pan, sauté the eggplants, and transfer to a casserole.
Heat 1 tbsp. of oil in the same pan, sauté the zucchini, and add to the casserole,
without stirring. Heat the remaining oil and sauté the tomatoes, peppers, and onions.
Add to the casserole. Lay fennel strips on top of the vegetables, add the garlic and
bouquet garni. Season with salt and pepper. Cover and simmer over very low heat for
1 to 1½ hours. You can, instead, bake for 1 to 1½ hours in a preheated oven at 200°F
(130°C). If there is too much juice, remove the lid for the last 45 minutes of the cooking.
Serve the ratatouille warm as a side dish with meat, or cold as a starter.

NOTE BY **ALAIN DUCASSE** I like to eat cold ratatouille with a warm poached egg. The contrasting temperatures
feel good in my mouth. The liquid egg yolk blends with the vegetable juice and gives
it a soft, mellow taste.

Zucchini Pies with Blossoms

Petites tourtes aux courgettes-fleurs

⌂ ⌂ ∞

Alain Ducasse

Serves 6 ✦ Preparation time : 30 minutes ✦ Resting time : 30 minutes ✦ Cooking time : 20 minutes ✦ 3⅓ cups (500 g) flour ✦ 1¾ cups (35 cl) olive oil ✦ salt and pepper ✦ 7 oz. (200 g) zucchini, with blossoms ✦ 2 oz. (50 g) spinach ✦ 1 onion, chopped ✦ 1 leek, white part only, washed and julienned ✦ 1 whole egg ✦ 1 egg yolk ✦ ¼ cup (30 g) Parmesan cheese, grated ✦ 1 cup (20 cl) chicken jus (page 323), lukewarm

Pour the flour into a large bowl and make a well in the center. Pour 1½ cups (30 cl) of oil, about ¾ cup (15 cl) of water, and a pinch of salt into the well. Mix and then knead until smooth, adding water if necessary. Cover the dough with a clean cloth and let rest in a cool place for 30 minutes. **P**reheat the oven to 400°F (210°C). **T**hinly slice the zucchini blossoms. Grate the zucchini, season with salt, drain in a colander for 10 minutes. Discard the spinach stems. Wash, dry and shred the spinach leaves. Peel and chop the onion. Wash the leek and cut into strips. In a bowl, combine all the vegetables with the whole egg, yolk, Parmesan cheese, and 1 tbsp. of olive oil. Season with salt and pepper and cover with a sheet of wax paper. **R**oll out the dough as thin as possible on a floured surface. With a pastry cutter, cut 12 circles, 5 to 6 in. (13 to 14 cm) in diameter. Save the extra dough for another use. Place 6 of the circles on a baking sheet. Spoon some of the vegetable mixture into the center of each one. Cover with another circle of dough and press the edges to seal. Brush the pies with oil and bake for 20 minutes. Drizzle with chicken jus and a little more oil. Serve with a mesclun salad, if desired.

This is a beautiful, very nourishing dish. Those of us who are weight-conscious may make open-face tarts rather than pies. Just reduce the ingredients for the dough by one third.

NOTE BY **FRANÇOISE BERNARD**

Eggs

Françoise Bernard has never forgotten the good, fresh eggs of her childhood. She would pierce a tiny hole in each end and swallow the egg raw and still warm. These pleasant memories of farm life account for her preference for almost-raw eggs. Her personal tastes have led her to wonder: Can the soft-boiled egg be served a starter for the family? Isn't it a rather individualistic dish, for which everyone has his or her own cooking standard? Some like their eggs when the white is still liquid; others will only eat them when over-cooked. Françoise Bernard eats eggs simply, with buttered *mouillettes*, or bread fingers—soft boiled eggs with caviar, scrambled eggs served in their shells. She doesn't think much of the sophisticated fantasies of chefs, except when she eats out. She remains loyal to family cuisine.

Bernard likes to serve warm hard-boiled eggs with a dash of olive oil on a crunchy romaine salad. The eggs must not be overcooked, however, or they turn grey, which spoils the pleasure. Poached eggs call for a sauce or a salad. Do not hesitate to trim those ugly white filaments with a pair of scissors. Make sure to remove the eggs from the water with a skimmer, not a fork, so as not to break them open.

Alain Ducasse is also quite talkative on the subject of eggs. For the most part, he prefers his eggs sunny-side up, either with fried croutons, bits of lemon, and capers, or straddled by a few crispy fries (this was a big hit in Madrid). He likes poached egg on a dandelion salad and a good Spanish omelet whose garnish is at least as important as the egg.

Not only is the egg indispensable in a thousand recipes, it also renders countless little services, says Françoise Bernard. Never caught off guard, she always keeps a dozen eggs in her refrigerator. For friends who show up unannounced, there can be a beautiful omelet. Served as a starter, stuffed eggs or shirred eggs en cocotte will extend a menu that is a little short. Chopped hard-boiled egg will liven up the most frugal hors d'oeuvre. Leeks in vinaigrette, for example, are so much more appetizing when sprinkled with specks of white and yellow.

Sorrel Omelet, Nevers-Style

Omelette nivernaise à l'oseille

⌂ ○

Françoise Bernard

Serves 4 ◆ **Preparation time : 15 minutes** ◆ **Cooking time : 15 minutes**
1 handful (50 g) of sorrel ◆ **3 tbsp. (40 g) butter** ◆ **8 eggs** ◆ **1 slice of cooked ham, shredded** ◆
1 tbsp. chopped chives ◆ **salt and pepper** ◆ **1 tbsp. oil**

Discard the sorrel stems. Wash, dry and coarsely chop the leaves. Sauté in 1½ tbsp. of the butter over low heat, stirring with a wooden spoon. Simmer, covered, for 5 to 7 minutes. **B**eat the eggs and add the sorrel, ham, chives, salt and pepper. Mix well. Melt the remaining butter in a skillet over low heat. Pour the butter into the beaten eggs. Heat the oil in the same skillet. When very hot, pour in the egg mixture. Cook for a few minutes over medium heat, stirring with a wooden spoon so that the eggs cook evenly. As soon as the edges of the omelet are dry, fold in half and slide onto a warm serving dish.

NOTE BY **ALAIN DUCASSE** You can turn this recipe into a truca, which is made in Nice—a flat omelet with Parmesan cheese, boiled ham, and herbs, such as borage, sorrel, and others. The *truca* is not an omelet in the traditional sense of the word because there is less egg than garnish—but served as a tapa (an hors d'oeuvre served with drinks), it makes a very nice snack. You can also vary it with some truffle, porcini, or chicken.

Soft-Boiled Eggs with Chanterelle Mushrooms

Oeufs mollets et girolles sautées

⌂ ∞

Alain Ducasse

Serves 4 ✦ **Preparation time : 25 minutes** ✦ **Cooking time : 20 minutes**
7 ounces (200 g) chanterelle mushrooms, cleaned and trimmed ✦ **8 tbsp. (100 g) butter** ✦ **6**
scallions, trimmed ✦ **12 fresh chicken eggs** ✦ **4 slices of country-style bread** ✦ **salt and white**
pepper ✦ **3 tbsp. juice from a roasted chicken, warm** ✦ **8 chives, roughly chopped** ✦ **grated black**
truffle, optional

Sauté the chanterelles in 1 tbsp. of the butter for 15 minutes. In another pan, sauté
and caramelize the scallions in about 4 tbsp. of butter for about 15 to 20 minutes.
Place the eggs in boiling salted water and cook for 3½ minutes—they should remain
soft inside. In the meantime, toast the bread slices, cut into sticks, and butter. Peel the
eggs, being careful not to damage them, and place in a deep serving dish. Season
with a few grains of salt and pepper. Spoon the chanterelles and scallions on the eggs,
add the chicken juice, and sprinkle with chives. Serve with the toast sticks. To make a
richer dish, add some grated black truffle, seasoned with a few grains of sea salt and
freshly ground pepper.

These eggs are so appetizing and easy to make. You might want to serve them with
a mesclun salad or with lamb's-quarter seasoned with chicken juice and an olive oil
vinaigrette. For an ordinary meal, the salad will suffice, and you can leave out the
chanterelles.

NOTE BY **FRANÇOISE BERNARD**

Fried Eggs with Bacon

Oeuf frit au bacon

⬆ ⬆ ∞

Françoise Bernard

Serves 4 ♦ Preparation time : 5 minutes ♦ Cooking time : 10 minutes
4 thin slices of bacon or smoked pork shoulder ♦ ½ cup (10 cl) oil ♦ 4 fresh eggs ♦ 2 small
tomatoes ♦ 1 tbsp. chopped parsley ♦ salt and pepper

Quickly sauté the bacon on both sides in 1 tbsp. of the oil. Remove and keep warm. Heat the remaining oil in a separate skillet. Break 1 egg into a cup, tip the skillet slightly, and slide in the egg. Add the other eggs the same way. When the clear egg whites begin to turn white, spoon them over the yolks with a wooden spoon. Fry over medium heat for another 2 minutes. **B**oil water in a saucepan. Drain the eggs on paper towels. Keep the eggs warm by placing them between 2 soup plates and setting the plates on a pot of boiling water. Halve the tomatoes and quickly sauté both sides in the skillet. Arrange the tomatoes on the serving platter. Sprinkle with parsley, salt and pepper. Place 1 slice of bacon and 1 fried egg on each tomato.

NOTE BY **ALAIN DUCASSE** You will really want to eat this dish with a few slices of grilled country bread. If you are cooking with pork shoulder, ask your butcher to slice it thin and be sure to cook it over high heat so that it will be very crispy.

Fried Eggs

Oeufs sur le plat

♙ ○

Alain Ducasse

**Serves 4 ♦ Preparation time : 20 minutes ♦ Cooking time : 15 minutes
4 slices of white sandwich bread, cubed ♦ 2 tbsp. olive oil ♦ 8 tbsp. (100 g) butter ♦ 4 tbsp.
small capers, drained ♦ 2 lemons, peeled, segmented, and diced ♦ salt and freshly ground pepper
♦ 8 eggs**

Preheat the oven to 400°F (210°C). **S**auté the bread in the oil. Melt the butter over low heat until it turns golden brown. Sauté the capers, then the diced lemon, and, at the last minute, the croutons. Season well. **S**prinkle salt and pepper into 4 individual porcelain gratin dishes. Break 2 eggs into each dish. Place the dishes over high heat for 2 to 3 minutes. Then put them in the oven in a pan of hot water. Bake 5 minutes or longer, depending on whether you want soft or hard cooked eggs. Serve in the individual baking dishes with the caper butter sauce. For those who prefer their eggs very well done, cook the eggs over easy on the stove before baking.

I knew that you could serve grenobloise sauce with fish—but here I've learned that you can also serve it with eggs, sunny-side up! This garnish gives the eggs a spicy flavor. The bitter lemon and capers, the crispy croutons, and the mellow dabs of butter will transform a classic recipe for a very reasonable price.

NOTE BY **FRANÇOISE BERNARD**

Pasta

Françoise Bernard was lucky enough to have known Mr. Panzani, the founder of the famous French company, Panzani, and "a charming, good-looking man." In his home, pasta was made every day. His wife, a stunning woman from the Vendée on the Atlantic coast, far from Italy, had totally embraced her husband's passion. She made pasta day after day with an ordinary little pasta machine, "a simple utensil to use," Françoise Bernard remembers. One evening, at *Le Alain Ducasse* restaurant, Bernard ordered *Pâtes mi-sechées aux rognons et crêtes de coq* (Half-dried Pasta with Kidneys and Cockscomb), a dish that, among others, earned him his third star. The dish reminded her of the friendly dinners she had often had at the Panzanis—and will remain forever in her memory. "Contrary to today's great chefs, I don't know how to rave about a dish," she says. "They are capable of expressing their feelings and talking at great length about one flavor, but I do have a good memory for dishes. That pasta, we ate it in total silence."

Françoise Bernard's own recipe for pasta was approved by Panzani himself. When buying pasta, she looks for authentic Italian pasta. What she does not like, positively hates, in fact, is unruly pasta, like spaghetti, that will not stay on the fork.

Alain Ducasse has found his dream pasta, but it is not made commercially. It is formed into the shape of a backward curving S and dried on a silk screen. This is no small matter for him, for Alain Ducasse loves sauce as much as he loves pasta. The rough surface of the silk renders the pasta porous, which makes it better able to absorb the sauce. In the course of his career, the chef has cooked all types of pasta: pappardelle, tagliatelle, spaghetti, spaghettini. Pasta and Alain Ducasse—now that is a passionate affair that is far from over.

Spaghetti Languedoc-Style

Spaghettis à la languedocienne

⌂ ∞

Françoise Bernard

Serves 4 ✦ **Preparation time : 30 minutes** ✦ **Cooking time : 30 minutes**
3 eggplants ✦ **1 tbsp. oil** ✦ **4 tomatoes, peeled and seeded** ✦ **8 oz. (250 g) white button mush-**
rooms, cleaned and diced ✦ **1 clove garlic, chopped** ✦ **salt and pepper** ✦ **8 oz. (250 g) spaghetti**
✦ **4 tbsp. (50 g) butter** ✦ **½ cup (50 g) grated Gruyère cheese**

Peel and cut the eggplants into rounds, sprinkle with salt, and drain. Pat dry with paper
towels. Sauté both sides in the oil over high heat. Add the tomatoes, mushrooms, and
garlic. Season with salt and pepper. Cover and simmer for 15 minutes. **P**reheat the
broiler. **B**oil a large pot of salted water. Add the spaghetti and cook about 15 minutes.
Drain, pour into a glass baking dish, add 2 tbsp. of the butter, and mix. Spoon the
vegetable mixture on top, sprinkle with the cheese, and dot with remaining butter.
Brown for 10 minutes under the broiler.

NOTE BY **ALAIN DUCASSE** Make sure that the eggplants do not soak up too much oil—the more you pour into
the pan, the more they will absorb. Add a little olive oil to the drained spaghetti to
keep it from sticking together. If you wish, substitute grated Parmesan cheese for the
gratin.

Spaghettini with Zucchini and Tomatoes

Spaghettinis aux tomates et aux courgettes

⌂ ◯◯

Alain Ducasse

Serves 4 ✦ Preparation time : 45 minutes ✦ Cooking time : 25 minutes
4 zucchini, preferably trumpet variety ✦ 2 oz. (50 g) sugar snap peas, tipped ✦ 2 oz. (50 g)
haricots verts **green beans, tipped ✦ 1 lb. (450 g) spaghettini ✦ ½ cup (10 cl) chicken stock**
(page 322) ✦ 6 tbsp. (80 g) butter ✦ 10 scallions, trimmed and thinly sliced on the diagonal ✦
¼ cup (5 cl) olive oil ✦ 6 zucchini blossoms, cut lengthwise into 3 pieces ✦ 6 Roma tomatoes,
peeled, seeded, and cut into strips ✦ coarse salt

Wash the zucchini. Peel the skin with a vegetable peeler to make curling swirls. Save the rest of the zucchini for another use, such as a stuffing or ratatouille. Boil the snap peas and *haricots verts* green beans in a large pot of salted water for 3 minutes. Remove with a slotted spoon and drain. **C**ook the spaghettini in boiling salted water for 5 minutes and drain. Boil the stock in the same pot and whisk in the butter. Add the drained pasta and cook for 3 to 5 minutes. **S**auté the zucchini swirls and scallions in 1 tbsp. of oil for 10 to 15 minutes. At the last minute, add the peas and *haricots verts*, and then add the zucchini blossoms. The vegetables should be crunchy and lightly caramelized. Fry the strips of tomato in the remaining oil and coarse salt. Serve the spaghettini on individual plates. Arrange caramelized vegetables around the pasta and place the tomatoes on top. You might also like to add a few oven-dried tomatoes (page 231) and some slivered black olives.

I like this dish very much. It's a good family dish, quick to make. The pasta finishes cooking in the bouillon, and the results are incomparably smooth. This is how the Spanish cook *fideos*, a kind of very thin spaghetti, that is inspired by paella recipes. NOTE BY **FRANÇOISE BERNARD**

Basil Pasta

Pâtes au basilic

⌂ ○

Françoise Bernard

Serves 4 ✦ **Preparation time : 10 minutes** ✦ **Cooking time : 15 minutes**
8 oz. (250 g) pasta, such as penne, fusilli, or shells ✦ **1 garlic clove** ✦ **15 fresh basil leaves** ✦ **3**
tbsp. olive oil ✦ **about ½ cup (50) grated Gruyère or Parmesan cheese** ✦ **coarse salt and pepper**

Boil a large pot of salted water. Drop the pasta into pot and cook, uncovered, for 10
to 20 minutes—3 to 5 minutes for fresh pasta. Mash the garlic and basil together in
a mortar. Pour a steady, thin stream of oil into the garlic-basil mixture, whisking vigorously. Whisk in the grated cheese and salt and pepper to taste. Drain the pasta and
immediately toss with the basil sauce. Serve very hot.

NOTE BY
ALAIN
DUCASSE
Pesto sauce is a real delight with pasta—but you must use good quality products.
Choose a good, aromatic, extra-virgin olive oil and freshly grated Parmesan cheese.
Stay away from packaged, grated Parmesan. Ask the cheese seller to grate it for you
or, better yet, grate it yourself. The small effort will be largely rewarded when it's time
to eat.

Macaroni Moulinier-Style

Macaronis à la façon du moulinier

⬠ ⬠ ○

Alain Ducasse

Serves 4 ✦ **Preparation time : 35 minutes** ✦ **Cooking time : 30 minutes**
10 sprigs basil ✦ **2 scallions, trimmed and cut on an angle** ✦ **1 onion, thinly sliced** ✦ **2 tomatoes,**
peeled and diced ✦ **1 large potato, sliced paper-thin** ✦ **4 tbsp. (50 g) butter** ✦ **5 tbsp. olive oil** ✦
1 lb. (50 g) macaroni ✦ **salt and pepper** ✦ **1 garlic clove** ✦ **1 quart (1 l) chicken stock (page**
322) ✦ **½ cup (50 g) grated Parmesan cheese**

Mince the basil leaves and tie the stems with string. Sauté the scallions, onion, tomatoes, and potatoes in the butter with 2 tbsp. of the oil. Add the macaroni, mix well,
and season lightly with salt and pepper. Add the garlic and basil stems and simmer
lightly for 20 minutes, adding the stock gradually. **W**hen the pasta is cooked al dente,
remove the garlic and basil stems, and mix in the Parmesan cheese. Sprinkle with the
minced basil leaves, add 1 tbsp. of oil to bind the sauce, and correct the seasoning.
Serve in mounded portions in individual soup plates. Drizzle 1 tbsp. of oil over each
serving and serve warm.

I like this way of cooking macaroni very much. Cook directly in the sauce, gradually
adding the bouillon so that the pasta can better absorb it. It reminds me of the technique for making risotto.

NOTE BY
FRANÇOISE
BERNARD

Rice

Once again, Alain Ducasse and Françoise Bernard are sitting across from each other in Ducasse's office, conversing comfortably. They are discussing rice and those modest yet indispensable varieties found at organic gourmet shops, the dry staples that have always nourished humankind. Alain Ducasse praises exotic rice, but also the rice cultivated in Camargue, north of Marseille. For him, the best recipe for rice is, first and foremost, risotto. His Monaco team prepares risottos in every possible color: saffron yellow, tomato red, even squid-ink black. They also prepare it with porcini and chanterelle mushrooms.

The success of risotto revolves around four basic elements: the rice, the fat, the bouillon, and the constant stirring of the broth with a wooden spoon. According to our master of risotto, you also need a special rice—the round Italian rice of Lombardia, unwashed and untreated. This type of rice can absorb a lot of liquid—and the more bouillon the rice absorbs, the more aromatic the risotto will be. Long Basmati rice would be unthinkable for a risotto—but Carnaroli rice, which is now easier to find, Vialone, Nano, Arborio, and the somewhat rarer Roma would all be fine. In the finished risotto, these shiny grains will be covered with a velvety film. Françoise Bernard is amazed by the advice in Alain Ducasse's book *Méditerranées: cuisine de l'essentiel* (*Essential Mediterranean Cuisine*). His chapter about rice reads like a gourmet thriller. When making rice pilaf or paella, look for a dry grain—it will cook by itself. Don't be tempted to stir paella while it is simmering.

Rice has many more secrets to reveal. The round varieties have inspired a number of desserts, including Condé Rice with Pears. In these dessert dishes, the rice is cooked in milk, which makes the grains taste creamy and sweet.

Royal Paella

Paella royale

☗ ☗ ◯◯◯

Françoise Bernard

Serves 8 ✦ Preparation time : 55 minutes ✦ Cooking time : 1 hour 45 minutes
about 2¼ lbs. (1 kg) mussels ✦ 24 langoustines or prawns ✦ 2 bouquets garnis ✦ 1 chicken,
3½ lbs. (1,5 kg) ✦ 5 oz. (150 g) veal tenderloin, diced ✦ 5 oz. (150 g) boneless pork, diced ✦
½ cup (10 cl) olive oil ✦ 2 onions, chopped ✦ 2 bell peppers, seeded, diced ✦ 1 tbsp. tomato
paste ✦ 4 tomatoes, peeled ✦ ½ tsp. saffron ✦ 3 garlic cloves, chopped ✦ 1 package frozen peas
✦ 2 quarts (2 l) boiling water ✦ salt and pepper ✦ 1 lb. (500 g) long-grain rice ✦ 7 oz. (200 g)
hot chorizo sausage, sliced ✦ 5 sprigs parsley, leaves, chopped

Scrub the mussels with a vegetable brush and wash thoroughly. Place in a covered
pot over low heat until the shells open. Strain the cooking juice. Remove the mussels
from their shells and reserve in the juice. Discard the shells. Place the langoustines in
a pot, cover with cold water, and add 1 bouquet garni. Slowly bring to a boil and
remove from the heat. Set aside, leaving the langoustines in the juice. Sauté the
chicken and meat in 3 tbsp. of the oil in a large pot. Add the onions, peppers, tomato
paste, tomatoes, saffron, and the remaining bouquet garni. Stir, cover, and cook over
medium heat for 10 minutes. Add the garlic, peas, mussel juice, langoustine juice, and
the boiling water. Season with salt and pepper to taste. Cover and cook over medium
heat for 45 minutes to 1 hour. Sauté the rice in the remaining oil in the serving pan.
Add 2 ladlefuls of the cooking juice. When the rice has completely absorbed the juice,
add 2 more ladlefuls. Continue adding juice in this way until the rice is cooked. Add
the meat and vegetables to the pan and cook for 15 more minutes. Add the mussels,
langoustines, sausage, and parsley, cook for 5 more minutes. Cover and let the paella
rest a few minutes before serving

NOTE BY **ALAIN DUCASSE** For this dish, I would prefer to sauté the rice in equal amounts of oil and butter rather
than only in oil, butter enhances the flavor of rice.

Condé Rice with Pears

Riz Condé aux poires

⭓ ⭓ ◯

Alain Ducasse

Serves 8 ✦ Preparation time : 1 hour ✦ Refrigeration time : 1 hour ✦ Cooking time : 45 minutes ✦ 1 cup (200 g) rice ✦ 1 quart (1 l) milk ✦ 2 vanilla bean pods, split ✦ salt ✦ 5 cups (940 g) sugar ✦ 4 cups (80 cl) water ✦ 1 lemon, zest peeled and juiced ✦ 8 pears ✦ 4 egg yolks ✦ ½ cup (10 cl) whipped cream ✦ 3 oz. (80 g) candied fruits ✦ 1½ tbsp. (20 g) butter ✦ 1 tbsp. kirsch ✦ 5 ounces (160 g) apricot jam, warm ✦ candied angelica and dark cherries, for garnish, optional

Preheat the oven to 350°F (180°C). Place the rice in a saucepan, cover with a lot of cold water, and boil for 1 minute. Rinse under cold water and drain. Boil the milk with 1 vanilla bean pod and 1 pinch of salt. Add the rice slowly and stir until the mixture boils. Transfer to a deep dish and bake, covered, for 25 to 30 minutes. In a saucepan, boil 4¼ cups (846 g) of the sugar, the water, lemon zest, and remaining vanilla bean pod. Peel and core the pears and sprinkle with lemon juice. Drop into the boiling syrup, cover the pan with parchment paper, and reduce heat. Poach, just under boiling, for 15 to 20 minutes. Whip the remaining sugar and egg yolks until the yolks lighten. Gently stir into the rice. Boil the rice mixture for a few seconds, remove from heat, and cool. Fold in the whipped cream and candied fruits. Butter a 9 in. (22 cm) round cake pan. Pour the mixture into the pan and refrigerate until set. Unmold the rice and top with the pears. Mix the kirsch into the apricot jam and serve on the side. If you'd like, garnish with candied angelica and dark cherries.

I would like to commend Alain Ducasse for giving a grandmother's dessert, once considered passé, a front-row seat. For this dessert, I would use round rice, which absorbs milk better and sweetens while baking.

NOTE BY **FRANÇOISE BERNARD**

Curried Rice

Riz au curry

⌂ ○

Françoise Bernard

Serves 4 ✦ **Preparation time : 15 minutes** ✦ **Cooking time : 30 minutes**
1 onion, chopped ✦ **3 tbsp. (40 g) butter** ✦ **1 cup (250 g) rice** ✦ **1 to 2 tbsp. curry powder** ✦ **salt**
and pepper ✦ **½ banana sliced, optional** ✦ **crème fraîche, for garnish, optional**

Sauté the onion in 1 tbsp. of the butter in a heavy saucepan. As soon as the onion is translucent, add the rice and curry powder, mixing well to coat the grains. Add 2 cups (40 cl) of water, season with salt and pepper. Cover and simmer over low heat until the liquid is completely absorbed—about 20 minutes. Remove from the heat and let rest for 5 minutes. **B**efore serving, fluff the rice with a fork and quickly stir in the remaining butter. To make the curry less spicy, you can add banana slices to the pan when you begin to cook the rice or some crème fraîche to the rice before you serve it.

NOTE BY **ALAIN DUCASSE**   I would love to give a Basque touch to this Andalusian dish, with a few sliced *pimentos del piquillo* an Espelette pepper. A Spanish chef might also add some *pimenton*, an astonishing paprika, which is sifted 10 times to yield a fine, slightly smoked flavor. It is the spice found in chorizo and paella.

Tomato Risotto

Risotto aux tomates

⚐ ⚐ ○

Alain Ducasse

Serves 4 ✦ Preparation time : 1 hour 15 minutes ✦ Cooking time : 1 hour
4 Roma tomatoes, peeled and chopped ✦ 6 tbsp. (6 g) olive oil ✦ 2 garlic cloves ✦ 2 sprigs
thyme, leaves only ✦ 7 oz. (200 g) zucchini, preferably violin variety, sliced ✦ 3½ cups (70 cl)
chicken stock (page 322) ✦ 6 tbsp. (80 g) butter ✦ 8 baby zucchini, with blossoms ✦ 1 oz.
(30 g) beef marrow, chopped ✦ 2 shallots, thinly sliced ✦ 7 oz. (200 g) rice ✦ ¼ cup (5 cl) white
wine ✦ 1½ oz. (40 g) mascarpone cheese ✦ ½ cup (50 g) Parmesan cheese, grated ✦ 2 tbsp.
whipped cream ✦ 8 oven-dried tomatoes (page 231) ✦ coarse sea salt and pepper

In a covered pot, simmer the tomatoes, garlic and thyme in 2 tbsp. of oil over low heat. Cook until the mixture resembles a thick jam. In a separate pan, sauté the zucchini in 2 tbsp. of oil and ½ cup (10 cl) of stock for 5 minutes. Add 1½ tbsp. (20 g) butter. Peel the skin of the baby zucchini with a vegetable peeler to make swirls. Thinly slice the blossoms. Slowly cook the blossoms, the curls, and the peeled baby zucchini, covered, in 2 tbsp. oil and ½ cup (10 cl) stock for 15 minutes. Cook the marrow in a few drops of oil in a covered pan over medium heat, add the shallots. Mix in the rice, season with salt and pepper. Deglaze the pan with the wine. Gradually add ladlefuls of warm stock to moisten, stirring constantly. After 15 to 18 minutes, add the mascarpone and Parmesan cheeses and about 4 tbsp. of butter. The rice should be very smooth and creamy. Stir in the tomato jam and the whipped cream. Arrange the risotto in soup plates. Top with the sautéed zucchini and oven-dried tomatoes. Garnish with zucchini blossoms and swirls.

Alain Ducasse is truly a risotto specialist. I used to be uneasy about stirring rice while it was cooking. Stirring is not recommended when cooking white rice or pilaf, however, because you want to keep the grains to be separate.

NOTE BY
FRANÇOISE
BERNARD

Apples

In the past few years, we have begun to take notice of the apple's many varieties. It would be a pity to settle for only one type in a country that has so many to offer! The Granny Smith apple's acidity sets Françoise Bernard's teeth on edge, but she has a weakness for the Reinette, a local variety that is not as pretty, but so good. The Calville apple, which is firm and crunchy, lasts a while, but there is a moment where it suddenly becomes overripe. She is also somewhat wary about the apples from abroad, especially American apples. She hates that the fruits are picked while still green so as to survive the long journey. She actually had to wander through the orchards of the French Southwest to convince herself of the virtues of the Golden Delicious. The Royal Golden apple, much more interesting than the Golden Delicious, is perfect for tatin tarts. The restaurant, *Le Henry IV*, in the Place des Vosges, offers this dessert only in season—and she wouldn't have passed it up for anything in the world. "The apple, for me, is above all a fruit for tarts," she says. "My mother knew how to prepare apple tarts in a jiffy, and my cousins and I still talk about them today. She would quickly prepare a short pastry crust and cook the tart during the meal, intoxicating us with the warm scents of the butter and fruit. I have never succeeded at making a tart as good as hers."

When she doesn't get her apples directly from the orchard, Françoise Bernard selects them carefully at the market—the Reinette, the Belle de Boskoop, and the Canada varieties. Alain Ducasse also prefers apples from the orchard. The correct choice of apples is essential to him—especially for his Cooked and Raw Apples, a very popular dessert. He likes the acidity of the Granny Smith, which he combines with foie gras. Although this chef is generally a purist, he may be unpredictable once in a while. The apple inspires him with eccentric ideas. "I want a square apple, a dessert that goes crunch, crunch, crunch," he requested one day from his baker, Frederic Robert—and there is just such a dessert today.

Apple Tart

Tarte aux pommes

⌂ ⌂ ○

Françoise Bernard

Serves 4 ◆ Preparation time : 25 minutes ◆ Resting time : 30 minutes ◆ Cooking time : 35 minutes ◆ 1 cup (150 g) flour ◆ ¼ tsp. salt ◆ 5½ tbsp. (75 g) butter, softened and cut into small pieces ◆ 1⅔ lbs. (750 g) apples ◆ 1 egg ◆ 3 tbsp. sugar ◆ 3 tbsp. crème fraîche or sour cream

Mix the flour, salt, and butter between the palms of your hands, squeezing and rubbing to obtain a pebbly texture. Sprinkle the dough with less than ½ cup (10 cl) of cold water and knead quickly, without overworking. Shape the dough into a ball, flatten with the palm of your hand, and reshape into a ball. Repeat 3 times to create a smooth dough. **B**utter a 9 in. (22 cm) tart pan. Thinly roll out the dough, line the pie plate, and refrigerate for about 30 minutes. **P**reheat the oven to 375°F (190°C). **P**eel and thinly slice the apples. Arrange in the dough so that they overlap. Bake for 20 to 25 minutes. Beat the egg with the sugar and crème fraîche. Pour the mixture over the apples and bake for another 10 minutes. Remove the tart as soon as you take the pan out of the oven. Serve hot or warm.

NOTE BY **ALAIN DUCASSE** You can spotlight the apple with many different cooking methods. This fruit can be quartered and sautéed, made into jam, or serve raw slices with lemon and pepper.

Cooked and Raw Apples

Pommes cuites et crues

⌂ ⌂ ○

Alain Ducasse

Serves 4 ◆ Preparation time : 1 hour ◆ Cooking time : 1 hour 10 minutes
8 Reinettes or Canada apples ◆ 9 tbsp. (120 g) butter ◆ 1 cup (200 g) granulated sugar ◆ 3
Granny Smith apples ◆ 1⅓ cups (200 g) flour ◆ 1 cup (200 g) brown sugar, softened ◆ ½ cup
(10 cl) *pommeau* (a drink made with cider and calvados brandy) ◆ 4 cups (75 cl) cider ◆ 4
gelatin leaves (8 g) or 1 envelope powdered gelatin

Preheat the oven to 350°F (180°C). Remove and reserve the cores and seeds of 4
Reinettes of equal size. Reserve the stems and end pieces. Melt 4 tbsp. of the butter.
Coat the apples with melted butter and roll in ¼ cup (50 g) of the sugar. Stand the
apples side by side in a deep dish and bake for 50 minutes. Remove from oven. Drain
and reserve the cooking juice and set the apples aside. Lower the oven temperature
to 200°F (90°C). Boil 1 cup (24 cl) water and ⅔ cup (133 g) sugar for 5 minutes. Wash
and thinly slice the Granny Smiths. Drop the slices into the hot syrup, remove with a
slotted spoon, and drain. Transfer to a baking dish and bake for 1 hour. Raise the
oven temperature to 350°F (180°C). Slice the remaining Reinettes into 8 rounds. Reheat the syrup. Combine the flour and brown sugar. Drop each apple round into the
syrup for 2 to 3 minutes, then drain. Dip the rounds into the flour-sugar mixture and
arrange on a baking sheet. Bake to form a crust—about 10 minutes. Sauté the reserved
cores, seeds, ends, and stems in 3 tbsp. of butter and the remaining sugar. Sprinkle
with the *pommeau* and cider, simmer for 40 minutes, and strain. If using gelatin leaves,
soak in cold water and pat dry with paper towels. Return the cider mixture to a boil
and stir in the gelatin. Refrigerate until set. Reduce the reserved cooking juice and stir
in the remaining butter. Set 1 baked Reinette on each plate. Cover with juice, the
baked Granny Smith slices, 2 apple rounds, and 1 tbsp. of the cider jelly. Serve.

Alain Ducasse has created an interesting idea here, with the contrast of cooked and
raw fruit. I love contrasts, especially hot and cold. The cold cider jelly goes very nicely
with the warm apples.

NOTE BY FRANÇOISE BERNARD

Roasted Venison with Apples

Rôti de chevreuil aux pommes

⬠ ⬠ ⚬⚬⚬

Françoise Bernard

Serves 4 ◆ Preparation time : 1 hour ◆ Cooking time : 1 hour 30 minutes ◆ Marinating time : 3 days ◆ 2 onions, sliced ◆ 2 carrots, sliced ◆ 2 shallots, sliced ◆ 2 tbsp. oil ◆ 2 garlic cloves, peeled ◆ 3 cups (75 cl) white or red wine ◆ ½ cup (10 cl) vinegar ◆ 1 celery stalk ◆ 1 bouquet garni ◆ 2 cloves ◆ 3 peppercorns ◆ 1 venison roast, 2¼ lbs. (1 kg), loin, haunch, or boneless ribs ◆ fine salt ◆ 2¼ lbs. (1 kg) Reinette or Granny Smith apples ◆ 4 tbsp. (50 g) butter

Three days before serving, sauté the onions, carrots, and shallots in the oil. Add the garlic, then the wine, vinegar, celery, bouquet garni, cloves, and peppercorns. Boil lightly, uncovered, for 30 to 40 minutes. Remove the marinade from the heat and cool completely. Marinate the venison in the refrigerator for 3 days, turning the meat in the morning and at night. About 1 hour before serving, preheat the oven to 425°F (220°C). Drain and salt the venison roast. Strain the vegetables and herbs from the marinade, place them in a buttered baking dish, and place the roast on top. Peel the apples, remove the cores and seeds with an apple corer. Place a dab of butter inside each of the apples and arrange them around the roast. Bake about 40 minutes (15 to 20 minutes per pound). Serve with a chestnut purée, a compote of unsweetened apples, cranberry sauce, or blueberry jam.

NOTE BY **ALAIN DUCASSE** If there are orchards near your house, do not hesitate to taste many different varieties before selecting the types of apples you'd like to use. The best ones are not mealy and will hold their shape when cooked.

Green Apple Sorbet with Warm Apples

Coupe glacée de pomme verte, pomme chaude au plat

⏡ ⏡ ○

Alain Ducasse

Serves 8 ✦ Preparation time : 1 hour ✦ Freezing time : 5 hours ✦ Cooking time : 30 minutes ✦ 3⅓ cups (630 g) granulated sugar ✦ 3 cups (70 cl) cider ✦ 1 tbsp. calvados brandy ✦ 4 small Reinette or Granny Smith apples ✦ 4 tbsp. (50 g) butter ✦ 4 tbsp. demerara sugar ✦ 4½ lbs. (2 kg) green apples ✦ juice of 1 lemon ✦ ⅓ cup (180 g) glucose or corn syrup

Boil ¾ cup (150 g) of the sugar in ½ cup (10 cl) water. Remove from the heat and cool. Mix in the cider and brandy, transfer to a shallow dish, and freeze. As the edges of the mixture start to freeze, scrape the iced pieces from the dish with a fork, and stir. Repeat as needed until the entire mixture has the consistency of sorbet—about 4 to 5 hours. **P**reheat the oven to 400°F (210°C). **P**eel and halve the Reinette apples. Cut thin slices and arrange in a rosette pattern in 4 ovenproof egg dishes, 4 in. (11 cm) diameter. Dot the apple slices with the butter and demerara sugar. Bake for 15 to 20 minutes. **W**ash the green apples, juice them, add the lemon juice to the purée. Boil the remaining sugar in 2 cups (50 cl) of water, remove from heat, and cool. Combine the apple purée, sugar water, and glucose. Spoon this compote into 4 stem glasses, leaving a hole in the center. Place the glasses high in the refrigerator so they get very cold. Just before serving, fill the hole in the compote with a scoop of sorbet. Serve the caramelized apples separately.

This inventive hot-cold dessert reveals the apple in three different forms: as a cold compote, a sorbet (granité), and caramelized slices. Each aspect has a different consistency and temperature, which creates surprising combinations. This dessert is characteristic of a grand chef, something you would expect to find at a restaurant—but it is very simple to make.

NOTE BY **FRANÇOISE BERNARD**

Apricots

When we think of the apricot, we immediately think of those delicious tarts of plump fruit halves that can turn any day of the week into a Sunday. Françoise Bernard and Alain Ducasse each have their own interpretations. Françoise Bernard gives the fruit a royal status by simply laying it on a thin pastry crust, where the flavor of the apricot can burst forth without interference. Alain Ducasse, on the other hand, cannot conceive of preparing apricots without almonds and pistachio.

Ducasse loves tangy flavors. He contrasts the acidity of the pulpy fruit with its soft texture. He makes simple *sablée* pastry tarts topped with apricots that have been lightly precooked with a little vanilla. The roundness of the fruit has inspired him to imagine it in dishes with rounded forms—an apricot half topped with a scoop of pistachio ice cream—what better color against the orange of the fruit?—or under a mound of almond cream. The apricot and the almond are very complementary flavors. This chef, almost without thinking, sprinkles a drop or two of bitter almond essence into all his apricot desserts.

In good growing years, Françoise Bernard makes jam. The apricot season is short—from late June to the end of August, depending on the variety—and the fruit must be utilized quickly. Apricot jam is her specialty. She adds flavor by leaving a few apricot kernels in the jam while it cooks. Apricot jam is a friend to every pastry chef—when heated and strained, it adds inimitable brilliance to their creations.

But, today, when sweet and savory are so often combined to make new flavors, why should the apricot belong only to the world of desserts? Have we forgotten the North African delights, the aromatic dishes in earthernware *tajines* that the apricot fills with its golden glow? Not quite. In Monaco, Alain Ducasse serves a shoulder of lamb with apricots, for which he has chosen the Jumbocot variety, a beautiful, luminous fruit from Languedoc and Provence, which reaches full maturity by the end of June. The apricot must be picked at its ripest, because once it's picked, it will not continue to ripen. The best fruits come from sunny regions—for example, the red apricot of Roussillon, which is flecked with vermillion spots, and the orange apricot of Provence, which has a musky aroma.

Puff-Pastry Apricot Tart

Tarte feuilletée aux abricots

⟳ ⟳ ⟳ ∞

Françoise Bernard

Serves 4 ✦ Preparation time : 1 hour 15 minutes ✦ Cooking time : 30 minutes ✦ Resting time : 45 minutes ✦ 1⅔ cups (250 g) flour ✦ ½ tsp. salt ✦ 12 tbsp. (175 g) butter ✦ about 1¼ lb. (500 g) fresh apricots ✦ 2 tbsp. sugar

Preheat the oven to 425°F (220°C). **W**orking on a flat surface, make a well in the flour. Pour in the salt and less than ½ cup (10 cl) water. Knead vigorously with your fingertips, without overworking the dough and making it rubbery. Roll into a ball and flatten with the palm of your hand. Roll and flatten 2 more times, then refrigerate for 15 minutes. **C**ream the butter until it has the same consistency as the dough. Roll into a square, ½ in. (1,5 cm) thick. On a floured surface, flatten the dough into a large square with your hand. Place the square of butter in the center of the dough. Fold the 4 sides of the dough to enclose the butter. Roll the folded square into a long, even rectangle. Fold the rectangle in thirds, first folding one end and then folding the other end on top. Turn the dough a quarter-turn, again roll out an even rectangle, and fold in thirds as before. Repeat this process 2 more times, refrigerating the dough for 15 minutes after each folding. **R**oll out the dough again and line a 9 in. (22 cm) tart pan. Halve and pit the apricots. Arrange the halves in the pastry dough, placing them close together. Bake about 30 minutes. Remove the tart from the pan and place on a wire rack to cool. Sprinkle with sugar before serving.

NOTE BY **ALAIN DUCASSE** For a very crisp pastry crust, bake dough on baking sheet and bake the apricots separately in a buttered and sugared earthenware baking dish. The juice of the cooking apricots always soaks into the pastry crust a little.

Ice Cream with Half-Candied Apricots

Coupe glacée à l'abricot mi-confit

♟ ♟ ○

Alain Ducasse

Serves 4 ♦ Preparation time : 1 hour 15 minutes ♦ Cooking time : 30 minutes
5 egg yolks ♦ 2¾ cups (480 g) sugar ♦ 3¼ cups (80 cl) almond milk, available in health-food
stores ♦ 1 drop almond extract, optional ♦ 9 oz. (250 g) ripe apricots ♦ 4 tbsp. (50 g) butter ♦
3 eggs ♦ 1 tsp. baking powder ♦ 1 cup (200 g) ground almonds ♦ zest of 2 lemons, finely
chopped or grated ♦ 1¼ cups (190 g) flour

Beat the egg yolks and about ¾ cup (150 g) sugar until the yolks lighten. Boil the almond milk, remove from heat, and cool slightly in the refrigerator. Stir the almond milk into the egg yolks. Cook over low heat, stirring until the custard sticks to the spoon—do not boil. Remove from heat, cool, and add the almond extract, if desired. Pour into an ice-cream maker and turn to make ice cream. Set aside in freezer. **P**reheat the oven to 350°F (180°C). **H**alve and pit the apricots. Roast them in the butter in a pan. Add about ½ cup (100 g) sugar and 1 tbsp. water and bake very slowly for 20 minutes. Be sure not to touch the apricots while they are baking. Remove from the oven. **R**aise the oven temperature to 425°F (220°C). **S**eparate the eggs. Beat the yolks and about 1 cup (200 g) sugar until the yolks lighten. Beat the egg whites until stiff, then stir in the remaining sugar, baking powder, ground almonds, chopped lemon zest, egg yolks, and flour. Roll out a very thin pastry dough on bake on a baking sheet for 10 minutes. With a pastry cutter, cut 4 circles out of the pastry dough—the circles should be the same diameter as the martini glasses in which you will serve your dessert. Fill 4 martini glasses about one third full of the almond ice cream. Cover each glass with a crisp pastry round and some warm—or cold—apricots. Serve.

I like the idea of contrasting hot and cold by placing the warm apricots directly on the ice cream. The crisp pastry could then be served on the side. To save some time, you could even buy a pastry crust from your baker, who, I am sure, makes excellent ones.

NOTE BY **FRANÇOISE BERNARD**

Apricot Jam

Confiture d'abricots

⌂ ○

Françoise Bernard

Makes five 8 ounce (250 g) jars ✦ **Preparation time : 10 minutes** ✦ **Soaking time :
12 hours** ✦ **Cooking time : 20 minutes** ✦ **2½ lbs. (1,1 kg) whole apricots or 2¼ lbs. (1 kg)
pitted apricots** ✦ **5 cups (1 kg) sugar** ✦ **juice of ½ lemon**

The day before serving, halve and pit the apricots. Reserve about 15 pits. Place the
halves in a large bowl, cover with the sugar, and let stand for about 12 hours. **T**he
next day, boil the fruit and sugar for 15 minutes. Crack open the reserved pits and
remove the kernels. About 5 minutes before the end of cooking, add the kernels and
lemon juice to the jam. **W**ash the jars and the lids carefully, sterilize in boiling water,
and let them dry on a clean cloth. As soon as the jam is cooked, remove the kernels,
ladle into jars, cover, and seal.

NOTE BY **ALAIN DUCASSE** To obtain an aromatic and tasty jam, you must choose ripe, sun-ripened apricots. You
can halve the quantity of sugar to preserve the fresh taste of the fruit. This jam will
keep in the refrigerator 3 months.

Apricot Tart

Tarte aux abricots

⇧ ⇧ ∞

Alain Ducasse

Serves 4 ◆ **Preparation time : 1 hour** ◆ **Resting time : 2 hours** ◆ **Cooking time : 40 minutes** ◆ 1½ cups (220 g) flour ◆ ½ tsp. baking powder ◆ 18 tbsp. (260 g) butter, softened ◆ 1½ cups (175 g) confectioners' sugar ◆ 3 eggs ◆ about 1¼ lb. (500 g) apricots ◆ 2 to 3 tbsp. granulated sugar ◆ ½ vanilla bean pod, split ◆ 1¼ cups (125 g) almond powder ◆ 4 tbsp. (60 g) pistachio paste ◆ 1 tbsp. kirsch ◆ about ½ cup (150 g) pastry cream (page 323) ◆ about 1 cup (100 g) sliced almonds ◆ about ½ cup (50 g) unsalted pistachios, crushed

The day before serving, combine 1⅓ cups (200 g) of flour, the baking soda, 8 tbsp. of the butter, ½ cup (50 g) of the confectioners' sugar, and 1 egg. When the dough forms a ball, cover with a cloth, and refrigerate. The next day, roll out a very thin dough on a floured surface. Line a buttered 6 in. (16 cm) tart pan with the dough. Refrigerate for 2 hours. Preheat the oven to 325°F (160°C). Cover the dough with a sheet of parchment paper. Add 2 to 3 cups of dried beans on top to keep the pastry flat while baking. Bake for 10 minutes. Raise the oven temperature to 350°F (180°C). Wash, halve, and pit the apricots. Melt 1 tbsp. butter over low heat in a skillet. Add the apricots, 1 tbsp. granulated sugar, and the vanilla bean pod. Cook over high heat for 5 minutes. With an electric mixer at low speed, mix 10 tbsp. of butter with the remaining confectioners' sugar. Add the almond powder, pistachio paste, kirsch, 2 eggs, and the pastry cream, in that order. Pour half of the mixture into the tart pastry, add the apricots, and pour the rest of the mixture on top. Bake for 8 minutes. Remove from oven and sprinkle with almonds and the remaining granulated sugar. Bake for 20 more minutes. Garnish with the crushed pistachios.

The apricot and the pistachio—what a good combination! Their flavors complement each other, and their colors do, too. I personally prefer apricot tarts made with a puff pastry, but this filling of almond and pistachio cream makes another crust unnecessary. NOTE BY **FRANÇOISE BERNARD**

Bananas

"A banana is as good for you as a steak." So said the posters in French schools in the old days. In the 1930s, Josephine Baker sang, "I like bananas because they have no bones." The banana sold itself back then. Today, it is one of the most popular fruits, along with apples and oranges. As a child, Françoise Bernard did not really like bananas, but people often offered her one after a meal because they thought the treat would make her happy.

The banana has become a favorite among the French. You will find it in a number of recipes, either as the main ingredient or as an addition. Alain Ducasse suggests that you add banana to a curry. Françoise Bernard makes the same suggestion. "The banana cools down the heat of spices and hot pepper," she says. You can serve the curry as those in India do—with some diced banana sprinkled with lemon juice and a pinch of salt and pepper. Those in West Indies serve the dish as a plantain fricassee. The banana's greatest success, however, is as dessert—including modest family desserts, like banana flambée or banana split. Yet the fruit also has a penchant for exotic flavors, which recall its origins. At *Le Louis XV*, Alain Ducasse serves it in fruit salad. "The ideal would be to eat it as is, at the foot of the tree," he adds. Yes, indeed! Even great chefs cannot, unfortunately, fulfill all our fantasies.

Choose your banana the way you prefer it. If the skin is yellow, the pulp will be firm and acidic. If the skin is speckled, it will be yellow, creamy, and aromatic. The banana has become very popular, and everybody can afford it—so much so that we forget that it is imported from the West Indies and Africa. A few varieties do have a slightly exotic look, like the pink-skinned, orange-pulp bananas from Asia and the short, plump bananas from Martinique, which are acidic and deliciously tender but slightly more expensive.

Banana Split

Banana Split

⌂ ∞

Françoise Bernard

Serves 4 ◆ **Preparation time : 15 minutes** ◆ **Cooking time : 2 hours**
1⅓ to 1¾ lbs. (600 to 800 g) fresh fruit, such as peaches, pears, strawberries, raspberries, etc.
◆ 5 tbsp. red currant or raspberry jelly ◆ 1 pint (50 cl) vanilla ice cream ◆ 1 pint (50 cl) raspberry
sorbet ◆ 1 pint (50 cl) pear or other sorbet ◆ 4 small bananas ◆ 1 cup (20 cl) whipped cream
◆ 2 tbsp. diced candied fruit ◆ 4 *crêpes dentelles* (thin dessert crêpes rolled into cigar shapes)

Peel the large fruits and cut into pieces. Leave the berries whole. Cook the jelly over low heat until it begins to liquify. Portion the fruit and berries into 4 small oblong dishes and cover with most of the softened jelly. Add a scoop of the ice cream and each sorbet. Peel the bananas and cut in half lengthwise. Arrange the halved bananas in the dishes. With a pastry brush, coat the bananas with the remaining jelly. Top with whipped cream and sprinkle with candied fruit. Serve immediately, with a *crêpe dentelle* on the side.

NOTE BY **ALAIN DUCASSE** Choose the small *figue-pomme* ("fig-apple") bananas from Martinique. They are rather expensive, but their acidic flavor will transform this classic dessert—and their small size is more pleasing to the eye.

Banana Bowl, Malibu Granité

Coupe de banane, granité Malibu

⌂ ⌂ ○

Alain Ducasse

Serves 4 ✦ **Preparation time : 50 minutes** ✦ **Freezing time : 5 hours** ✦ **Cooking time : 10 minutes** ✦ **1¼ cups (250 g) sugar** ✦ **2 tbsp. (60 g) glucose, or corn syrup** ✦ **3 lbs. (1,3 kg) bananas** ✦ **1 cup (20 cl) Malibu coconut liqueur** ✦ **juice of 1 lemon**

Boil ½ cup (100 g) of the sugar, the glucose, and 1¾ cups (35 cl) of water. Remove from heat and cool in the refrigerator. Peel 1¾ lbs. (800 g) of the bananas and purée in a food processor. Combine the syrup and purée. Pour into an ice-cream maker and turn to make the sorbet. Set aside in freezer. **B**oil the remaining sugar and 2½ cups (60 cl) water for 5 minutes. Remove from the heat and cool in the refrigerator. Stir the coconut liqueur into the syrup, transfer to a deep dish, and freeze. As soon as ice forms at the edges of the mixture, scrape it back into the mixture with a fork. Repeat as needed until the entire mixture has the consistency of a granité—about 4 to 5 hours. **P**eel and slice the remaining bananas and sprinkle with lemon juice. Spoon into large ice-cream dishes and top with the banana sorbet and coconut granité. Serve at once.

Bananas and coconut are a perfect match—maybe because both are products of the islands. I would pour a dash of Malibu coconut liqueur (or Martinique rum) into the bowls before serving. Or I would suggest the idea to my guests.

NOTE BY **FRANÇOISE BERNARD**

Bananas Martinique-Style

Banane à la martiniquaise

⌂ ∞

Françoise Bernard

Serves 4 ✦ **Preparation time : 15 minutes** ✦ **Cooking time : 10 minutes**
4 under-ripe bananas ✦ **2 tbsp. (30 g) butter** ✦ **¼ cup (50 g) granulated sugar** ✦ **2 tsp. vanilla**
sugar ✦ **juice of 1 orange** ✦ **3 tbsp. rum** ✦ **1 cup (100 g) raisins** ✦ **1 clove**

Peel the bananas and halve lengthwise. Melt the butter over low heat. Sauté the banana halves in the foamy butter for a few minutes. Brown both sides, turning with a slotted spoon. Place the granulated sugar, vanilla sugar, orange juice, rum, raisins, and clove in the skillet. Bring to a boil and immediately flambé, being careful that the flame doesn't get too high. Remove the clove and serve hot.

NOTE BY **ALAIN DUCASSE** For a more caramelized flavor and a nicely colored syrup, use brown sugar or powdered molasses. These sugars will coat the bananas with a beautiful amber color. You can find brown sugar in any grocery store and powdered molasses in a health-food store.

Oven-Roasted Martinique Bananas

Banane de Martinique rôtie au four

⌂ ∞

Alain Ducasse

Serves 4 ◆ **Preparation time : 45 minutes** ◆ **Cooking time : 30 minutes**
½ cup (50 g) raisins ◆ 1¼ cups (30 cl) rum ◆ 4 bananas ◆ 4 vanilla bean pods, split ◆ 3 tbsp.
(40 g) butter ◆ 3 tbsp. granulated sugar ◆ ½ cup (100 g) confectioners' sugar ◆ One 4 ounce
(100 g) puff-pastry dough ◆ 1 cup (20 cl) pastry cream (page 323) ◆ ½ cup (10 cl) whipped
cream ◆ ¾ cup (15 cl) Malibu coconut liqueur

Macerate the raisins in the rum. **P**reheat the oven to 325°F (160°C). **P**eel the bananas
and split them two thirds along their length. Place a vanilla bean pod inside each
banana. Caramelize the butter and the sugar in a skillet and sauté the bananas, rolling
to cover evenly. Transfer to a baking dish and bake for 10 minutes. **R**emove the raisins
and deglaze the baking dish with the rum. Boil to reduce for 5 minutes and add ⅔
cup (15 cl) water. Add the raisins and boil for 5 more minutes. **R**aise the oven temperature to 375°F (200°C). **O**n a surface sprinkled with the confectioners' sugar, roll
out the puff-pastry dough as thin as possible. Cut into 4 long strips. Lightly press the
center of each strip with your finger to make an indentation, where you will later place
the banana. Bake about 10 minutes. **C**ombine the pastry cream and whipped cream.
Gently stir in the coconut liqueur. Spoon some of the cream into 4 oval plates. Arrange
the puff pastries on top and garnish with more cream. Rest a banana in each groove
in the pastry. Sprinkle with the rum syrup and a few raisins.

What a delight! This is a devilishly gourmet recipe. Although the presentation is playful, this dish is not for children. The roasted bananas, vanilla beans, and whipped cream should be enough to make them happy. They won't miss the liqueur.

NOTE BY **FRANÇOISE BERNARD**

Cherries

"My soft sour-cherry and almond clafoutis [fruit baked in batter] is definitely not an old-fashioned dessert, one of Grandma's recipes—but it is an excellent home-style dessert," Alain Ducasse says. What actually makes a dessert a traditional favorite? Alain Ducasse first offered his clafoutis in 1981 at his *La Terrasse* restaurant in Juan-les-Pins. He still likes this classic fruit dessert, served as an afternoon snack when he was a child—the wonderful aroma would fill the whole house. He enjoys playing with the lively colors and fruity flavors of this spring pastry with a summer fragrance.

As for Françoise Bernard, she is totally impervious to the charms of the cherry, sung unanimously by one and all. Maybe it's because of the pits. Or maybe it's because, once, as a child, while she was eating a basketful of cherries, she discovered with horror that there were worms in her fruit. Today, she has grown to love cherry jam and cherry clafoutis. According to her, this fruit is better suited as a dessert than as an entrée. For her clafoutis, she prefers the English varieties of cherries, which are unfortunately difficult to find in France. Or she chooses black cherries or the sour Montmorency cherries. "If you make your clafoutis for young children, remember to pit the fruit. You should know, though, that the pits of the cherries give the clafoutis an incomparable flavor," this wise cook adds.

The *Cœur de Pigeon* cherry, which really does resemble a pigeon's heart, and the morello are Alain Ducasse's favorites. In his Paris restaurant, he serves pigeon in jus flavored with cherry pits. Sweet-and-sour morello cherry jam, served with a slice of rump steak, was his very first "sauce to eat," meant to be enjoyed as part of the dish, not just as a condiment left on the plate. This concept, which has given sauces their original status, has been imitated by many since. Alain Ducasse is, at present, the only chef who can use the term "saucing up" without sounding vulgar. In fact, there is nothing pejorative about it. On the contrary, "saucing up" is the expression of a connoisseur who smacks his lips in anticipation, without the slightest tinge of remorse.

Candied Cherry *Rigodon*

Rigodon aux cerises confites

⌂ ∞

Françoise Bernard

Serves 4 to 6 people ✦ **Preparation time : 20 minutes** ✦ **Cooking time : 35 minutes**
4 tbsp. chopped candied fruit ✦ **2 tbsp. rum or kirsch** ✦ **3 cups (75 cl) milk** ✦ **5 tbsp. sugar** ✦ **2**
pinches of salt ✦ **½ tsp. ground cinnamon or vanilla extract** ✦ **5 oz. (150 g) leftover cake, such**
as sponge or pound cake ✦ **6 eggs** ✦ **3 oz. (100 g) candied cherries** ✦ **2 tbsp. (30 g) butter** ✦ **1**
cup (20 cl) apricot jam, for decorating

Preheat the oven to 425°F (220°C). **M**acerate the chopped candied fruit in the rum.
Cook the milk, sugar, salt, and cinnamon in a saucepan over low heat. As soon as the
mixture boils, crumble the cake into the pan and mix well. Beat the eggs with a whisk,
beating constantly. Halve and pit the cherries. Add the candied fruit to the mixture.
Generously butter an 8 in. (20 cm) soufflé dish. Pour the fruit mixture into the dish,
dot with butter, and bake for about 30 minutes. **R**emove from oven and let cool.
Unmold the *rigodon*, place on a round serving platter, and frost the top with a layer
of apricot jam.

NOTE BY **ALAIN DUCASSE** For a more homogenous mixture, I would incorporate the cherries as a jam, lightly
cooked over low heat with a little sugar. I would then serve the *rigodon* with more of
this cooled cherry compote on the side.

Sautéed Bigarreau Cherries with Kirsch and Pistachio Ice Cream

Bigarreaux poêlés au kirsch, glace à la pistache

⌂ ⌂ ○

Alain Ducasse

Serves 4 ✦ Preparation time : 50 minutes ✦ Freezing time : 1 hour ✦ Cooking time : 35 minutes ✦ 3 tbsp. (40 g) butter ✦ 60 Bigarreau cherries, pitted ✦ ¾ cup (145 g) sugar ✦ 1 tbsp. kirsch ✦ 4 egg yolks ✦ 2 cups (50 cl) milk ✦ 3 tbsp. pistachio paste or ½ cup (100 g) unsalted pistachios, ground ✦ ¼ cup (5 cl) heavy cream

Melt the butter over low heat until hazelnut brown. Add the cherries, sprinkle with 1 tbsp. of the sugar so they render some of their juice, then drizzle with kirsch. Simmer over very low heat for 10 minutes. **B**eat the egg yolks with the remaining sugar. Boil the milk and slowly pour over the egg yolks, whisking vigorously. Transfer to the saucepan and cook over low heat—stirring constantly until the custard coats the spoon. Remove from heat. **S**train the custard, stir in the pistachio paste, and let cool. Whisk in the heavy cream. Pour into an ice-cream maker and turn into ice cream. **W**hen the ice cream is ready, portion the cherries into 4 small, individual dishes and add a scoop of pistachio ice cream to each.

The base of this ice cream is a light custard, which is very unstable. Check the cooking by tracing a line on the cream-covered spoon with your finger. When the line remains well marked, the cream is ready. If the cream becomes a little grainy, it is slightly overcooked—whip it with an electric beater for a few seconds to make it smooth again.

NOTE BY **FRANÇOISE BERNARD**

Cherry Clafoutis

Clafoutis aux cerises

⌂ ○

Françoise Bernard

Serves 4 ◆ Preparation time : 15 minutes ◆ Cooking time : 45 minutes
2½ tbsp. (35 g) butter ◆ 1⅓ cups (30 cl) milk ◆ 2 to 3 tbsp. sifted flour ◆ 3 eggs ◆ 4 tbsp. sugar
◆ 2 pinches of salt ◆ 1.2 lb. (500 g) cherries, preferably dark, stemmed but not pitted ◆ sugar,
for sprinkling, optional

Preheat the oven to 375°F (190°C). **M**elt 2 tbsp. of the butter in a small saucepan over low heat. In a separate pan, warm the milk. With an electric mixer, mix together the flour, eggs, sugar, salt, melted butter, and milk to form a smooth batter. Grease a baking dish with the remaining butter and add the whole cherries. Pour the batter on top. **B**ake for about 40 minutes on the middle rack of the oven. **S**erve in the baking dish, warm or cold. If desired, sprinkle with sugar before serving.

NOTE BY **ALAIN DUCASSE** For clafoutis, I prefer the morello cherry, which adds a pleasant acidic flavor. You can also add an equal amount of almond powder to the flour.

Morello Cherry Clafoutis with Cherry Granité

Clafoutis aux griottes, granité de cerise

⌂ ○

Alain Ducasse

Serves 8 ✦ **Preparation time : 1 hour 30 minutes** ✦ **Freezing time : 5 hours** ✦ **Cooking time : 30 minutes** ✦ 3¾ cups (725 g) granulated sugar ✦ 4½ lbs. (2 kg) sweet cherries, pitted ✦ 1 lb. 3 oz. (540 g) butter, softened ✦ 5 cups (500 g) almond powder ✦ 5 eggs ✦ ¾ cup (90 g) cornstarch ✦ 1¾ cups (40 cl) milk ✦ 5 egg yolks ✦ 1¾ lbs. (800 g) morello cherries, pitted ✦ 2 tbsp. confectioners' sugar

The day before, prepare the sorbet. Boil 1 cup (25 cl) water and 1 cup plus 2 tbsp. (125 g) granulated sugar for 5 minutes. Remove from heat and cool. In a food processor, purée the sweet cherries and add to the cooled syrup. Transfer to a bowl and freeze. When ice begins to form, scrape the base and sides of the bowl with a fork. Repeat as needed until the mixture has the consistency of a sorbet (granité), about 4 to 5 hours. The next day, preheat the oven to 375°F (190°C). Cream 1 lb. plus 4 tbsp. (500 g) of butter with 2½ cups (500 g) granulated sugar and the almond powder. Beating constantly, add the whole eggs, one at a time. Add ½ cup (60 g) cornstarch. Reserve one fifth of this butter cream for another recipe. Boil the milk, beat the egg yolks with the remaining sugar and cornstarch. Slowly pour the milk over the egg yolks, stir constantly. Transfer to the saucepan and heat, stirring. Twenty-five seconds after the custard starts to boil, remove from heat, pour into bowl, and let cool completely. Combine the butter cream, custard, and morello cherries. Pour into 8 buttered earthenware or ceramic molds, 2 in. (6 cm) deep. Bake 20 minutes. Check the cooking by pricking with a metal skewer—if it comes out clean, the clafoutis is cooked. Sprinkle with confectioners' sugar and serve with a scoop of cherry granité.

You can recognize the masterful touch of the chef in the sorbet that accompanies this rich and refined dessert. Inspired by the classic family dessert, this clafoutis is elegant and, at the same time, easy to make. The granité almost makes itself.

NOTE BY **FRANÇOISE BERNARD**

Grapes

Although she likes sweet-and-sour recipes, Françoise Bernard rarely cooks with fruit—except grapes. Because this fruit is less sweet than others, or at least seemingly less so because of its tartness, she thinks it is an excellent addition to savory dishes. But what a job! Fresh grapes requires peeling and pitting. So, when Bernard cooks, she chooses the larger grape varieties, like the Italia, which is much easier to peel. This golden yellow fruit is not as delicate as the Chasselas grape, but it's tender and crunchy and has a beautiful appearance. "It is often simpler to use raisins," she adds. As an example, she mentions her Breton Baked Custard, made with raisins that she has soaked in rum to mellow the flavor.

Alain Ducasse favors quality local products. The Chasselas de Moissac-to date, the only variety worthy of a label of guaranteed origin-is his favorite grape. Cultivated on the sloping vineyards of Moissac, a small town in Tarn-et-Garonne, this is the first grape to appear in the markets. The leaves that cover each cluster vouch for their freshness. Alain Ducasse cooks grapes mostly with game or with apples and a piece of foie gras.

Alain Ducasse adds apples to his grape jelly, which he serves with brioche as a dessert. For him, the grapes are simply an addition and shouldn't overpower the dish. He prefers the fruit of the vine in its freshest form—in a bunch, with their joyous taste of wine.

Quail with Grapes on Toast Canapés

Cailles aux raisins sur canapé

⌂ ⌂ ∞∞

Françoise Bernard

Serves 4 ✦ **Preparation time : 30 minutes** ✦ **Cooking time : 30 minutes**
8 slices white sandwich bread ✦ **9 tbsp. (120 g) butter** ✦ **10 oz. (300 g) muscat grapes** ✦ **8 trussed and barded quail** ✦ **3 oz. (100 g) chicken livers, cleaned and chopped** ✦ **½ cup (10 cl) cognac** ✦ **Salt and pepper**

Sauté the bread with 4 tbsp. of the butter. Peel the grapes with a small, sharp knife and slip a few inside each quail. Melt 2 tbsp. of butter in a casserole and sear the quails over high heat. Cover and cook over low heat for 10 minutes. Quickly sauté the chicken livers in 2 tbsp. of butter. Sprinkle half of the cognac on the liver and flambé, being careful that the flame doesn't leap too high. Mash the liver with the remaining butter. Season with salt and pepper. Spread the liver paté on the toasted bread, arrange on a serving platter, and set aside in a warm place. **R**emove the quails from the casserole and remove the bard. Skim the grease off the juice and return the quails to the casserole. Sprinkle with the remaining cognac and flambé. Add the peeled grapes, cover, cook over low heat for 3 minutes. Arrange the quails on the canapés. Top with the cooking juice and garnish with grapes.

NOTE BY **ALAIN DUCASSE** Here's a tip for seeding grapes more easily: Bend the end of a paper clip into a loop. Slip the loop into the grape to remove the seeds. This tool is more modern than the Bar-le-Duc goose feather and quite as efficient! To enhance the taste of grapes, soak them in port wine or cognac.

Fried Foie Gras with Apples and Grapes

Foie gras poêlé aux pommes et aux raisins

⭡ ⭡ ⭡ ◯◯◯

Alain Ducasse

Serves 4 ⬦ **Preparation time : 40 minutes** ⬦ **Cooking time : 40 minutes**
11 ounces (330 g) Chasselas grapes ⬦ **1¾ lbs. (750 g) fresh duck foie gras** ⬦ **coarse sea salt**
and freshly ground pepper ⬦ **3 Granny Smith apples** ⬦ **½ cup (10 cl) red port wine** ⬦ **1 cup**
(20 cl) duck jus (page 323) ⬦ **¼ cup (50 g) sugar** ⬦ **6 tbsp. (80 g) butter**

Wash the grapes and reserve 40. Purée the rest in a food processor, strain the juice, and set aside. Blanch the reserved grapes for a few seconds, cool under running water, and peel. **T**rim the foie gras. Cut 4 slices, 5 oz. (150 g) each, and reserve the last piece. Season all the slices with salt and pepper. **P**eel and core the apples. Dice 1 apple and cut the other 2 into 6 wedges each. Sauté the unsliced foie gras, without adding fat, and then brown the diced apple. Do not skim the fat. Add the port wine and reduce by half over high heat. Add the grape juice and reduce by half. Add the duck jus and reduce by half again. Strain into a bowl, pressing down to extract as much sauce as possible. **I**n a very hot skillet, sauté the apple wedges and sugar in 5 tbsp. of butter. In a separate hot skillet, sauté the sliced foie gras for 3 minutes on each side, without adding fat. Reheat the strained sauce, adding the reserved grapes and butter. The more syrupy this juice is, the tastier it will be. Arrange 3 apple wedges on each plate and place a slice of foie gras on top. Drizzle with the sauce and decorate with grapes. Add pepper and a few grains of salt.

Do not confuse fresh foie gras, which is raw, with cooked or semi-cooked, which does not require any preparation. I am being precise about this because I know from experience that there are many people who make the mistake.

NOTE BY FRANÇOISE BERNARD

Breton Baked Custard with Raisins

Far breton aux raisins secs

⌂ ○

Françoise Bernard

Serves 4 to 6 ✦ **Marinating time : 1 hour** ✦ **Preparation time : 30 minutes** ✦ **Cooking time : 1 hour** ✦ **¾ cup (125 g) raisins** ✦ **4 tbsp. rum** ✦ **5 tbsp. flour** ✦ **½ tsp. salt** ✦ **3 tbsp. sugar** ✦ **3 eggs** ✦ **2 cups (50 cl) milk, warm** ✦ **1½ tbsp. (20 g) butter**

Macerate the raisins in rum for 1 hour. Preheat the oven to 400°F (210°C). Beat together the flour, salt, sugar, and eggs in a large bowl. Add the warm milk and mix until smooth. Add the raisins and rum. Generously butter a medium-size baking dish. The mixture should fill the dish halfway. Bake for 30 minutes. Lower the oven temperature to 350°F (180°C). Bake for 20 to 30 more minutes. Serve the custard warm. It's rather difficult to remove it, so serve it directly from the baking dish.

NOTE BY **ALAIN DUCASSE** For a dessert with unforgettable flavor, prepare this dish, in season, with dark grapes that you have dried yourself. To dry the grapes, just "forget" them in a 175°F (70°C) oven. Keep the door ajar until they are wrinkled like raisins.

Grape Jelly

Gelée de raisin

⚜ ⚜ ○

Alain Ducasse

Serves 4 ◆ **Preparation time : 40 minutes** ◆ **Cooking time : 40 minutes**
2½ lbs. (1,2 kg) grapes ◆ **10 oz. (300 g) apples** ◆ **1 lemon, zest peeled and juiced** ◆ **⅔ cup (15 cl) water** ◆ **4 cups (800 g) sugar** ◆ **1½ tbsp. (10 g) pectin**

Stem all the grapes. Wash and quarter the apples, without removing the skins or seeds. Dice the lemon zest, boil, and drain. **B**oil 7 oz. (230 g) of the grapes, the apples, lemon juice, and water. Purée the mixture in a food processor. Return the purée to the pot, add the sugar, and cook for 20 minutes. Peel and seed the remaining grapes. Add the pectin to the pot, bring to a boil, and add the grapes and lemon zest. Reduce heat and simmer until syrupy—about 10 minutes. Pour into ramekins. This jelly is delicious on slices of brioche.

This autumn recipe will be very tasty made with muscat grapes. You can replace the pectin with canning sugar, which is easier to find in large quantities. Equivalent amounts should be indicated on the package.

NOTE BY **FRANÇOISE BERNARD**

Oranges

What would Alain Ducasse's cuisine be without the orange? This fruit adds a deliciously acidic touch and contrasting flavor to his recipes. The man has no culinary taboos—he does not hesitate to combine lamb or roasted sea bream with the fruity aroma of the orange. More traditionally, he adds orange to daube stew in his Monaco restaurant.

The orange is also suited to gourmet desserts—Alain Ducasse's Warm Tart with Orange Wine, for example, and Françoise Bernard's Orange Crêpes, one of her favorites dishes because it is so easy to make. This excellent cook is also proud of her orange preserves, which rival English marmalades, although she uses sweet oranges and the English swear by the bitter. She precooks the fruit, cuts it into pieces, processes it, then cooks it in water for 20 minutes to lessen the bitter taste, which she decidedly dislikes. The next day, she adds sugar. She also dislikes the bitter Seville orange, but is very fond of the blood orange, a small round fruit with sweet, juicy red pulp. The Navel orange, easy to recognize because of its ingrown navel, is also very juicy and aromatic. It's the best variety to eat fresh. Alain Ducasse holds the bergamot orange, which flavors Earl Grey tea, in high esteem. A few drops are enough to flavor an entire dish.

You sometimes see oranges with green skins, which are, nevertheless, ripe. In tropical climates, the chlorophyll in the skin does not change color. Whether bitter or sweet, orange or green, this fruit can add a classic or exotic touch to a thousand exuberant recipes.

Orange Soufflé

Orange soufflée

⌂ ⌂ ○

Françoise Bernard

Serves 6 ◆ Preparation time : 50 minutes ◆ Cooking time : 25 minutes
6 large, thick-skinned oranges ◆ 2 eggs ◆ ⅓ cup (60 g) sugar ◆ 1 tbsp. cornstarch ◆ 1 tsp. cointreau

Preheat the oven to 400°F (210°C). **S**crub the oranges with a vegetable brush under cold water. Cut off a small cap from the top of each and discard. Scoop out the pulp with a grapefruit knife, making sure not to pierce the skins, and set aside. Cut a thin slice off each base, without exposing the pulp, so that the oranges will stand upright while baking. Or support them in the baking dish with a large piece of crumpled aluminum foil **E**xtract the juice from the pulp of 4 oranges. Save the remaining pulp for another recipe. Separate the eggs. Beat the egg yolks and sugar with an electric mixer until the yolks lighten. Add the orange juice and cornstarch. Transfer the mixture to a saucepan and bring to a boil over low heat, stirring constantly. Remove from the heat, add the cointreau, and place the pan in cold water to cool quickly. Be careful not to splash any water into the mixture. **B**eat the egg whites to stiff peaks and gently fold into the cooled mixture. Spoon the orange mousse into the reserved orange skins. Place the oranges close together in a small baking dish and bake for 15 to 20 minutes. Serve immediately—while the mousse is still inflated by the heat—because these soufflés fall very quickly.

NOTE BY **ALAIN DUCASSE** For more flavor, replace the sugar with 2 sugar lumps that have been rubbed over the skin of well-washed oranges or tangerines. Dissolve the lumps by mixing them, but not cooking them, with the egg yolks, stirring constantly.

Warm Tart with Orange Wine

Fine tartelette tiède au vin d'orange

⇧ ○

Alain Ducasse

Serves 4 ✦ Preparation time : 1 hour 15 minutes ✦ Drying time : 2 days ✦ Resting time : 12 hours ✦ Cooking time : 1 hour ✦ 1 pink grapefruit, zest peeled ✦ 1 cup plus 2 tbsp. (220 g) sugar ✦ 2 tbsp. (30 g) lard ✦ 8 tbsp. (100 g) butter ✦ 1⅔ cups (250 g) flour ✦ fine salt ✦ 1 cup (20 cl) alcohol ✦ 1 quart (1 l) rosé wine ✦ juice of 2 oranges ✦ juice of ½ lemon ✦ ½ tsp. vanilla extract

Three days before serving, roll the grapefruit zest in 4 tbsp. of the sugar. Let dry in a warm place 85°F (30°C) for 48 hours. In a food processor, grind the zest into a grapefruit sugar. Set aside in a dry place. The day before serving, cut the lard and 4 tbsp. of butter into 1⅓ cups (200 g) flour. Gradually add about ½ cup (10 cl) water and 3 pinches of salt. Flatten the dough with the palm of your hand and roll into a ball. Repeat. Refrigerate the dough overnight. The day of serving, preheat the oven to 325°F (170°C). To make the orange wine, pour the alcohol, wine, 1 cup (200 g) of the sugar, vanilla orange, and lemon juice, into a saucepan. Bring to a boil, remove from heat, cool, and refrigerate. Mix the grapefruit sugar with 4 tbsp. of flour. Butter four 4 in. (11 cm) tart pans. Roll out the dough on a floured surface, cut 4 circles, and line the tart pans. Sprinkle the dough with the sugar-flour mixture, add a dab of butter, and bake 20 to 25 minutes. Add the orange wine to the tarts halfway through the baking. Remove from the oven and tart pans. Place on a cake rack to cool. Serve warm.

I encourage you to buy ring molds which you can find in specialty shops. They are more practical than tart pans with removable bases—and they take up less space in your kitchen. Rather than keeping an assortment of tart pans, buy ring molds of different diameters and place them directly on the baking sheet.

NOTE BY **FRANÇOISE BERNARD**

Orange Crêpes
Crêpes à l'orange

⌂ ○

Françoise Bernard

Serves 4 ✦ **Preparation time : 10 minutes** ✦ **Cooking time : 10 minutes**
8 crêpes ✦ **6 tbsp. confectioners' sugar** ✦ **4 tbsp. (50 g) butter** ✦ **2 oranges** ✦ **1 tbsp. orange**
liqueur

Sprinkle the crêpes with 3 tbsp. of sugar and fold in four. Heat half of the butter over
low heat in a large skillet. When the butter turns golden brown, add 4 folded crêpes,
sauté for 30 seconds. Turn, without unfolding, cook on other side. Remove from pan
and set aside in a serving dish, keeping them warm. Brown the remaining butter and
sauté the remaining 4 crêpes in the same way. Place in the serving dish with the others.
Wash and scrub 1 of the oranges with a vegetable brush and grate the zest. Juice
both oranges. Add the juice, orange liqueur, remaining sugar, and grated zest to the
crêpe skillet. Simmer over low heat, stirring with a wooden spoon, until the mixture
starts to boil. Pour the syrup over the warm crêpes and serve immediately.

NOTE BY **ALAIN DUCASSE** This recipe is a variation of the celebrated Crêpes Suzette. Surprise your guests by
changing the recipe even a little bit more—spread a generous layer of orange mar-
malade over the crêpes. The bitter citrus fruit accents the sugary crêpes.

Citrus Fruit Salad in Sauternes Jelly

Salade d'agrumes en gelée de sauternes

⌂ ∞

Alain Ducasse

Serves 4 ◆ Preparation time : 50 minutes ◆ Maceration time : 7 hours ◆ Cooking time : 1 hour 30 minutes ◆ Refrigeration time : 1 hour ◆ 5 oranges ◆ 2 lemons ◆ 2 pink grapefruits ◆ 1¾ cups (350 g) granulated sugar ◆ 1 bunch of lemon thyme, leaves only, minced ◆ 1⅓ cup or 7 oz. (220 g) sugar cubes ◆ 3 cups (75 cl) sauternes ◆ 10 gelatin leaves (20 g) or 1 envelope powdered gelatin

Wash the fruit and pat dry with paper towels. Peel 2 of the oranges, lemons, and grapefruits in strips, top to bottom, removing some pulp with the peel. Quarter the 2 oranges and 2 grapefruits. Place the peels in a saucepan with just enough water to cover. Add ¾ cup (150 g) granulated sugar and cook over low heat until the skins are half candied—about 1 hour 30 minutes. **B**oil 3¼ cups (80 cl) water with 1 cup (200 g) granulated sugar. Remove from heat, add the lemon thyme leaves, and cool. Macerate the quartered fruit in the thyme syrup for at least 6 hours. **R**ub the sugar cubes over the skin of the 3 remaining oranges. Boil the cubes in the sauternes. Soak the gelatin leaves and pat dry. Stir, one by one, into the sauternes to dissolve. Strain and refrigerate until set—at least 1 hour. Combine the candied peels and quartered fruit, spoon the mixture into individual dishes. Top with pieces or spoonfuls of sauternes jelly.

A lot of English desserts contain fruits that are coated in jelly. I prefer to dot the fruit with little dabs of jelly or serve it in a jelly that has not completely set. I think the fruit looks more alive and more appetizing.

NOTE BY **FRANÇOISE BERNARD**

Peaches

The white, the yellow, and the purple "vineyard" peach all have beautiful days ahead of them. The culinary successes of this fruit are countless. It has always been popular in tarts and clafoutis, and today it is served with savory dishes, too. For Françoise Bernard, it all began with Duck with Peaches, a dish she ate at a restaurant one day, which convinced her that the peach and duck were meant for each other. Chefs have since grown bolder and have begun to combine this fruit of the orchard with the fruit of the sea. Françoise Bernard praises Alain Senderens's lobster with peaches. Alain Ducasse's iced lobster bisque is made with peaches that have baked for a long time under thin rounds of lemon. The lobster is particularly well suited to gourmet adventures—sometimes, it is even paired with vanilla. Today, the trend is toward roasted peaches—cooked in the oven or a pot—and served as a garnish for game or as a dessert. One particularly trendy dessert is a peach fricassee served with French toast and eggnog.

Alain Ducasse treats the peach as he does the apricot. Indeed, the two fruits are similar in their general shape and aromatic acidity. Before roasting them in butter, he garnishes peach halves with apricot compote and pistachios to give them a hazelnut aroma. The great chef is always in the vanguard, but he does not forget the classics. His Peach Melba with Caramelized Almonds has the taste of eternity, and his peach *tarte Tatin* will take you straight to seventh heaven. Warm and caramelized flavors mix well with the peach, as does the coldness of ice cream.

Françoise Bernard is very fond of peaches. She eats fresh white peaches whole and slices them to make salads, alone or with other fruits. Yellow peaches hold their shape better while cooking, so she poaches them in vanilla syrup, poaches the yellow peach in vanilla syrup, because it holds its shape better during cooking. She remains impervious, however, to the trend that pushes us blindly toward every product of nature. She has never liked the *pêches de vigne*, or "vineyard peaches," which is available in Porquerolle, her vacation spot. As far as she is concerned, there are many other fruits that taste better than these purple peaches. To her, the pulp looks as if it has broken veins—too bad if it is more in vogue to praise their bucolic charms!

Peach Charlotte

Charlotte aux pêches

⌂ ◯

Françoise Bernard

Serve 4 ✦ **Preparation time : 30 minutes** ✦ **Cooking time : 5 minutes** ✦ **Refriger-**
ation time : 10 hours ✦ **1 can peaches in syrup (8 halves)** ✦ **1 vanilla bean pod, split** ✦ **juice**
of ½ lemon ✦ **¼ cup (5 cl) kirsch** ✦ **1 sponge cake, 6 to 7 in. (15 to 17 cm) diameter** ✦ **½ cup**
(10 cl) heavy cream, very cold ✦ **4 tbsp. confectioners' sugar**

Drain the can of peaches into a saucepan. Add the vanilla bean and most of the lemon
juice. When the syrup begins to boil, add the peaches. Reduce the heat, cook 2 to 3
minutes, then remove. Let the peaches cool in the syrup. **S**tir the kirsch into 1 cup
(20 cl) of the cooled syrup. Cut the sponge cake horizontally into 2 or 3 layers. Drizzle
the layers with the syrup. Cut the peaches into ½ in. (1 cm) slices. In a charlotte mold
or soufflé dish, alternately layer cake and peaches, starting and finishing with a layer
of cake. Place a heavy plate on top to weight the mixture and refrigerate for 10 hours.
Whip the cream and add the confectioners' sugar and a dash of lemon juice. To serve,
unmold the charlotte on a round plate and decorate with whipped cream.

NOTE BY **ALAIN DUCASSE** If you have some extra time, make lady fingers. Sprinkled with sugar, they can be
substituted for the sponge cake. Lady fingers are quick to make and keep well in a
tightly sealed container.

Roasted Peaches and French Toast

Pêche rôtie et pain perdu

� ᵕ ∞

Alain Ducasse

Serves 4 ◆ **Preparation time : 40 minutes** ◆ **Cooking time : 30 minutes**
½ cup (50 g) chopped almonds ◆ 4 large, ripe white peaches, peeled, halved, and pitted ◆ 1 cup (200 g) sugar ◆ 11 tbsp. (160 g) butter ◆ ½ cup (50 g) green pistachios, unsalted ◆ 4 green cardamom seeds ◆ 1¼ cups (30 cl) peach wine ◆ 4 whole eggs ◆ 2 egg yolks ◆ 2 cups (50 cl) milk ◆ ½ vanilla bean pod, split ◆ 4 slices stale brioche

Preheat the oven to 325°F (160°C). **S**auté the chopped almonds in a dry skillet for 1 minute. Roll the peach halves in ½ cup (100 g) sugar. Sauté the peaches in about 4 tbsp. of butter to lightly brown and transfer to baking dish. In the same skillet, caramelize the pistachios, cardamom seeds and almonds. Add the peach wine and reduce to one third its volume. Pour the syrup over the peaches and oven-roast for about 10 minutes. **W**hisk the whole eggs and yolks into the milk. Add the remaining sugar and vanilla bean. Melt the remaining butter in a skillet over low heat and sauté the bread on both sides. Place 1 slice of bread on each plate and top with 2 peach halves and syrup. If the syrup is too thin, reduce slightly to thicken.

You can dust French toast with confectioners' sugar and serve it simply—which is good, but very ordinary. Why not revive this family dessert with Alain Ducasse's recipe, which combines the different flavors of sautéed and roasted fruits.

NOTE BY **FRANÇOISE BERNARD**

Peach Cake

Biscuit moelleux aux pêches

⌂ ⌂ ∞

Françoise Bernard

Serves 6 to 8 ✦ **Preparation time : 1 hour** ✦ **Cooking time : 1 hour** ✦ **Cooling time : 2 hours** ✦ **5 to 6 large, ripe, yellow peaches** ✦ **¾ cup (150 g) granulated sugar** ✦ **2 tsp. vanilla sugar** ✦ **1 tbsp. rum** ✦ **3 whole eggs** ✦ **salt** ✦ **½ cup (75 g) flour** ✦ **½ cup (75 g) cornstarch** ✦ **1 tsp. baking powder** ✦ **1 lemon** ✦ **4 tbsp. (50 g) butter** ✦ **1 cup (100 g) confectioners' sugar** ✦ **1 egg white** ✦ **candied fruit of different colors, such as cherry and angelica**

Preheat the oven to 375°F (190°C). **P**eel and halve the peaches and remove their pits. To make the cake batter, put the granulated sugar, vanilla sugar, rum, whole eggs, and 2 pinches of salt in the top of a double boiler. Place over simmering water. Beat the mixture with an electric beater until it becomes white and fluffy and doubles in volume. Remove from heat and continue to beat until full volume and cool. Sift together the flour, cornstarch, and baking powder. Add to the batter. **G**rate the zest from half the lemon and juice the whole lemon. Melt the butter. Brush a deep, 8 in. (20 cm) cake pan with butter on the sides and bottom. Add the remaining butter, half the lemon juice, and the grated zest into the cake batter. Mix quickly and well. Lightly flour the mold and pour in the batter. Submerge the peach halves in the batter and bake for 40 minutes. **U**nmold the cake while still warm and let cool on a wire rack. With a wooden spoon, make an icing by vigorously whipping the confectioners' sugar, egg white, and the remaining lemon juice. With a metal spatula or large knife, immediately frost the entire cake, top and sides, with icing. Decorate with candied fruit.

NOTE BY **ALAIN DUCASSE** The combination of cooked and raw fruit is always effective. To heighten the flavors, sprinkle sugar and lemon juice on a few raw peaches and add them to the cake as a garnish.

Peach Melba with Caramelized Almonds

Pêche Melba aux amandes caramélisées

⌂ ⌂ ∞

Alain Ducasse

Serves 4 ✦ Preparation time : 30 minutes ✦ Cooking time : 25 minutes
2½ cups (500 g) granulated sugar ✦ 4 white peaches, peeled and halved but not pitted ✦ 1½ cups (150 g) slivered almonds ✦ 10 oz. (300 g) red currants ✦ ½ vanilla bean pod ✦ ⅔ cup (150 g) heavy cream, very cold ✦ ½ cup (50 g) confectioners' sugar ✦ 1 quart (1 l) vanilla ice cream

Preheat the oven to 350°F (170°C). Boil the granulated sugar in a 1 quart (1 l) water for 5 to 8 minutes. Add the peaches, poach for 15 minutes, and remove from heat. Let the peaches cool in the syrup and remove the pits. Drain the peach halves on paper towels. Refrigerate. Reheat the syrup. Drop the almonds into the syrup, quickly remove with a slotted spoon, and drain. Spread on a nonstick baking sheet and toast in the oven until brown. Set aside in a cool, dry place. Stem the currants. Purée the fruit in a food processor and strain the juice. Split the vanilla bean pod lengthwise and scrape the seeds into the cream. Whip the cream, adding the confectioners' sugar at the end. Place 2 large scoops of vanilla ice cream in each of 4 individual stem glasses. Top with 2 peach halves and some currant juice. Garnish with a dollop of whipped cream and a sprinkling of caramelized almonds.

This dessert was created in the mid-nineteenth century by the great French chef Georges Auguste Escoffier for the opera diva Nellie Melba. It has since remained a classic. In the original version—presented in a silver terrine between two swan wings carved out of ice—the peaches were arranged on a bed of vanilla ice cream and covered with a raspberry purée and spun sugar.

NOTE BY **FRANÇOISE BERNARD**

Pears

Françoise Bernard's Malakoff Pear Sponge Cake is one of her greatest hits. "It's always surprising to see how one recipe turns into a success story. It happens unexpectedly, like a musical hit. This pear cake, which is topped with chocolate icing and served cold, is very simple indeed. I invented it one day when my pears were threatening to turn bad. That gave me the idea of poaching them in syrup and making a cake with them. Since then, my friends have never stopped talking about it." In general, Françoise Bernard prefers to eat pears cooked because they are easier to digest. She fans the slices, sprinkles them with bits of macaroon, and bakes them. The flavors of almond and pear combine to perfection—which is how you achieve the aromas of a fancy tart in a dessert much easier to make.

Alain Ducasse often cooks pears—either alone or with cooked apples, raw apples, or following a principle dear to his heart, cooked and raw apples. He just cannot resist combining a tender caramelized pear with a fresh raw one. "I enjoy a difference in textures in my desserts and in my dishes," he says. This inclination gave him the idea for Caramelized and Raw Pear Tart, a variation on *tarte Tatin*. It is very easy to make, and its success depends solely on the quality of the pears, he claims. Years ago, pears were prepared *en Moscovite*. During the 1960s, they were often served as a mousse. Today, they are served as an ice cream. The ice mousse, which is called a parfait in classical cuisine, is a hybrid of the mousse and ice cream. Most chefs completely neglect this recipe, because they often associate it with coffee—although it can be made in many flavors. To make up for this long period of neglect, Alain Ducasse has invented his own recipe for Pear Parfait.

Ducasse does not restrict the pear to desserts. He also features the fruit, cooked in Colonna pork fat, with a dramatic *à la grecque* vegetable salad. And to introduce an unusual flavor, an insolent touch of freshness, he sprinkles a few swirls of raw pear on a vegetable casserole.

Pears with Macaroons

Poire aux macarons

⌂ ∞

Françoise Bernard

**Serves 4 ◆ Preparation time : 25 minutes ◆ Cooking time : 20 minutes
3 tbsp. (40 g) butter ◆ 4 very ripe pears, peeled, halved, and cored ◆ ⅓ cup (7 cl) apricot jam
◆ 3 large almond macaroon cookies**

Preheat the oven to 400°F (190°C). Butter a round, 8 in. (20 cm) baking dish. Lay the pear halves on a cutting board. Slice each one into thin, lengthwise strips, leaving the strips attached at the stem end. Gently push the fanned strips of each half back together. Place the pears close together in the buttered baking dish core side up. Fill the hollow left by the core of the pear with some of the jam. Finely chop the macaroons and sprinkle on top. Dot with butter and bake for about 20 minutes. Remove from heat and cool. Serve directly from the baking dish.

NOTE BY **ALAIN DUCASSE** As a final touch, I would sprinkle this dessert with some grated raw pear (choose a firm variety), as you would sprinkle a truffle. The contrasts of cooked and raw, warm and cold, are always a pleasant surprise.

Pear Parfait

Parfait aux poires

Alain Ducasse

Serves 8 • Preparation time : 45 minutes • Freezing time : 6 hours • Cooking time : 15 minutes • 3 pears, peeled and cored • 2¼ cups (250 g) sugar • 1 vanilla bean pod, split • 1 quart (1 l) heavy cream • 8 large egg yolks • ½ cup (10 cl) Poire William brandy

Combine the pears, sugar, vanilla bean pod, and 1 quart (1 l) of water in a saucepan. Vigorously boil for about 5 minutes and remove from heat. Let the pears completely cool in the syrup. **W**hip the cream and refrigerate. Purée the pears in a food processor. Set aside ⅔ cup (150 g) of the purée and save the rest for another recipe. Transfer 1 cup (20 cl) of the syrup to a pan and cook until it leaves a thread when you raise the spoon—230°F (110°C) on a candy thermometer. **B**eat the egg yolks until lemon-colored and stir in the hot syrup. Continue stirring until the mixture leaves a smooth ribbon when you raise the spoon. Fold in the pear purée, whipped cream, and brandy. Spoon the mixture into a charlotte mold and freeze at least 6 hours.

The parfait is a simple and delicious frozen dessert. It's very rich in cream but, unlike traditional ice cream, it doesn't require an ice-cream maker. Serve this dessert to your guests in autumn.

NOTE BY **FRANÇOISE BERNARD**

Malakoff Pear Sponge Cake

Pavé de poire Malakoff

⌂ ○

Françoise Bernard

Serves 6 to 8 ✦ **Preparation time : 30 minutes** ✦ **Cooking time : 10 minutes** ✦ **Refrigeration time : 15 hours** ✦ **1 large can of pears in syrup** ✦ **13 tbsp. (175 g) softened butter** ✦ **¾ cup (150 g) granulated sugar** ✦ **1 cup (100 g) ground almonds** ✦ **2 tbsp. kirsch or pear brandy** ✦ **2½ oz. (75 g) dark chocolate** ✦ **½ cup (50 g) confectioners' sugar, sifted**

The day before serving, carefully drain the pears, reserving the syrup, and cut into thin slices. Put the 10½ tbsp. (150 g) butter and granulated sugar into a large, warm bowl. Cream the butter and sugar with an electric mixer. Mix in the almonds and the kirsch. Gently fold the pear slices into the almond mixture, being careful not to break them. With a pastry brush, coat the inside of a 9 in. (24 cm) cake pan with some of the pear syrup. Place the batter in the pan, packing it down by tapping the pan on the surface of the table. Refrigerate overnight. The next day, place the bottom of the cake pan in hot water and unmold onto a serving dish. Break the chocolate into 2 pieces and melt in a double boiler over medium heat. Add the confectioners' sugar, stirring vigorously. Cut the remaining butter into small pieces and mix into the chocolate frosting. Remove from heat and stir in 3 tbsp. of pear syrup, stirring vigorously until smooth and shiny. Pour the frosting over the cake and refrigerate for at least 3 hours before serving.

NOTE BY **ALAIN DUCASSE** You can enliven this dessert by adding a cold pear coulis with vanilla and lemon. Poach a few pears in a light syrup flavored with 1 vanilla bean and purée in a blender with some of the syrup and lemon juice.

Caramelized and Raw Pear Tart

Tarte aux poires caramélisées et crues

⇧ ⇧ ○

Alain Ducasse

Serves 4 ◆ Preparation time : 45 minutes ◆ Resting time : 1 hour 20 minutes ◆ Cooking time : 30 minutes ◆ 1½ cups (230 g) flour ◆ 2 tsp. baking powder ◆ 2 pinches of salt ◆ 9 tbsp. (140 g) softened butter ◆ 2 egg yolks ◆ ½ cup plus 1 tbsp. (110 g) sugar ◆ 1 tsp. vanilla extract ◆ 3 juicy pears ◆ juice of 2 lemons

Mix 1⅓ cups (200 g) flour, the baking powder, salt, and 8 tbsp. of butter with your fingertips until the mixture has a grainy texture. Beat the egg yolks with ½ cup (100 g) sugar and the vanilla until the yolks lighten. Mix into the dough and refrigerate for 1 hour. **O**n a floured surface, roll the dough into a rectangle, 8 × 3 in. (20 × 8 cm) and ¼ in. (4 mm) thick. Line a baking sheet with parchment paper. Place the dough on top, prick with a fork, and refrigerate for 20 minutes. **P**reheat the oven to 350°F (180°C). **C**over the dough with a second sheet of parchment paper, weight with dried beans, and bake for 20 minutes. Remove the pastry crust from the oven and cool on a wire rack. **P**eel and core 2 of the pears. Slice and drizzle with lemon juice. Grate the remaining pear and drizzle with lemon juice. Melt the 1 tbsp. butter in a nonstick pan. When it turns golden brown, add the remaining sugar. Add the pear slices and coat evenly with the caramel. Sprinkle the grated pear on the pastry crust, arrange the caramelized pears on top, and drizzle the rest of the caramel over the tart. Serve with pear sorbet or pistachio ice cream.

The raw, grated pear beneath the caramelized slices is a surprise. This dessert is a fresh and delicious reinvention of the classic apple *tart Tatin*.

NOTE BY
FRANÇOISE
BERNARD

Pineapple

Françoise Bernard associates pineapples with Christmas because, not long ago, this fruit was considered rare and very special. Today, it is an ingredient in many sweet-and-sour dressings. Françoise Bernard is very fond of duck with pineapple, for example, a classic of Asian cuisine. Except in these exotic dishes, she prefer the fruit fresh, with some sugar. Because the quality of this fruit has improved so much in the past few years—as she remarks sensibly—there is no reason to mask its taste with alcohol or spices. It is picked ripe and transported by air to destinations around the world.

The pineapple has one problem, however. It is not easy to peel, and few people have mastered the art. That is why Françoise Bernard, the author of the legendary *Recettes faciles* (*Simple Recipes*), always includes preparation tips in her books. First, cut off both ends. Then, stand the pineapple upright and slice off the skin from top to bottom to "undress" the fruit. Finally, carve out the "eyes" with the tip of your knife. It seems that the pineapple likes to play practical jokes: It is sweeter at the base than at the top. If you serve it in slices, cut it lengthwise to ensure equal proportions of sweetness in each slice. If you would like to preserve the decorative skin, first cut the fruit in half. Remove the pulp and refill the pineapple half with a mixed salad that includes pineapple cubes. This method of preparation is especially popular among caterers because the presentation is attractive on the table.

Alain Ducasse likes the acidic freshness of pineapples. He is not crazy about those *salades composées* (mixed salads) that are considered exotic because a few pineapple cubes are tossed in. He does, however, appreciate the inclusion of pineapple in fresh fruit salads. The pineapple also cooks well—when caramelized, the little Victoria pineapple gives out an unexpected flavor. Alain Ducasse has created a dessert with thin slices of pineapple baked in a puff pastry that resembles its own skin. His Crisp Roasted Pineapple recipe is most certainly famous, because many chefs are now putting pineapple slices in pastry crusts in their restaurants.

Pineapple *à la Belle de Meaux*

Ananas à la belle de Meaux

♙ ♙ ∞

Françoise Bernard

Serves 4 ✦ **Preparation time : 40 minutes** ✦ **Marinating time : 30 minutes**
1 pineapple, 3 to 4 lbs. (1,5 to 2 kg) ✦ **8 oz. (250 g) strawberries** ✦ **4 tbsp. granulated sugar** ✦
¼ cup (5 cl) kirsch ✦ **1 cup (250 g) crème fraîche, very cold** ✦ **2 to 3 tbsp. cold milk** ✦ **1 tbsp.**
vanilla sugar

Slice the pineapple in half lengthwise. Remove the pulp with a sharp knife, cutting at
least ½ in. (1 cm) away from the outer skin to avoid damaging the scales. Reserve the
hollowed pineapple skins. Dice the pulp and place in a bowl. Quickly rinse the strawberries in cold water. Reserve a few for the garnish and stem the rest. Add to the bowl.
Dissolve the sugar in the kirsch, pour over the fruit, and mix. Refrigerate for 30 minutes.
Begin whisking the crème fraîche into the milk with wide, slow movements, to incorporate as much air as possible into the cream. Then beat rapidly to thicken the cream.
When the cream is firm enough to cling to the whisk, stop beating and stir in the
vanilla sugar. Spoon the fruit mixture into the pineapple skins. Top with whipped cream
and the reserved strawberries.

NOTE BY **ALAIN DUCASSE** Many people prefer heavy cream to crème fraîche because it is readily available in
supermarkets. Heavy cream can just as easily be beaten into a whipped cream.

Hot and Cold Pineapple

Ananas en froid et chaud

⬆ ⬆ ⬆ ∞

Alain Ducasse

Serves 4 ✦ Preparation time : 50 minutes ✦ Resting time : 2 hours ✦ Cooking time : 30 minutes ✦ 1 cup (20 cl) syrup, made from 2 cups (50 cl) water and 1¼ cups (250 g) sugar ✦ 1⅔ cups (260 g) flour ✦ 1 cup (160 g) potato flour ✦ 1 tsp. baking powder ✦ 1¾ cups (35 cl) water ✦ 1 large pineapple ✦ 3 tbsp. (40 g) butter ✦ ¼ cup (50 g) sugar ✦ ½ cup (10 cl) rum ✦ 1 cup (20 cl) pineapple juice ✦ about 6 cups (1,5 l) vegetable oil, for frying ✦ 1 pint (50 cl) pineapple sorbet

Preheat the oven to 225°F (100°C). **T**o make the syrup, boil the water and sugar for 5 minutes. Remove from heat and set aside. **T**o make the batter for the fritters, mix the flour, potato flour, and baking powder in about 1½ cups (35 cl) water. Let rest for 2 hours. **S**kin the pineapple, cut it in half lengthwise, and remove the core. Reserve one half and cut the other lengthwise into 4 slices. Roast the slices in the butter and sugar. When golden brown, deglaze the pan first with rum and then with pineapple juice. **V**ery thinly slice the other half-pineapple lengthwise—ideally with a mandolin or meat slicer. Arrange the thin leaves on a nonstick baking sheet, cover with syrup, bake until crisp and golden brown. **H**eat the frying oil to 350° (180°C) in a deep fryer. Remove the pulp from the reserved pineapple half. Cut into large cubes and pat dry with a paper towel. Dip the cubes in the batter and fry. **L**ine each dish with crisp pineapple leaves and place 1 large scoop of pineapple sorbet on top. Insert another leaf in each scoop of sorbet, add 1 slice of roasted pineapple, and cover with syrup. Serve with the pineapple fritters.

This dessert is certainly the work of a chef. The fruit is prepared in three forms: roasted, deep-fried, and frozen in a sorbet. This dish is the ultimate gourmet dream for those who love the mixture of sweet and sour flavors and the contrast of temperatures. If you don't have a meat slicer, freeze the half-pineapple until it is firm—it will then be easier to cut into thin slices.

NOTE BY **FRANÇOISE BERNARD**

Pineapple Tart

Tarte aux ananas

⌂⌂ ⌂   ∞

Françoise Bernard

Serves 4 ◆ Preparation time : 1 hour ◆ Resting time : 1 hour ◆ Cooking time : 25 minutes ◆ 7 tbsp. (90 g) butter, softened ◆ ¾ cup (150 g) sugar ◆ 3 egg yolks ◆ fine salt ◆ 1¼ cups (180 g) flour, sifted ◆ 1 cup (20 cl) milk ◆ 5 thin slices of pineapple, fresh or canned ◆ 2 tbsp. kirsch ◆ Candied cherries or red currant jelly, warmed, for decorating

With an electric mixer, cream 4 tbsp. (60 g) butter with half the sugar. Mix in 1 egg yolk and a pinch of salt. Sprinkle 1 cup (150 g) sifted flour onto a flat surface. Quickly work the butter mixture into the flour, rubbing the dough between your hands until it has a grainy texture. Knead as little as possible. Roll into a ball and refrigerate for 1 hour. **P**reheat the oven to 350°F (180°C). **R**oll out the dough with a rolling pin on a floured surface. Line a buttered 8 to 9 in. (20 to 22 cm) tart pan, prick the crust with a fork, and refrigerate for 10 minutes. **B**ake the pastry for 15 to 20 minutes. Let cool and remove from the tart pan. **Q**uarter the fresh pineapple slices. (Halve the canned slices.) **T**o make the pastry cream, boil the milk with a pinch of salt in a saucepan. Beat the remaining yolks and sugar in a bowl until the yolks lighten. Whisk in the remaining flour. Gradually add the boiling milk. Return the mixture to the pan and cook over low heat, stirring until the cream thickens. Boil for 1 or 2 minutes, add the kirsch, remove from heat, and cool. **S**pread the pastry cream on the tart crust and top with pineapple slices or halves. Decorate with candied cherries or brush with red currant jelly.

NOTE BY **ALAIN DUCASSE** Be sure to drain the canned pineapple well so that the syrup does not dilute the kirsch cream. Vary the flavor by replacing the kirsch with rum. I would decorate the tart with flowering thyme or fresh mint rather than candied cherries.

Crisp Roasted Pineapple

Ananas rôti en écailles croustillantes

☆ ☆ ☆ ∞

Alain Ducasse

Serves 4 ◆ Preparation time : 1 hour ◆ Cooking time : 25 minutes
4 oz. (100 g) puff-pastry dough ◆ 1¼ cups (100 g) confectioners' sugar ◆ 1 large pineapple ◆
6 tbsp. (80 g) butter ◆ ½ cup (100 g) granulated sugar ◆ ⅔ cup (15 cl) rum ◆ 1 cup (20 cl)
pineapple juice ◆ ½ cup (100 g) pastry cream (page 323) ◆ ½ cup (100 g) whipped cream ◆ 4
sprigs mint

Preheat the oven to 400°F (210°C). Sprinkle confectioners' sugar on a flat surface and thinly roll out the puff-pastry dough. Place the dough on a baking sheet and bake until golden brown—about 8 minutes. With a pastry cutter, cut four 3 in. (7 cm) rounds. Cut the remaining pastry into 1 in. (2 cm) rounds. Skin the pineapple, halve it lengthwise, and cut ½ in. slices (1 cm) from each half. Cook the butter and granulated sugar in a skillet over low heat. When the mixture turns a light caramel color, sauté the pineapple slices on both sides and remove to a dish. Deglaze the cooking juice with ½ cup (10 cl) rum and flambé, being careful that the flame doesn't leap too high. Boil to reduce slightly, add the pineapple juice, and reduce the syrup to half its volume. Combine the pasty cream and whipped cream. Sprinkle with rum to taste. Place the large pastry round in the center of the serving platter and ladle the cream on top. Stud the cream with pineapple slices and small pastry rounds, alternately. Pour the syrup around the edges and decorate with sprigs of mint. Serve immediately.

For fear of breaking the pastry, I would cut the dough rounds before baking them. When skinning the pineapple, don't be afraid to remove a thick layer of the skin. In order to carve out the pineapple "eyes," which are hard to digest, you'll have to sacrifice some of the pulp. NOTE BY **FRANÇOISE BERNARD**

Plums

Imagine standing in an orchard, grabbing the greengage plums that are all around you. They are letting themselves be picked without any resistance. They are so gorged with sugar that the skin bursts, allowing you a glimpse of their warm, golden pulp. No wonder Françoise Bernard loves these plums when they split open—it means that they have reached their full maturity. Only then do these fruits reveal all of their flavor, while some people wrongly believe that they are too damaged to eat.

Tiny balls of yellow mirabelle plums make the most beautiful tarts of all, but their season is really too short. Quetsche plums are also magnificent in a brioche tart, crystallized in sugar. Françoise Bernard only likes the pointed quetsches, which are sweeter than the others. She once tried to make them into a jam, but the results were not encouraging, so she abandoned the idea. Greengage plums, on the other hand, make deliciously tangy compotes. The plum is simply perfect for home-style desserts.

Alain Ducasse, born in Castelsarrasin, has introduced the red plum in his version of a pastis recipe from the Landes region. Dried for many hours in low heat, the plum turns into a prune. You will also find it in Françoise Bernard's recipe for Swedish Stuffed Pork with Prunes, pork and plums go very well together. In the north of France, where she spent her vacations as a child, women prepared splendid plum yeast dough tarts, which they brought to the baker's oven to be baked for the holidays. Everybody looked forward to the moment when they came out of the oven, and they all longed to have the most beautiful one.

Swedish Stuffed Pork with Prunes

Porc farci aux pruneaux à la suédoise

⌂ ⌂ ◯◯

Françoise Bernard

Serves 4 ✦ Preparation time : 40 minutes ✦ Cooking time : 1 hour 30 minutes
1 pork roast, 2¼ lbs. (1 kg) ✦ 20 prunes ✦ 4 tbsp. (50 g) butter ✦ salt and pepper ✦ 2¼ lbs.
(1 kg) Reinette or Granny Smith apples

Preheat the oven to 400°F (210°C). **A**sk the butcher to pierce a hole the roast from end to end—or do this yourself with the handle of a wooden spoon. **P**it the prunes. Insert 6 to 8 into the hole in the meat, forcing them deeper with the handle of the wooden spoon. In a skillet over high heat, sear the meat on all sides in 2 tbsp. of the butter. **T**ransfer the meat and juice to a large baking dish, season with salt and pepper, and roast in the oven for 10 minutes. Boil ½ cup (10 cl) of water, add to the cooking juices, and lower the oven temperature to 350°F (180°C). Bake for 40 minutes, basting frequently. **P**eel and core the apples, leaving them whole. Insert 1 or 2 prunes and a dab of butter in each apple. Arrange the apples around the roast and bake for 40 more minutes. **T**urn off the heat and let the roast rest inside the oven for about 10 minutes. Carve the meat and serve with the apples.

NOTE BY **ALAIN DUCASSE** Ask your butcher to prepare a roast from the shoulder blade. I would roast it for a shorter period of time to preserve the tenderness of the meat. Long cooking times are not beneficial to pork.

Landes-Style Prune Pastis with Herb Liqueur

Pastis landais aux prunes confites, liqueur d'herbes

⬆ ⬆ ∞

Alain Ducasse

Serves 4 ◆ **Marinating time : 15 days** ◆ **Preparation time : 1 hour** ◆ **Waiting time : 30 minutes** ◆ **Cooking time : 1 hour 10 minutes** ◆ ¾ cup (140 g) sugar ◆ 1 cup (20 cl) brandy or alcohol ◆ 5 sprigs mint or sage, leaves only ◆ 10 oz. (300 g) Reinette or Granny Smith apples ◆ ½ pear ◆ 10 oz. (300 g) red plums ◆ ½ vanilla bean pod, split ◆ juice of ½ orange ◆ 2 cups (45 cl) port wine ◆ ¾ cup (130 g) flour ◆ 2 tbsp. ground almonds ◆ 5 tbsp. (70 g) butter, softened ◆ 1 egg

Two weeks before serving, make the herb liqueur. Boil ¼ cup (5 cl) water with 2 tbsp. of the sugar for 2 minutes. Remove from the heat, cool in the refrigerator, and add the brandy. Soak the mint leaves in the liqueur for 2 weeks in the refrigerator. On the day you will serve the dish, peel the apples and the pear and wash the plums. Dice all the fruit. Add ½ cup (100 g) sugar, the vanilla bean pod, orange juice, and 1 cup (20 cl) of the port wine. Cook over low heat to form a dry compote—about 35 minutes. Remove from the heat and cool. Remove the vanilla bean pod. With your fingertips, mix the remaining sugar, ⅔ cup (100 g) flour, the ground almonds, and 4 tbsp. of the butter. When the mixture has a grainy texture, mix in the egg and form into a ball. Let the dough rest for 30 minutes. Preheat the oven to 350°F (180°C). Cut the dough in half and, on a floured surface, roll each half into an 8 in. (20 cm) circle. Butter a tart pan of the same size and line with one of the dough circles. Spread the compote on top and cover with the other dough circle, pressing the edges to seal. Bake for 25 to 30 minutes. Let the pastis cool in the oven. Reduce the remaining port wine until it forms a syrup—about 20 minutes. Cut the pastis into four pieces and serve on individual plates. Pour some port syrup alongside and serve the herb liquor separately.

This is really a dessert from the orchards, combining the plum, the pear, and the apple. It's unusual to reduce port wine by itself to make a sauce—but the taste of this cooked wine matches the red plums perfectly.

NOTE BY **FRANÇOISE BERNARD**

Brioche Tart with Quetsche Plums

Tarte briochée aux quetsches

⇞ ⇞ ∞

Françoise Bernard

Serves 4 ✦ **Preparation time : 1 hour** ✦ **Waiting time : 1 hour 30 minutes** ✦ **Cooking time : 35 minutes** ✦ **about 1 cup (125 g) flour** ✦ **3 tsp. confectioners' sugar** ✦ **salt** ✦ **3 tbsp. milk** ✦ **1 package dry yeast** ✦ **4 tbsp. (50 g) butter** ✦ **1 egg** ✦ **1 lb. (500 g) plums** ✦ **4 tbsp. granulated sugar** ✦ **1 tsp. ground cinnamon**

Mix the flour, 1 tsp. of confectioners' sugar, and 3 pinches of salt in a large mixing bowl. Warm the milk and stir in the yeast. Melt the butter in a 9 in. (24 cm) cake pan. With the bread hook of an electric mixer, mix the melted butter, flour mixture, diluted yeast, and egg. Beat the dough vigorously until it becomes elastic and detaches from the sides of the mixing bowl—about 10 minutes. If the dough is too soft, add a little flour and beat for a few more seconds. Cover with a clean cloth and let rise in a warm place for 1 hour. **P**unch down the dough and place it in the cake pan. Spread it with your hands, pushing it up against the sides of the plate. Let it rise again in a warm place for 30 minutes. **P**reheat the oven to 450°F (240°C). **W**ash, halve, and pit the plums. Arrange on top of the pastry dough, skin side down and close together. Bake for 25 to 30 minutes. Fifteen minutes before the baking is done, sprinkle granulated sugar on top to caramelize. **M**ix the confectioners' sugar with the cinnamon and put into a fine strainer. Remove the tart from the pan while still hot and sprinkle with the cinnamon sugar. Serve hot or warm.

NOTE BY **ALAIN DUCASSE** You can completely transform the appearance of this dessert by molding the dough as you would a Bresse brioche—that is, like a flat pizza crust. Make a few holes in the dough with a spoon, dot with butter, and cover with heavy cream and granulated sugar. Serve the plums separately as a warm compote.

Mirabelle Plum Clafoutis

Clafoutis aux mirabelles

⌂ ∞

Alain Ducasse

Serves 6 to 8 ✦ **Preparation time : 55 minutes** ✦ **Cooking time : 45 minutes**
9 tbsp. (130 g) butter, softened ✦ **1 cup (100 g) ground almonds** ✦ **1 cup (120 g) confectioners'**
sugar ✦ **¼ cup (35 g) cornstarch** ✦ **1 egg** ✦ **1 cup (20 cl) milk** ✦ **2 egg yolks** ✦ **¼ cup (50 g)**
granulated sugar ✦ **14 oz. (400 g) pitted mirabelles, halved**

Preheat the oven to 350°F (180°C). **C**ream 8 tbsp. of the butter. Set aside 1 tbsp.
confectioners' sugar then sift together the ground almonds and sugar. Add one third
of the cornstarch. With a whisk or pastry blender, cut the butter into the almond
mixture. Add 1 egg and mix well. **B**oil the milk in a saucepan. Beat the yolks with the
granulated sugar. Add the remaining cornstarch. Pour milk into the egg mixture, beating as you pour. Return to the saucepan, over medium heat stirring vigorously to
prevent the cream from burning. When the mixture has thickened, remove from heat,
pour into a lightly buttered bowl, and cool quickly on ice. **G**ently mix the almond butter
and pastry cream with the mirabelles. Pour into a buttered earthenware baking dish
and bake for 25 to 30 minutes. Check for doneness by pricking with the tip of a knife—
when the blade comes out clean, the clafoutis is done. Sprinkle with confectioners'
sugar just before serving. Serve warm.

The composition of this clafoutis, with almond butter and pastry cream is quite unexpected in a home-style dessert. I would have simply worked with a mixture of eggs,
flour, sugar, and milk—but I will try to be more innovative now.

NOTE BY
FRANÇOISE
BERNARD

Strawberries

Strawberries remind Françoise Bernard of the desserts of her childhood-the Sunday tarts and strawberry sponge cakes— and the summer lunches of plain strawberries topped with crème fraîche. Her tastes have not changed, although now she sometimes replaces the crème fraîche with some cold whipped fresh cheese to maintain her waistline, without diminishing the treat. She also loves freshly picked strawberries just as they are.

The strawberry, sweet and tender, is also one of Alain Ducasse's childhood favorites. He features it in sweet desserts—bonbons, ice creams and sorbets, syrups (just cooked with a little sugar in a double boiler), French toast, and *vacherins* (meringues with fruit and whipped cream). In his recipes, the strawberry becomes pure delight. His recipe for Wild Strawberries with a Mascarpone Sorbet has traveled around the world. You can experience it in Bangkok or New York. Of course, the strawberry is not only a dessert delicacy. Anything is possible with this dark red berry. Alain Ducasse dares to put a dash of olive oil on fried strawberries. Françoise Bernard feels no qualms imagining the decorative fruit in her mixed savory salads.

Their favorite variety? The wild Mara strawberry. Alain Ducasse choose it for his French toast with strawberries. This ever-bearing variety has also seduced Françoise Bernard. "When we began to find the wild Mara strawberry in the marketplace, I was so pleasantly surprised by the flavor that I refused to buy any others," she says. Of course, advances in agronomy have made strawberry production possible year-round—but this small fruit, with its shiny colors and delicate fragrance, will always be a symbol of nature's perpetual renewal.

Frozen Strawberry Mousse

Mousse glacée aux fraises

⊓ ∞

Françoise Bernard

Serves 4 ✦ **Preparation time : 35 minutes** ✦ **Refrigeration time : 3 hours**
1 lb. (450 g) strawberries, washed and stemmed ✦ **½ cup (100 g) granulated sugar** ✦ **3 tsp.**
vanilla sugar ✦ **juice of ½ lemon** ✦ **⅔ cup (150 g) crème fraîche or sour cream, cold** ✦ **about**
½ cup (12,5 cl) milk, cold

In a food processor, purée the strawberries, granulated sugar, vanilla sugar, and lemon juice until smooth. Whisk the crème fraîche and milk to make a whipped mousse cream. With a rubber scraper, gently fold the strawberry purée into the whipped cream. Freeze for at least 3 hours. Place a serving of strawberry mousse into individual ice-cream dishes and serve.

NOTE BY **ALAIN DUCASSE** To enhance the presentation, first garnish the plates with finely sliced strawberries topped with strawberry jelly—then add spoonfuls of mouse on top.

French Toast with Strawberries and Mint Salad

Pain perdu aux fraises, salade de menthe

⬠ ⬠ ○

Alain Ducasse

Serves 4 ◆ Preparation time : 30 minutes ◆ Cooking time : 15 minutes
1½ lbs. (600 g) Mara strawberries ◆ 4 whole eggs ◆ 2 egg yolks ◆ 2½ cups (50 cl) milk ◆ ⅔ cup (130 g) granulated sugar ◆ ½ vanilla bean pod, split ◆ 4 large slices of brioche ◆ 11 tbsp. (150 g) butter ◆ 2 handfuls (50 g) mint leaves ◆ 3 tbsp. extra-virgin olive oil ◆ ¼ cup (25 g) confectioners' sugar ◆ juice of 1 lemon

Quickly wash the strawberries without removing the stems, drain on a clean cloth, and set aside. Combine the eggs, yolks, milk, ⅓ cup (65 g) granulated sugar, and the vanilla bean pod. Soak the slices of brioche in the mixture. Melt 8 tbsp. of the butter in a skillet over low heat and brown both sides of the brioche slices. Set aside, keeping warm. Melt ¼ cup (50 g) granulated sugar in a saucepan over low heat, without stirring. When it turns golden brown, add the remaining butter. Add the strawberries and cook for 3 to 4 minutes. Wash the mint leaves and season with the oil, confectioners' sugar, and lemon juice. On individual plates, serve the brioche, surrounded by strawberries, and the mint salad alongside. You can also serve this dish with vanilla ice cream.

I am surprised to find olive oil in this recipe. Indeed, this sunny oil has multiple uses, in both sweet and savory recipes—but in this combination of strawberry and brioche, I prefer the natural flavor of the mint, without the oil.

NOTE BY **FRANÇOISE BERNARD**

Strawberries Romanoff

Fraises Romanoff

⬆ ⬆ ⬁

Françoise Bernard

Serves 4 ⬩ Preparation time : 20 minutes ⬩ Marinating time : 2 hours juice of 1 lemon ⬩ juice of 1 orange ⬩ 3 tbsp. curaçao ⬩ 2 tbsp. granulated sugar ⬩ 1 lb. (450 g) strawberries, washed and stemmed ⬩ 1 cup (200 g) heavy cream, very cold ⬩ 1 tbsp. vanilla sugar

Mix the lemon and orange juices, curaçao, and granulated sugar in a bowl. Gently mix in the strawberries. Cover and refrigerate for 2 hours. **W**hip the cream with vanilla sugar until it is clings to the whisk. Refrigerate. Pour the whipped cream over the strawberries just before serving.

NOTE BY **ALAIN DUCASSE** With this kind of fruit dessert, I prefer that the whipped cream be soft, not stiff—more like cream than like a mousse.

Iced Strawberry Meringue

Vacherin glacé aux fraises

♙ ∞

Alain Ducasse

Serves 8 ✦ Preparation time : 1 hour ✦ Cooking time : 1 hour 15 minutes ✦ Freezing time : 20 minutes ✦ 6 egg whites ✦ 1¾ cups (320 g) granulated sugar ✦ 2 cups (240 g) confectioners' sugar, sifted ✦ 2¼ lbs. (1 kg) strawberries, washed and stemmed ✦ 1¼ cups (30 cl) heavy cream, very cold ✦ 3 tsp. vanilla sugar ✦ 1½ pints (75 cl) vanilla ice cream

Preheat the oven to 250°F (120°C). **S**et aside 1½ tbsp. of confectioners' sugar. Beat the egg whites to form stiff peaks, gradually adding 1 cup (200 g) of the granulated sugar and the confectioners' sugar. Fill a pastry bag and squeeze the meringue onto a baking sheet, in thin strips 2 in. (5 cm) long. Sprinkle with some confectioners' sugar and bake for 1 hour 15 minutes. **B**oil the reserved granu lated sugar with ½ cup (10 cl) water, remove from heat, and cool. Reserve ½ lb. (250 g) of the strawberries and purée the rest in a food processor. Combine the strawberry purée and syrup. Pour into an ice-cream maker and turn into sorbet. **W**hip the cream and fold in vanilla sugar and the reserved confectioners' sugar. Spoon layers of strawberry sorbet and vanilla ice cream into individual ring molds, 2 in. (5 cm) high. Freeze for 20 minutes. (If you don't have individual molds, make a 9 in. (24 cm) mold with strips of cardboard, stapled together, end to end.) **P**lace the molds on serving plates, remove the rings. Lay 5 meringue sticks on each. Top with the whipped cream, squeezed through a pastry bag with a fluted tip. Decorate with the reserved strawberries. You can also drizzle with a few drops of strawberry sauce.

Need I mention that you can make this *vacherin* with a good-quality store-bought ice cream? You can also, to make things even easier, buy the meringue sticks at a bakery. This dessert is also delicious with a homemade strawberry coulis, made from strawberries blended with a little granulated sugar and lemon juice. **NOTE BY FRANÇOISE BERNARD**

Basic Recipes of Alain Ducasse

White Chicken Stock

6½ (3 kgs) chicken carcass ✦ 1 medium (150 kg) onion, peeled ✦ 2 stalks (150 g) celery ✦ 4 medium (200 g) carrots, peeled ✦ 1 large (100 g) leek, green part ✦ 3 medium tomatoes, ripe ✦ 3 shallots, peeled ✦ 3 parsley stems ✦ 3 tbsp. black peppercorns, crushed ✦ 1 tbsp. coarse sea salt

Wash the vegetables and cut them in large pieces. Chop the bones into pieces. In a large pot blanch the bones by covering them with cold water, bring to a boil, cook 5 minutes to remove the blood. Drain, discard the cooking liquid and wash the bones under cold water. Clean the pot, return the bones to the pot, cover with cold water, add the vegetables, pepper and salt. Cook over very low heat 1½ to 2 hours. Skim occasionally during the cooking to remove impurities. Strain and reserve in refrigerator or freezer.

White Veal Stock

4¼ lbs. (2 kg) veal bones, leg or tail, 2 in. pieces ✦ 1¾ qts. (1,5 l) chicken stock

In a large pot blanch the bones by covering them with cold water, bring to a boil, cook 10 minutes to remove the blood. Drain, discard the cooking liquid and wash the bones under cold water. Clean the pot, return the bones to the pot, cover with chicken stock and cook over very low heat approximately 3 hours. Skim occasionally during cooking to remove the impurities. Strain and reserve in refrigerator or freezer.

Veal Jus
and other meat jus

⅔ cup (150 cl) olive oil or chicken fat ♦ 4¼ lbs. (2 kg) veal rump, cut 1 inch pieces ♦ 1 clove garlic, cut lengthwise ♦ 10 tbsp. (150 g) butter

In a heavy enamel coated cast iron pot, heat the olive oil, add the veal and sauté until golden, discard the fat, then add in the butter with a wooden spoon to incorporate with the cooking juices. Cover the meat with water and cook over medium heat until the liquid evaporates. Add more water halfway up the pot and reduce again until it becomes the consistency of syrup. One more time add water halfway then simmer approximately 2 hours. Remove from heat, strain and cool. If you keep your "veal jus" in the refrigerator the butter will solidify on the top and protect your jus. You can repeat this process for poultry or meats.

Tomato Confit

8 tomatoes ♦ 1 sprig thyme ♦ 1 lemon, sliced ♦ 3 garlic cloves, unpeeled ♦ coarse salt ♦ olive oil

Preheat oven to 175°F (70°C). Blanch and peel the tomatoes, cut them in half vertically, remove the seeds. Place in a *gratin* baking dish with the thyme leaves, lemon slices and garlic cloves. Sprinkle with salt and pour olive oil over the dish to cover the tomatoes. Bake in oven for 2 hours.

Pastry Cream

1 cup (25 cl) milk ♦ 3 egg yolks ♦ ¼ cup (50 g) granulated sugar ♦ 3 tbsp. (20 g) cornstarch

In a heavy bottom saucepan bring the milk to a boil. Whip the yolks in a bowl with the sugar and cornstarch until they are light. Pour the milk over the yolks mixture, stir to incorporate. Return the mix to the saucepan. Over high heat bring back to a boil stirring constantly, count to 15 and remove from the heat.

Index of Recipes

Françoise Bernard thanks all those—too many
to be named—who participated in the creation
of all her books (especially at Hachette).
She particularly wishes to thank Janine Pelouard, her assistant
forever, whose loyal friendship and rare
professional qualities have been most precious.

Alain Ducasse especially thanks Didier Elena
for the time and work that he spent creating
this book, and pays tribute to his precious and
loyal collaboration.

Valerie Lhomme thanks for their valuable
collaboration: The French Company of Orient and China,
the Palais Royal China Co., Quartz, Kitchen Bazaar,
Dehillerin, Terre de Sienne, Muriel Grateau, Le Creuset,
Françoise Saget.

The Publisher thanks Larousse Publishing for all
the drawings in this book which are extracted from
the *Larousse Universel* in two volumes, under the
direction of Claude Augé, © Librairie Larousse, 1922.